Socialist, Anti-Semite, and Jew

Socialist, Anti-Semite, and Jew

*German Social Democracy
Confronts the Problem of Anti-Semitism
1918-1933*

DONALD L. NIEWYK

Louisiana State University Press
Baton Rouge

ISBN 0-8071-0531-7
Library of Congress Catalog Card Number 79-137123
Copyright © 1971 by Louisiana State University Press
All rights reserved
Manufactured in the United States of America
Printed by The TJM Corporation, Baton Rouge, Louisiana
Designed by J. Barney McKee

To his mentor
JOHN L. SNELL
*the author dedicates this book
in gratitude and admiration*

Ein Unglueck erkennt man
Nicht an der Nase, sondern daran, dass
Man einen Schaden hat dadurch. Es sind nicht die Nasen
Die das Unglueck sind, sondern die Taten. Es braucht einer
Da doch keine besondere Nase, um
Das Volk berauben zu koennen . . .

—Brecht
Der Jude, ein Unglueck fuer das Volk

Preface

This book could not have been completed without the generous assistance and cooperation of numerous individuals and institutions. I want to acknowledge a special debt of gratitude to Professor John L. Snell, now of the University of North Carolina, who first suggested to me the need for this study and who patiently provided expert advice and guidance through most of its development. I should also like to thank Professors Pierre H. Laurent, Radomir Luza, and Hans A. Schmitt for their helpful suggestions in the writing of an earlier version of this study at Tulane University.

Writing about the history of a delicate and complex topic in recent times is difficult without knowledge of the personal experiences and impressions of some of the surviving participants. In this respect I was extremely fortunate in receiving gracious aid from several men and women who were active in Socialist and Jewish organizations during the Weimar years and with whom lengthy and repeated correspondence or interviews were possible. For their invaluable help I am particularly indebted to Rudolf Callmann, Dr. Rudolf Coper, Dr. Ernst Fraenkel, Martin M. Gleisner, Dr. Ernest Hamburger, Dr. Alfred Hirschberg, Dr. Hans Hirschfeld, Dr. Wilhelm Hoegner, Dr. Carl Landauer, Walter M. Lowe, Walter G. Oschilewski, Dr. Eva Reichmann, Gerhart H. Seger, Hedwig Wachenheim, and Jeanette Wolff.

I am also indebted to Dr. Peter Loesche of the Otto Suhr Institute in Berlin and to Dr. Henryk Skrzypczak of the Berlin Historical Commission for guiding me to a number of Socialist sources in the free sector of that divided city. I also want to thank Dr. M. Trumpp of the *Bundesarchiv* in Koblenz and the staffs of the Tulane University Library, the Wiener Library (London), the International Institute of Social History (Amsterdam), and a number of German libraries and archives, especially the library of the Free University of Berlin, the municipal archives in Hamburg and Leipzig, the state archives in West Berlin and Munich, and the SPD Archive in Bonn, for their aid and cooperation. And to Tulane University, the Free University of Berlin, Ithaca College, and the College Center of the Finger Lakes I am grateful for the financial assistance granted during the course of my research.

D.L.N.

Ithaca, New York

Contents

Abbreviations

ADGB   Allgemeiner Deutscher Gewerkschaftsbund
(General German Trade Union Federation)

CV   Centralverein deutscher Staatsbuerger
juedischen Glaubens
(Central Association of German Citizens
of the Jewish Faith)

DDP   Deutsche Demokratische Partei
(German Democratic Party)

DNVP   Deutschnationale Volkspartei
(German National People's Party)

DVP   Deutsche Volkspartei
(German People's Party)

KPD   Kommunistische Partei Deutschlands
(Communist Party of Germany)

NSDAP   Nationalsozialistische Deutsche Arbeiterpartei
(National Socialist German Workers' Party—
Nazi Party)

SPD   Sozialdemokratische Partei Deutschlands
(Social Democratic Party of Germany)

USPD   Unabhaengige Sozialdemokratische Partei
Deutschlands
(Independent Social Democratic Party of Germany)

Socialist, Anti-Semite, and Jew

Chapter I

Introduction

Nazi anti-Semitism ultimately led to the extermination of more than five million European Jews. There can be no doubt that the German people must, in some degree, share responsibility for this crime. While Hitler never publicly advocated the murder of Jews, he flooded Germany with intensely anti-Semitic propaganda during the rise of nazism to power as well as after 1933. Yet it remains uncertain whether the Nazis themselves are chiefly responsible for animosity toward the Jews in Germany or whether they merely appealed to a virulent anti-Semitic sentiment already deeply rooted in German society. Such historians of National Socialist ideology as Peter Viereck, Rohan D'O. Butler, and George L. Mosse,[1] proponents of the latter view, have identified racism and authoritarianism as features of a uniquely German "national character." Many popular accounts, including that by William L. Shirer,[2] have done the same thing. There have been, meanwhile, few studies of pre-1933 opposition to anti-Semitism in Germany.

[1] Viereck, *Metapolitics: The Roots of the Nazi Mind* (New York, 1965); Butler, *The Roots of National Socialism* (New York, 1942); George L. Mosse, *The Crisis of German Ideology: Intellectual Origins of the Third Reich* (New York, 1964).
[2] Shirer, *The Rise and Fall of the Third Reich: A History of Nazi Germany* (New York, 1960).

This study will portray the attitudes and actions of the Social Democratic Party of Germany (SPD) toward Jews and anti-Semitism during the years of the Weimar Republic, with special emphasis on the decisive period 1929–33. It will assess the causes and results of those attitudes and, indirectly, assist in evaluating contentions that Germans in general possess an abiding affection for racist ideas. Although the SPD never enjoyed an electoral majority, it remained the largest party in Germany from 1912 until July, 1932, and it appears to have retained the firm allegiance of most working-class Germans throughout the Weimar period. The attitudes of this Party toward Jews and anti-Semitism reflected the feelings of its leaders and influenced the thinking of millions of ordinary workers and other supporters of the German republic. To determine if the SPD forewarned Germans by supplying them with a realistic view of Nazi Judeophobia, attention will be given to the Socialists' theoretical explanation of anti-Semitism in the Weimar period. The effectiveness of the Party's opposition to anti-Semitism will be assessed on the basis of its day-to-day responses to hatred directed toward Jews.

Although the German Socialists correctly have been regarded as consistent enemies of all the right-wing parties, and especially of the Nazis, little study has been made of their reactions to virulent Judeophobia in the period after World War I. Richard N. Hunt has noted only in passing that German Socialists opposed anti-Semitism.[3] Hans-Helmuth Knuetter, in a brief essay on relations between the leftist parties and the Jews in 1932, has correctly concluded that the SPD underestimated Nazi anti-Semitism but has not fully accounted for that Socialist attitude.[4]

[3] Hunt, *German Social Democracy, 1918–1933* (New Haven and London, 1964), 40.

[4] Knuetter, "Die Linksparteien," in Werner E. Mosse and Arnold Paucker (eds.), *Entscheidungsjahr 1932: Zur Judenfrage in der Endphase der Weimarer Republik* (Tuebingen, 1965), 323–45.

Marxian socialism and anti-Semitism are theoretically incompatible. The former acknowledges but one enemy, the
bourgeoisie as guardian of the capitalist system; individuals,
ethnic groups, and nations are mere pawns in the inexorable
march of impersonal economic forces. Anti-Semitism, on the
other hand, places the guilt for human woes on a "race," the
Jews. German Socialists before World War I frequently exposed and condemned anti-Semitism in every area of German
society. At the same time, however, a few of them were suscep-
tible to anticapitalist anti-Semitism; insisting that all Jews were
morally obligated to work for the general emancipation of
all the oppressed through the Social Democratic Party, they
singled out non-Socialist Jews for special criticism. An examina-
tion of whether or how these attitudes changed during the
Weimar era and an assessment of the infiltration of anti-Jewish
views into the SPD after 1918 will suggest the intensity and
spread of Judeophobia in Weimar Germany.

The discomforts experienced by Jews in the Weimar Republic were not without historical precedent. In medieval Germany, as elsewhere in Europe at that time, Christians regarded
Jews with suspicion as "Christ-killers" and deliberate un-
believers. Legally the Jews found refuge with the Imperial
Crown of the Holy Roman Empire, although in practice they
were considered the protected property of the local princes. In
return the rulers were assured an important source of liquid
revenue, for they could levy all manner of special taxes on the
Jewish communities or simply demand that debts owed to
Jews be paid into the royal coffers instead. These monarchs not
infrequently thought of "their Jews" only as commodities to be
exploited to the point of indigence and then expelled. On occasion whole Jewish communities were exchanged to pay royal
debts.

Strong anti-Semitism was aroused as a corollary to the religious fervor of the Crusades. Bands of zealots destined for Palestine sometimes thought it desirable first to deal with the "infidels" living among them, and each of the Crusades was accompanied by a wave of popular massacres that spread from France into the Rhineland. The fact that some of these deeds began with the burning of records of indebtedness suggests that more than purely religious motives prompted this violence. During the First Crusade in 1096 more than twelve thousand Jews were slaughtered in Germany alone. While subsequent Crusades were not as disastrous for the Jews, 1096 marked the end of whatever security German Jews had enjoyed. Previously Christians and Jews had lived together in harmony, isolated moments of tension notwithstanding, but the Crusades poisoned these relationships and forced the Jews to withdraw into shells from which they emerged only to perform necessary business transactions. This isolation spawned mutual hostility. In the twelfth and thirteenth centuries the Jews were accused of committing the ritual-murder of Christian youths, desecrating the Host, and inspiring heretical movements within the Church. In 1348, when the Black Death swept across Europe, killing at least a quarter of the population, the Jews were denounced for entering into a conspiracy with lepers to poison the wells. Almost every German community massacred the Jews or forced them to flee. Large numbers of Germany's Jews migrated into thinly populated areas of Eastern Europe—especially Poland—that afforded relative safety from these pogroms.

During subsequent centuries the descendants of many German Jews who had fled to the East returned to crowded ghettos to live once more as moneylenders, petty traders, and artisans. For hundreds of years their condition remained barely comfortable, but at least they were relatively unmolested in Germany. In contrast, the Jews of France were expelled at the end of the fourteenth century, and those of Spain and Portugal were similarly uprooted a hundred years later. Not until the

Napoleonic period was any general move made toward emancipating German Jewry. In much of French-occupied Europe, Jews were then given equal rights, and many ghetto walls were demolished by French engineers. The reaction that followed Waterloo did not completely reverse the movement toward Jewish emancipation. The names of German Jews slowly became prominent in business, literature, and politics. Jewish intellectuals and political activists generally tied their political fortunes to the liberal movement, and Jews played prominent roles in the Revolution of 1848. In 1850 Frederick William IV of Prussia reaffirmed the right of Jews to vote, to own land, and to enter the professions. In 1869 the North German Confederation freed Jews of every civic restriction, and this was extended throughout the German Empire after its creation in 1871 under Bismarck's leadership.[5]

Legal emancipation did not bring social equality. It was virtually impossible for a Jew to become an officer in the Prussian army, nor could one aspire to a position of importance in the bureaucracy. It was unusually difficult for Jews to attain prestigious positions in the academic world. Anti-Semitism in Imperial Germany arose in reaction to the industrialization, secularization, and liberalization of society. Conservative intellectuals like Heinrich von Treitschke, Paul de Lagarde, and Julius Langbehn regarded Jews as typical representatives of the

[5] The best short general histories of the Jews are: James Parkes, *A History of the Jewish People* (London, 1962), and Cecil Roth, *A History of the Jews* (New York, 1961). More detailed information may be gleaned from Israel Abrahams, *Jewish Life in the Middle Ages* (Rev. ed.; London, 1932); Salo W. Baron, *A Social and Religious History of the Jews* (12 vols.; New York, 1952–67); Guido Kisch, *The Jews in Medieval Germany: A Study of Their Legal and Social Status* (Chicago, 1949); Marvin Lowenthal, *The Jews of Germany: A Story of Sixteen Centuries* (New York, 1936); Jacob R. Marcus, *The Rise and Destiny of the German Jew* (Cincinnati, 1934); and Jakob Toury, *Die politischen Orientierungen der Juden in Deutschland. Von Jena bis Weimar* (Tuebingen, 1966). A detailed and well-written popular account that is not entirely free from errors is Howard Morley Sachar, *The Course of Modern Jewish History* (Cleveland, 1958).

forces that were breaking down traditional German values. Their grievances were echoed on a less sophisticated level by the petty bourgeois victims of capitalist expansion.[6] Political Judeophobia found expression in Court Chaplain Adolf Stoecker's Christian Social Movement during the 1880's. In 1893 anti-Semitic parties won 3.4 percent of the votes and elected sixteen representatives to the Reichstag. Imperial Germany's post-1900 prosperity, however, robbed anti-Jewish parties of much of their appeal, and in 1912 they mustered a mere 0.9 percent of the votes and only three Reichstag seats.[7] Notwithstanding efforts to inspire political anti-Semitism, outrages against Jews were rare in Imperial Germany. The country witnessed no Dreyfus Affair or crowds of enraged citizens roaming the streets shouting, "Death to the Jews!" Before 1914 the Jews of Germany were treated as well as, or better than, those of any large country in continental Europe.[8]

World War I and the Revolution of 1918–19 brought both new opportunities and new impediments to German Jews. The war shattered the prosperous, complacent world of Imperial Germany and offered defeat, inflation, hunger, and humiliation in its stead. Among right-wing Germans it became popular to trace these and subsequent problems to the Jews. Anti-Semites irrationally blamed Jews for the German collapse, holding them responsible for all antiwar propaganda that had been distributed in Germany from 1914 to 1918. They asserted that Jews had profited financially from the war and had dodged

[6] Peter G. J. Pulzer, *The Rise of Political Anti-Semitism in Germany and Austria* (New York, 1964), 18–86; Fritz Stern, *The Politics of Cultural Despair* (Berkeley and Los Angeles, 1961), 61–64, 139–43.

[7] Koppel S. Pinson, *Modern Germany: Its History and Civilization* (New York, 1954), 573.

[8] Paul W. Massing, *Rehearsal for Destruction: A Study of Political Anti-Semitism in Imperial Germany* (New York, 1949), 21–36. Peter G. J. Pulzer unconvincingly maintains that pre–World War I anti-Semitic parties "succeeded in their object" by having "impregnated wide sections of the [German] population with anti-Semitic ideas." Pulzer, *The Rise of Political Anti-Semitism*, 290.

their military obligations, while all other Germans had made the greatest sacrifices for the Fatherland.[9] The Weimar Republic's acceptance of Jews into the government service led to charges that they had glutted the bureaucracy; as a result, the republic was defamed as the "Jew Republic."[10] Jewish leadership in left-wing revolutions in Russia, Hungary, and Germany stimulated the identification of Jews with bolshevism.[11] In the minds of many Germans, traditional Jewish ties with capitalism and intellectual pursuits associated the Jews with deceitful profiteering, heartless intellectualism, and scheming rationalism. Relative Jewish prosperity during the difficult Weimar years stimulated jealousy and resentment among some Germans. In 1929 the per capita income of Berlin Jews was almost twice that of the city's non-Jews, while at the same time German universities were educating a number of Jewish students that was nearly four times as great as the proportion of Jews in Germany (figured on a percentage basis).[12] For fanatical anti-Semites these conditions meant one thing—that the Jews were indeed guilty of the cold-blooded exploitation of Germany's economy. In particular, Jewish support for liberalism, democracy, and socialism stimulated political reactionaries to accuse the Jews of underwriting the importation of a "foreign" system of government that Germans could neither understand nor accept.

[9] Waldemar Gurian, "Antisemitism in Modern Germany," in Koppel S. Pinson (ed.), *Essays on Antisemitism* (New York, 1946), 240.

[10] Walter Gross, "Das politische Schicksal der deutschen Juden in der Weimarer Republik," in Hans Tramer (ed.), *In Zwei Welten: Siegfried Moses—zum fuenfundsiebzigsten Geburtstag* (Tel Aviv, 1962), 536–55.

[11] The identification of Jews and bolshevism was a basic element of Hitler's anti-Semitism. Hitler, however, also used a conspiracy theory to unite it with assertions of Jewish proclivity for capitalism. The Jewish capitalists, he argued, used Marxism to harness the workers to the struggle against the national economy, which the Jews wanted to destroy "in order that the international stock-exchange can triumph over its dead body." Adolf Hitler, *Mein Kampf*, trans. Ralph Manheim (Boston, 1943), 61–65, 319, 320–24.

[12] Arthur Ruppin, *The Jews in the Modern World* (London, 1934), 152, 313.

Hence, although the Weimar Constitution guaranteed equal rights to all citizens, the lot of German Jews deteriorated in the years following World War I. The most violent anti-Semites formed small but active *voelkisch* organizations that demanded an end to Jewish equality.[13] The most successful of them, the Nazi Party, absorbed most of its competitors after 1929. In addition, the Nationalist Party (DNVP), the party of the old ruling classes, made anti-Semitic appeals throughout the period 1919–33. Jews who for decades had pridefully regarded themselves as being Germans who belonged to the Jewish *faith* frequently reacted with incredulity; only a few were direct victims of racist attacks, and the majority doubted the existence of any real threat to their security. As late as 1932 wealthy Jews who were asked to contribute funds to combat Hitler told Prince Hubertus zu Loewenstein: "First of all you are too pessimistic, secondly—well, and what if Hitler did come to power?" [14]

Like the Jews, German Socialists had begun their political existence as pariahs, gradually became assimilated into German society, and finally fell victim to the National Socialists. The SPD was the child of two parent organizations: the General German Workers' Association, founded in 1863 by Ferdinand Lassalle, and the Social Democratic Labor Party, organized by August Bebel and Wilhelm Liebknecht in 1869. Lassalle preached that the German proletariat should work to gain political power through universal suffrage. He saw no reason why the Prussian monarchy and the workers should not ally against their common enemy, the bourgeoisie. State socialism

[13] The German adjective *voelkisch* cannot satisfactorily be translated into a single English word; at once it means "nationalistic," "racist," "pure German," and "anti-Semitic," and it is therefore used in its German form on these pages.

[14] Loewenstein, *Conquest of the Past: An Autobiography* (Boston, 1938), 284–85.

was his goal. Bebel and Liebknecht, however, were strongly influenced by the class-conscious dogmas of Marxism and looked to the day when the monarchy would be overthrown, capitalism would collapse, and the proletariat would build a socialist utopia on its ruins. They rejected cooperation with the state and sneered at "reformism." The repressive attitude taken by Bismarck toward both socialist parties after 1872 facilitated their merger in 1875 under the terms of the Gotha Program, which included many of the long-term aims of Marx along with demands for more moderate and immediate political reforms. This combination of revolutionary theory and practical reformism was to mark the history of the SPD until World War I, at the end of which the intransigent Marxist revolutionaries formed the German Communist Party (KPD).

In 1878 Bismarck decided to crush the newly unified Socialist Party. To do so he unjustly accused the Socialists of attempting to assassinate the emperor and engineered anti-Socialist legislation that gave the government authority to take repressive measures against the Party and all organizations connected with it. Bismarck also attempted to wean the workers from socialism by introducing the first comprehensive social security system in the world. He was not able to eliminate the Socialist movement. On the contrary, his repressive acts only increased the workers' alienation from the state and the Socialists' receptivity to the revolutionary dogmas of Marxism. In 1890 Bismarck was dismissed as chancellor, the anti-Socialist laws were permitted to lapse, and the Socialists returned from exile, acknowledging the Marxist Karl Kautsky as their theoretical mentor after the death of Engels in 1895. The SPD grew rapidly until in 1912 it became the largest party in the Reichstag with 110 mandates and almost 35 percent of the votes. By that time, too, it had attracted fully a million members and built a network of 110 daily newspapers, one in virtually every industrial center in Germany, with *Vorwaerts* in Berlin as the central organ.[15]

Notwithstanding the dominance of orthodox Marxism in SPD theory, strong new reformist impulses were provided during the 1890's by Eduard Bernstein. In a series of articles in the theoretical periodical *Die neue Zeit*, Bernstein pointed to the prosperity of Imperial Germany and offered it as evidence that Marx had erred in predicting the sure deterioration of capitalism and corresponding intensification of class hatred. He urged German Socialists to set aside their revolutionary jargon, acknowledge the essentially reformist character of their activities, and ally freely with nonsocialist parties in the interest of passing legislation favorable to the workers. Kautsky, Bebel, and other more orthodox Marxists were quick to attack these ideas. But Bernstein was not alone in holding such convictions, and he and his friends—"revisionists," as they were called—developed their ideas more fully in the independent periodical *Sozialistische Monatshefte*. Revisionism had two powerful allies: the bureaucratization of the Party machinery and the growth in size and power of the Socialist trade unions, both of which served to moderate the temper of the SPD by emphasizing the immediate problems of Party organization, electoral success, and better wages and working conditions for the proletariat. Bebel was a diplomatic leader, and the coalition of orthodox Marxists and revisionists continued to function until after his death in 1913.[16]

German Social Democrats alternately supported the gradual

[15] George Douglas Howard Cole, *A History of Socialist Thought* (New York, 1953), II, 86-271; Vernon L. Lidtke, *The Outlawed Party: Social Democracy in Germany, 1878-1890* (Princeton, 1966); Pinson, *Modern Germany*, 194-218; Carl E. Schorske, *German Social Democracy, 1905-1917: The Development of the Great Schism* (Cambridge, Mass., 1955), 1-16.

[16] Peter Gay, *The Dilemma of Democratic Socialism: Eduard Bernstein's Challenge to Marx* (New York, 1962), 19-252; Schorske, *German Social Democracy*, 16-330.

reformation of the monarchy and its overthrow until 1918. In that year, power was thrust into their inexperienced hands by the collapse of the Imperial Government. Rather than force socialism on a bleeding nation, the SPD leaders chose to place Germany's fate in the hands of a popularly elected Constituent Assembly, in which the Socialists were the largest but by no means the controlling element. German Communists, disgusted over the SPD's failure to establish a left-wing dictatorship and inspired by events in Russia, revolted against the SPD-dominated provisional government in January, 1919. They were joined by the left wing of the Independent Social Democratic Party (USPD), which had seceded from the SPD in 1917 to oppose the latter's support for the German war effort. The bloody suppression of this uprising by the Majority Socialists and the army permanently alienated leftist radicals from the Party and turned part of the proletariat militantly against the Weimar Republic. Social Democrats, however, became the mainstay of the democratic republic, though they failed to win the electoral majority that would have permitted them to build socialism.

The domestic policies of German Socialists during the Weimar era were consistently moderate, aimed at the creation of a free, democratic, and humanitarian society that would provide a smooth transition to socialism. They advocated a foreign policy that was equally responsible, favoring international peace and reconciliation. To implement these goals the Socialists willingly participated in bourgeois-dominated governments and, after 1930, tolerated the Bruening-Hindenburg government to prevent Hitler from coming to power. But their moderate program could not appeal to Germans seeking radical answers to difficult problems, and the SPD declined in membership and popular support, especially from 1920 to 1924 and again after 1929. After Hitler became dictator the Party's activities were sharply restricted. On June 22, 1933, the SPD was outlawed and its members forced to conform, to flee, or to take the struggle underground.[17]

A number of influences with roots deep in the pre-1919 period helped to shape the specific treatment of the Jewish question in German Social Democracy during the Weimar years. One of the most important of these was Karl Marx's treatment of the subject. Marx's father, born a Jew, had become a Christian. Marx himself professed atheism. In his work *Zur Judenfrage* ("On the Jewish Question"), Marx commented in 1843: "What is the foundation of the Jew in our world? Practical necessity, private privilege." Here, too, he stated that "the social emancipation of Jewry is the emancipation of society from Jewry." [18] These terse comments have led some to conclude that Marx was an anti-Semite. Dagobert D. Runes calls him a vitriolic enemy of the Jews.[19] Edmund Silberner[20] goes even further by calling pre–World War I SPD leader Franz Mehring an anti-Semite for having said that Marx was completely free from prejudice against the Jews.[21]

A careful reading of *Zur Judenfrage* in the light of Marxian materialism shows that it is incorrect to identify its author with racial or political anti-Semitism. Marx understood that the preoccupation of the Jews with "money and the bill of exchange" resulted from historical factors. It was the capitalistic system,

---

[17] The best source of information about the SPD during the Weimar period is Carl Landauer, *European Socialism: A History of Ideas and Movements* (Berkeley and Los Angeles, 1959), I, 809–64, 912–1007; II, 1279–321, 1349–400. See also Hunt, *German Social Democracy*, 26–259.

[18] Marx, *Zur Judenfrage* (1843), quoted in Dagobert D. Runes, *A World Without Jews* (New York, 1959), 37.

[19] Runes, *A World Without Jews*, vi; cf. Wanda Kampmann, *Deutsche und Juden: Studien zur Geschichte des deutschen Judentums* (Heidelberg, 1963), 324–32.

[20] Silberner, "German Social Democracy and the Jewish Question Prior to World War One," *Historia Judaica*, XV (April, 1953), 9; Silberner, *Sozialisten zur Judenfrage*, trans. Arthur Mandel (Berlin, 1962), 202–203.

[21] Mehring, *Geschichte der deutschen Sozialdemokratie* (Stuttgart, 1919), I, 206.

said Marx, that made the Jew an outcast, for he argued that the Jew was not the creator of capitalism, but its victim. "The organization of society so as to abolish the preconditions of usury, and hence its possibility, would render the Jew impossible. His religious conviction would dissolve like a stale miasma under the pressure of the real life of the community. On the other hand, should the Jew recognize his materialistic nature as valueless and work for its abolition, he would be working for simple human emancipation and the shedding of his development to date, thus rejecting the highest practical expression of human self-alienation." [22]

Marx's economic-determinist explanation was both naive and open to misinterpretation. His rejection of religious and ethnic differences as factors in Judeo-Christian relations displayed deep misunderstanding of the Jewish question. And his strong language, intended for an educated group of readers, could be misinterpreted when taken out of context. But to call Marx an anti-Semite is to misjudge his thoughts. He may have oversimplified the matter, but he never permitted his analysis to descend to hatred for anything but capitalism. More revealing of Marx's attitude toward anti-Semitism is an outright defense of the persecuted Jews of Jerusalem that he wrote for the New York *Daily Tribune* in 1854.[23]

A second determinant of the attitude of German Socialists toward the Jewish question was their view of religion in general and its relation to the class struggle. The SPD frequently expressed its official position with the sentence: "Religion ist Privatsache" ("Religion is a private affair"). But traditionally the Party had displayed antipathy for organized religion and had encouraged its members to leave the churches. Marx had described religion as the "opiate of the masses," a deliberate fabrication by the ruling classes to make the workers accept

22 Marx, *Zur Judenfrage*, 37.
23 New York *Daily Tribune*, April 15, 1854.

their plight on earth. In 1906 one Social Democrat expressed a fairly common SPD opinion when he wrote: "The free-thinker need not necessarily be a Socialist, but a Socialist must be a freethinker." [24] SPD opposition to organized religion sub-sided somewhat during the Weimar period. Socialists who were also Christians formed small groups that sought to exert leftist influences within the churches;[25] Socialist Roman Catholics in the Rhineland published their own monthly newspaper, *Das Rote Blatt*;[26] a leading Protestant theologian, Paul Tillich, became an active Social Democrat, spreading the message that socialism and Christianity were necessary to each other.[27] But Socialist hostility against religion by no means disappeared dur-ing the period 1919–33. Nor was it confined to Christianity alone; it extended to all faiths, Judaism included.[28] Most Social-ists of Jewish backgrounds were radically assimilationist and would have nothing to do with the Hebrew religion.

Yet another influence shaping German Socialist treatment of the problem posed by anti-Semitism in the period 1919–33 was the large number of Jews in the SPD, many of whom held positions of leadership. Why did many Jews join what had been the chief party of opposition in Imperial Germany? Prob-ably the most important reasons were the relative insecurity and the social inequality of the Jews. Their position in society pre-vented them from regarding social and political conditions with equanimity.[29] Secondly, socialism in Germany was primarily an urban movement, and most Jews lived in cities.[30] Moreover,

[24] H. Salzmann, "Partei und Religion," *Die neue Zeit*, XXIV (1906), 644.

[25] *Vorwaerts*, February 10, March 13, 1919; January 22, 1921.

[26] Nachlass Wilhelm Sollmann, fol. 11, no. 2.

[27] *Vorwaerts*, July 29, 1930.

[28] Jewish sensitivity to Socialist hostility for Judaism was openly expressed by the *Centralverein Zeitung*, which doubted an SPD spokesman's claim that his party was not opposed to religion. "Die S.P.D. nicht Gegner der Reli-gion," *Centralverein Zeitung*, XI (1932), 434, hereinafter cited as *CV Zeitung*.

[29] Landauer, *European Socialism*, I, 282.

[30] Eduard Bernstein, "Jews and German Social Democracy," *Die Tukunft*,

the Socialists welcomed Jews into their ranks, offering them more equality than they could find in other German political parties. It is important to remember, however, that it was primarily members of the Jewish intelligentsia who came to identify themselves with the final goals of socialism; the majority of ordinary Jews appear to have supported bourgeois-democratic parties both before and after 1919 or came to the SPD because it demanded democratization and fought anti-Semitism.[31]

In any case, Jewish intellectuals and political activists joined the SPD in numbers disproportionate to the size of the Jewish population of Germany. The Jews of Germany composed 0.9 percent of the total population in 1925, and by 1933 the figure had fallen to less than 0.8 percent.[32] The number of Jewish leaders in the Party is unknown, but a rough estimate may be obtained from available data. Eduard Bernstein contended in 1921 that roughly 10 percent of the participants in Party conferences were Jews.[33] Of the 153 Socialists elected to the Reichstag in 1928, at least 17 were of Jewish descent (11 percent).[34]

XXVI (March, 1921), 145 ff., quoted in Massing, *Rehearsal for Destruction,* 329.

[31] Toury, *Die politischen Orientierungen,* 212–29; Paucker, "Die juedische Abwehrkampf," *Entscheidungsjahr,* 457.

[32] *Statistisches Jahrbuch fuer das Deutsche Reich* [1928] (Berlin, 1928), XLVII, 18; *ibid.,* [1934] (Berlin, 1934), LIII, 14. These figures refer only to Jews who associated themselves with the Hebrew religion.

[33] Bernstein as quoted in Massing, *Rehearsal for Destruction,* 329.

[34] *Reichstags-Handbuch, IV. Wahlperiode, 1928* (Berlin, 1928). Only three of the seventeen indicated that they were Jewish by religion or background: Hugo Heimann, Ludwig Marum, and Julius Moses. The descent of the others was determined from E. G. Lowenthal, "Die Juden im oeffentlichen Leben," in Mosse and Paucker (eds.), *Entscheidungsjahr,* 51–86; Siegmund Kaznelson (ed.), *Juden im deutschen Kulturbereich* (Rev. ed.; Berlin, 1959), 556–87, 1043–60; F. O. H. Schulz, *Jude und Arbeiter: Ein Abschnitt aus der Tragoedie des deutschen Volkes* (Berlin, 1944), 148–70; *Die Juden in Deutschland* (Munich, 1939), 137–62. The last two sources are products of the Nazi "Institute for the Study of the Jewish Question" and must be used cautiously because of their tendency to turn non-Jews into Jews. Schulz is especially exhaustive.

Ten of the 121 SPD delegates elected to the Reichstag in November, 1932, had Jewish origins, (just over 8 percent).[35] Several Jews held positions of special importance in the Party as editors and journalists, political leaders, and technical experts. Friedrich Stampfer was editor-in-chief of *Vorwaerts*, and he was assisted on its editorial board by Erich Kuttner, Curt Geyer, Victor Schiff, Richard Bernstein, Josef Steiner, and Ludwig Lessen, while Max Hochdorf was the Party organ's respected fine arts critic. Adolf Braun founded and directed the SPD Press Service, served as secretary for the Party Central Committee, and edited *Die Gesellschaft* as well. Josef Bloch, a leading revisionist of pro-Zionist sentiments, was editor of the *Sozialistische Monatshefte*. In addition to contributing regularly to *Vorwaerts*, Alexander Rubinstein edited *Die Buecherwarte*. Rudolf Hilferding, the Party's best mind on financial problems and author of *Das Finanzkapital*, was Finance Minister in the first Stresemann cabinet in 1923 and in the Mueller cabinet from 1928 to 1929. The "uncrowned king of Prussia," Ernst Heilmann, was longtime chairman of the SPD delegation in the Prussian Parliament, while his close friend Paul Hertz was secretary of the delegation. Eduard Bernstein remained active in the Reichstag until 1928 and was regarded as the "grand old man" of German socialism until his death four years later. Paul Hirsch was the first Minister-President of Prussia in 1919–20 and later was elected mayor of Dortmund, while Otto Landsberg was the first postwar Minister of Justice and, subsequently, a prominent member of the Socialist Reichstag delegation. Oscar Cohn, a leader of the SPD left wing in the Reichstag, was an undersecretary of state in the Prussian Ministry of Justice.

---

[35] *Reichstags-Handbuch, VII. Wahlperiode, 1932* (Berlin, 1933). Only one of the three Socialist delegates who in 1928 acknowledged their Jewish descent was reelected in November, 1932, and he (Ludwig Marum) no longer indicated his Jewish background in the official *Reichstag Handbook*. Again, the descent of the remaining nine was verified in the Lowenthal essay and the two Nazi volumes, cited in the previous footnote.

Three talented Jewish leaders of the Socialist women's movement were Wally Zepler, Toni Sender, and Mathilde Wurm. Otto Friedlaender directed the League of Socialist Student Groups, while Kurt Loewenstein led various Socialist teachers' organizations and was the Party's expert on education. The SPD's leading specialist in municipal administration was Hugo Heimann; in matters relating to the national economy it was Fritz Naphtali. Chief legal adviser to *Vorwaerts* was Fritz Juliusberger, and Ernst Fraenkel filled a similar function for the Metal Workers' Union. Siegfried Aufhaeuser headed the Socialist white-collar union, the *Allgemeiner freier Angestelltenbund* (General Free Federation of Salaried Employees), and Berlin professor Emil Lederer was its economic expert. Hugo Sinzheimer advised the Socialist trade unions on tariffs and price policies. This, it must be added, is only an incomplete list of Jews prominent in German Social Democracy.[36]

That Jewish intellectuals chose the Social Democrats in preference to other political parties is shown in a comparison of the numbers of Jews who represented the various parties in the Reichstag. It has been estimated that sixty Jews served at one time or another in the German Reichstag from 1871 to 1930 and that thirty-five of these were Socialists; the rest were Progressives, National Liberals, and Communists.[37] This hardly suggests that there were many anti-Semites in the SPD. Indeed, this evidence of substantial participation of Jews in the leadership of the SPD was sufficient to cause the right-wing Jewhaters of Weimar Germany to castigate Social Democracy as the Party of the Jews.

A final element that shaped SPD attitudes toward anti-Semitism after 1918 was the tradition of opposition to it that

36 Bernstein as quoted in Massing, *Rehearsal for Destruction*, 325–28; Kaznelson, *Juden im deutschen Kulturbereich*, 556–87; Schulz, *Jude und Arbeiter*, 126–70.
37 Sachar, *Modern Jewish History*, 286.

the Party had established in the period 1875–1918. German anti-Semitism first threatened to achieve organized political expression between 1878 and 1885 in the form of Court Chaplain Adolf Stoecker's Christian Social Party. Stoecker was convinced of the need to create a nonsocialist mass movement that would appeal to the workers with a broad program of social reform, including protective labor laws and legislation governing the length of the workday and setting minimum wages. At the same time he sometimes was critical of what he considered Jewish domination over the German economy, a factor to which he tended to trace the abuses of capitalism. Stoecker's followers even more than he turned anti-Semitism into a conspicuous political weapon. In meeting after meeting they lashed out at laissez-faire economic liberalism and at the Jews who, it was said, both originated and managed the system. The effort of the Christian Social Party to merge "German socialism" and anti-Semitism made it an early forerunner of Adolf Hitler's National Socialism.[38]

Although Stoecker received substantial support from the Conservative Party, his Christian Social Movement never succeeded in attracting many workers to anti-Semitism. Stoecker was himself too closely associated with the German government, which in those days of the anti-Socialist law inevitably aroused strong suspicions among the working class. Even more decisive was the forceful opposition of the SPD, which regarded the defeat of Stoecker's movement as a matter of life or death. The Socialists called meetings to denounce the chaplain's agitation and passed resolutions committing German labor to combat discrimination against Jews with all its strength. Social Democrats took over anti-Semitic meetings sponsored by the Christian Social Party and turned them into demonstrations for the outlawed SPD. Stoecker's offers of electoral support and

[38] Pinson, *Modern Germany*, 166–67; Pulzer, *The Rise of Political Anti-Semitism*, 91–97.

assistance against the continuation of the anti-Socialist laws in return for compromises on the subject of social reform were contemptuously rejected. In a militant gesture of resistence the Socialists nominated a Jewish candidate, Paul Singer, in the Berlin municipal election of 1883, and he was elected on the first ballot. In the Reichstag election held the following year the Social Democrats made an exception to their rule of abstaining from voting in districts where they were hopelessly outnumbered in order to support a bourgeois candidate against Stoecker in Berlin. Stoecker lost, and his movement declined rapidly thereafter.[39]

The radical political anti-Semitism of the 1890's, led by Otto Boeckel and Hermann Ahlwardt, differed considerably from that of the Christian Social Party. It was more overtly racist, and it was more "democratic" in that it attacked aristocratic privileges as well as capitalism. Instead of threatening to steal the workers from the SPD, it appeared to appeal primarily to the rural population and to dissatisfied groups within the bourgeoisie. Finally, this new form of political anti-Semitism met with substantially greater electoral success, winning its greatest victory in 1893 when it sent sixteen delegates to the Reichstag.

By the 1890's the SPD also had undergone notable changes. The anti-Socialist laws had been allowed to lapse in 1890, and leading Socialists had returned from exile abroad, now acknowledging a disciple of Marx, Karl Kautsky, as their theoretical leader, second only to the aged Engels. The Party's 1891 Erfurt Program for the first time outlined a specifically Marxist theoretical analysis of political, economic, and social conditions. The SPD's new Marxist complexion also produced an orthodox Marxist response to the animosity toward Jews. Marx had insisted that anti-Semitism was a direct result of capitalism and could not disappear until the collapse of that system. Thus there seemed no reason for German Marxists to single out Judeo-

[39] Massing, *Rehearsal for Destruction*, 170–74.

phobia for special treatment. In fact, the Socialists reasoned that this new wave of anti-Semitism might ultimately work to the advantage of socialism; since it was partly anticapitalist, it would arouse the laziest and those least politically aware to social consciousness. As an 1893 resolution of the SPD Party Congress put it: "The urban and rural petty bourgeois groups which are being aroused by the anti-Semitic leaders against the Jewish capitalists will finally understand that their enemy is not only the Jewish capitalist but the capitalist class itself and that only the success of Socialism can liberate them from their distress." [40]

Franz Mehring, writing in 1891, could thus comment on the struggles between the opponents and defenders of Jews by calling Marx's *Zur Judenfrage* the "secure bulwark of knowledge [from which] one may watch with a calm smile how the furious fighters in both camps storm against and beat one another." [41] Later he added that Marx's essay was "the fundamental inquiry which . . . does not need any comment, because any comment would weaken it." [42] The Socialists, therefore, did not duplicate in the 1890's their head-on confrontation with the political anti-Semitism of the Stoecker movement. Rather, they took a wait-and-see attitude, secure in the conviction that this wave of Judeophobia would disappear, but not before it had awakened new groups of hitherto apathetic Germans to the evils of capitalism. While it was not anti-Semitic, Marxist economic dogma thus inspired an apathetic SPD attitude toward anti-Semitism in the 1890's.

During the last years before the outbreak of World War I, as the wave of political anti-Semitism that had begun in the 1890's slowly faded into the background, German Social Demo-

---

[40] *Ibid.*, 182.
[41] *Ibid.*, 158.
[42] Edmund Silberner, "Was Marx an Anti-Semite?" *Historia Judaica,* XI (April, 1949), 26; Silberner, *Sozialisten zur Judenfrage,* 123.

crats, and especially those who formed and reflected Socialist opinion in the Party press, became increasingly impatient with the disabilities under which the Jews of Germany and Eastern Europe functioned. Orthodox Marxism's apathetic attitude was repeated occasionally by Party theoreticians, but it did not significantly influence the practical, day-to-day responses of Socialists to anti-Semitism in Imperial Germany's last years. Typical of the new SPD attitude toward Judeophobia was continuing concern over the status of Jewish civil rights in all areas of German life. *Vorwaerts* gave unfavorable publicity to trials in which Jews were treated unfairly or disrespectfully; at the same time, it bristled over the judicial judgments that let anti-Semites off lightly. It also criticized laws that discriminated against Jewish aliens in Germany, and it influenced public opinion against the adoption of further discriminatory measures. Socialists were also highly critical of Judeophobia in the government bureaucracy and in German student organizations. Nor did they neglect to denounce the persecution of Jews in the armed forces or their exclusion from the officers' corps.[43]

The SPD attributed the persistence of anti-Semitism in part to the toleration and encouragement given it by German officialdom. Without such assistance the Socialists were certain that Judeophobia would soon disappear, for they noted with satisfaction that political anti-Semitism was slowly dying out, and they were confident it would eventually vanish altogether. They believed, however, that some of what remained had penetrated other political parties; the Catholic Center Party came in for special SPD condemnation for harboring anti-Semitism. On the other hand, a sure way to arouse Socialist ire was to accuse the SPD itself of sheltering Jew-haters.

---

[43] For details of the SPD's sensitivity to infringements upon Jewish civil rights during this period, consult my "German Social Democracy and the Problem of Anti-Semitism, 1906–1914" (M.A. thesis, Tulane University, 1964).

In addition to its forceful opposition to anti-Semitism in Imperial Germany's last years, the SPD devoted much sympathetic attention to the fate of millions of luckless Jews in the Russian Empire and Rumania. The Social Democrats pictured them as hideously persecuted minorities, the targets of repeated pogroms sponsored by governments that needed the Jews as scapegoats for myriad problems and failures. There was considerable passionate discussion inside the SPD over the means appropriate to the emancipation of these unfortunates. Some Socialists favored the program of the General League of Jewish Workers, which advocated cultural autonomy for Eastern European Jews as a prelude to eventual assimilation. Others, principally a group of revisionists in the circle of the *Sozialistische Monatshefte*, actively espoused Zionism. Orthodox Marxists, on the other hand, had no use for Zionism and urged the Jews of Eastern Europe to participate actively in the class struggle to work for the day of general socialist emancipation. Each group displayed equal eagerness to achieve civil rights for Eastern European Jews, but each propounded a solution most nearly in accord with its own socialist *Weltanschauung*.[44]

While German Socialists were outspoken advocates of equal rights for Jews during the last years before World War I, it is possible to find evidence of a very few, isolated instances of anti-Semitism in the SPD. Writing of this period, Gustav Noske noted in 1947 that in the SPD "anti-Semitism was very rarely expressed openly, although it was not entirely missing 'under the rug.' " He offered only one concrete example—that of Richard Fischer, who was in the prewar years a Socialist Reichstag delegate, as well as managing director of *Vorwaerts* and the Socialist printing house "Paul Singer and Company."[45] Ac-

[44] One may take exception to Edmund Silberner's contention that Socialist opposition to Zionism represented "contempt for Jewry as a corporate body." Silberner, "German Social Democracy and the Jewish Question," 40–41; Silberner, *Sozialisten zur Judenfrage*, 213.

[45] *Reichstags-Handbuch, 13. Legislaturperiode* (Berlin, 1912), 245.

cording to Noske, Fischer "gave frequent, drastic expression to his anti-Semitic sentiments against many party members." [46] It is perhaps significant that this was the same Richard Fischer who in 1911 was accused by the *Berliner Tageblatt* of having uttered an anti-Semitic statement during a meeting of the Reichstag Budget Commission.[47] This suggestive evidence is hardly enough to convict Fischer of Judeophobia, and his editorship of *Vorwaerts* did not prevent the central organ of the SPD from opposing anti-Semitism. But, as is noted below, *Vorwaerts* under Fischer's leadership also was critical of bourgeois Jews.

Evidence linking a prominent Social Democratic leader with anti-Semitic opinions before 1918 is found only in the case of Dr. Eduard David, the SPD's revisionist expert on agrarian matters, who after 1903 was a member of the Reichstag and during the war was a leader of those Socialists who believed the German war effort was basically defensive and ought to be given at least limited Socialist support. David's *Kriegstagesbuch* contains unflattering comments about some of the Jews among his Party colleagues. In his entry for July 4–11, 1915, he noted that Karl Kautsky, Anton Hofrichter, and Gustav Eckstein had attacked his new book, *Die Sozialdemokratie im Weltkriege*, and he designated these critics "loud Austrian Jews." [48]

[46] Noske, *Erlebtes aus Aufstieg und Niedergang einer Demokratie* (Offenbach, 1947), 148.

[47] See *Vorwaerts*, February 26, 1911. The Socialist organ vehemently denied the charge. Dr. Hans Hirschfeld, who knew Fischer and worked with his son on the *Fraenkische Tagespost* immediately after the war, believes Fischer could have made statements that sounded anti-Semitic without meaning them to seem so; not only was Fischer a prickly personality, but he was frequently exasperated over the lack of business sense displayed by his editorial staff and may have hurled ironic "anti-Jewish" comments at them. Interview with Dr. Hans Hirschfeld, February 16, 1967. Cf. Emil Unger-Winkelried, *Von Bebel zu Hitler: Vom Zukunfts-Staat zum Dritten Reich. Aus dem Leben eines sozialdemokratischen Arbeiters* (Berlin, 1934), 95.

[48] Erich Matthias and Susanne Miller (eds.), *Das Kriegstagesbuch des Reichstagsabgeordneten Eduard David, 1914 bis 1918* (Duesseldorf, 1966), 136. Kautsky, of course, was a non-Jew.

On March 16 of the following year, he commented that his Reichstag colleague Georg Gradnauer was the last Jew in whom he still had confidence.[49] A few months later, when Socialist Oscar Cohn protested discrimination against Jews in the armed services, David observed impatiently: "The Jews Cohn, Haase, and Davidsohn once again radically see to the business of the anti-Semites."[50] Immediately after the war David was for a time president of the Weimar National Assembly and held ministerial posts in the Scheidemann, Bauer, and Mueller cabinets. He also represented Mainz in the Reichstag until his death in 1930. There is, however, no evidence that he openly expressed his anti-Semitic views at any time before or after 1918.[51]

Other men who held responsible positions in the SPD before 1918—including Emil Kloth, August Winnig, and Emil Unger-Winkelried—later broke with the Party and exhibited clearly anti-Semitic opinions. It is impossible to determine whether such opinions were the products of conditions during and after the war or whether they found expression before 1918, but the leaders and organs speaking for the Party consistently opposed and discouraged anti-Semitism.

While a few individual Social Democrats may have kept Socialist anti-Semitism alive "under the rug" before 1918, large numbers of SPD members tended to identify Jews with capitalism. Karl Kautsky explained: "The great mass of the Jews constituted for two thousand years an exclusive, hereditary caste of urban merchants, financiers, intellectuals, including some artisans, and developed, by practice and accumulation

---

[49] *Ibid.*, 165.

[50] *Ibid.*, 181. The entry is for June 6, 1916. Hugo Haase and Georg Davidsohn had not joined Cohn in the debate.

[51] A much less important pre-Weimar Socialist, one R. Cronheim, who was an editor of the *Berliner Volksblatt* in 1884, won the animosity of August Bebel by privately admitting to anti-Semitic opinions. Lidtke, *The Outlawed Party*, 148.

from generation to generation, more and more of the traits peculiar to all these strata, as opposed to the peasant masses of the rest of the population." [52] The close identification of Jews with capitalism sometimes made them a target for the Socialists in their anticapitalist agitation. The Social Democrats identified Jewish capitalists as anti-Semitic allies of the Tsarist government who provided it with loans and prevented Jewish workers from organizing. Socialists were similarly critical of Jews who supported the liberal-democratic Progressive Party in Germany, especially when it formed anti-Socialist electoral alliances with allegedly anti-Semitic candidates. They also castigated wealthy German Jews who refused to lend assistance to indigent Eastern European refugees among their coreligionists or who worked closely with their anti-Jewish German government for personal gain.

These SPD attacks against Jewish capitalists, while by no means typical of the Party's attitude toward anti-Semitism, kept alive among the workers the stereotype of Jews as grasping capitalists who were interested only in personal gain. In 1957 Jewish SPD leader Friedrich Stampfer wrote that before 1918 even "many Jewish Social Democrats acknowledged a certain relative justification in anti-Semitism." [53] Stampfer reflected the assumption that Jews, as a minority deprived of full social equality, had a special obligation to support the SPD, the party of all the oppressed. The persistence of most ordinary Jewish voters in supporting bourgeois political parties can only have intensified Socialist annoyance.[54]

Because they were unwilling to spare Jewish capitalists from

---

[52] Kautsky, *Rasse und Judentum* (Rev. ed.; Stuttgart, 1921), 67.
[53] Stampfer, *Erfahrungen und Erkenntnisse: Aufzeichnungen aus meinem Leben* (Cologne, 1957), 86.
[54] Ernest Hamburger, *Juden im oeffentlichen Leben Deutschlands: Regierungsmitglieder, Beamte und Parlamentarier in der monarchischen Zeit 1848–1918* (Tuebingen, 1968), 129–32, 145–48; Toury, *Politischen Orientierungen der Juden*, 212–29.

their general condemnation and, indeed, explicitly criticized Jewish capitalists, German Socialists occasionally contributed to anti-Semitism in Germany. But throughout the period before World War I, the overwhelming preponderance of Socialist comment on the Jewish question in Germany was devoted to the unambiguous defense of Jewish rights and the condemnation of anti-Semitism in all levels of public life. These actions reflected the opinions of SPD leaders and also educated the German workers against anti-Semitism.

Chapter II

Socialist Explanations and Refutations
of Anti-Semitism
1918-1928

The year 1918 brought Germany military defeat and revolution. These in turn helped to produce anti-Semitism of greater violence than any experienced in Germany since the Middle Ages, as men sought to assign blame for disasters on specific groups of citizens. Prewar Social Democratic predictions of the extinction of political anti-Semitism were belied as the DNVP and a rash of smaller *voelkisch* movements openly embraced and circulated strongly anti-Jewish opinions. Although this early postwar agitation reached its greatest intensity from the revolution through the Kapp putsch and again during the inflationary crisis of 1923, it remained a serious irritant throughout the period 1918–28. The SPD was forced to realize that occasional denunciations of discrimination against Jews would no longer suffice at a time when pogroms after the Russian model threatened to add to Germany's postwar chaos.

The majority of German Social Democrats interpreted this post-1918 intensification of Judeophobia as a reactionary tool to divert public attention from the failures of the capitalist economy and from defeat on the battlefield, and the critical situation these engendered. Anti-Semitism was first employed in this sense by the army in 1918 to "explain" Germany's military collapse, said the Socialists,[1] and then it was embraced by all of

[1] *Vorwaerts*, April 24, 1923.

the parties of the right until it became a "typical, representative pattern in the political struggle." [2] Above all, the Social Democrats believed that political reaction used the Jews in general and Jewish capitalists in particular as collective scapegoats for the sins of all capitalists. *Vorwaerts* satirized these efforts in 1923: "Stinnes buys and buys; perhaps before long all of Germany will belong to him. 'Certainly not Stinnes! The Jews!' And with that Stinnes disappears from the scene; he does not exist, except in the imagination of the Jews and their associates." [3] A year later a Party pamphlet alerted the workers: "The proletariat recognizes in religious, economic, political, and racial anti-Semitism a well calculated Fascist maneuver to divert attention from their criminal hatred for the workers to a minority of the German people, the one percent of Jews, and to hold this minority responsible for all the misery and distress of our day. Therefore working people who are politically aware and mature reject Jew-hate in all its forms." [4]

Most German Social Democrats also regarded postwar anti-Semitic agitation as part of a plot engineered by political reactionaries for the purpose of mobilizing the masses against the SPD and the fledgling republic it supported. In 1919 Socialist Karl Brammer warned that the old powers displaced by the revolution were planning to regain their lost privileges by using anti-Semitic propaganda to create a "pogrom mood, . . . which we must combat under all circumstances." [5] A year later the readers of *Vorwaerts* were advised that this agitation against the Jews was "part of a great plan to lead the Republic to col-

---

[2] Conrad Schmidt, "Ein neues Schlagwort," *Sozialistische Monatshefte*, XXIX (1923), 648.

[3] *Vorwaerts*, August 5, 1923.

[4] *Was muss das schaffende Volk vom politischen, wirschaftlichen, religioesen Juden— und Rassenhass des reaktionaeren Faschismus wissen? Fuer Redner und Funktionaere herausgegeben von der Sozialdemokratischen Partei Deutschlands, Ortsverein Hannover* (Hanover, [1924]), 8.

[5] Brammer, *Das Gesicht der Reaktion 1918–1919* (Berlin, 1919), 26–27.

lapse and clear the way for an armed dictatorship." [6] At that time, too, the Social Democrats accused the DNVP and the DVP of employing Judeophobia as a means of ruining the two parties with which most German Jews had associated themselves, the SPD and the DDP. Later Hermann Mueller agreed that the purpose of this agitation was "to mobilize the lowest instincts of the patriotic mob against the Social Democratic and Democratic Parties." [7] The Socialists accused their right-wing opponents of using anti-Jewish appeals to take advantage of the millions of politically inexperienced Germans who were utterly unschooled in social problems; as one of their anti-Nazi pamphlets put it in 1922, anti-Semitism was for the Hitlerites "the most effective means of political agitation since it can appeal most quickly to the masses of unenlightened people." [8] An SPD appeal to women voters in the 1921 Prussian Landtag election stated the case most bluntly: "The dark powers of reaction depend upon confused, unthinking women and, to put it plainly, gamble specifically on their stupidity. Therefore, comrades, think about this matter constantly and remember: whoever instigates Jew-baiting works hand in hand with the counter-revolution." [9]

As the Socialists analyzed it, postwar anti-Semitism in Germany was not primarily aimed at the Jews at all—they were merely convenient scapegoats. Its real objective was the destruction of the SPD and the Weimar Republic. According to the brilliant young Socialist journalist Carlo Mierendorff: "The racially pure, black-white-red cliche-mongers attack 'the Jews' but they mean 'the republicans.' They know very well that the 'Jews' who presently occupy seats of authority in the nation

[6] *Vorwaerts*, May 19, 1920.

[7] Hermann Mueller-Franken, *Die November Revolution: Errinerungen* (Rev. ed.; Berlin, 1931), 108; *Vorwaerts*, January 7, 1920.

[8] NSDAP Hauptarchiv, fol. 1894.

[9] Erna Buesing, "Duerfen wir Antisemiten sein?" *Die Waehlerin*, February 6, 1921, p. 3.

and the provinces are not the real power-factors in the German Republic, but the millions of organized workers, employees, and civil servants. The 'Aryan' struggle against Jewry is nothing other than a veiled struggle for the empire and the monarchy." [10]

The Social Democrats found nothing new in this exploitation of anti-Semitism by political reactionaries. They equated it with the entire history of Judeophobia in modern times. The artisans of the mid-nineteenth century and the petite bourgeoisie of more recent times had been injured by the capitalist system but had stupidly allowed themselves to be led against the Jews rather than against the real source of their troubles. Now these same groups were letting the "wire-pullers of anti-Semitism," whose "real targets" were "democracy and Socialism," mislead them in just the same way.[11] The Social Democrats also observed that the Jews traditionally had been regarded as the bearers of new and "subversive" ideas. Such slurs had been hurled at the proponents of liberal principles in 1848, and later Adolf Stoecker had pictured the Jews as the originators and principal supporters of materialistic Social Democracy. After 1918 the reactionaries continued to rail against the Jews, but this time they meant the republic.

The Social Democrats who subscribed to this "plot theory" of anti-Semitism concluded that a concerted attack against anti-Semitism was less a moral duty than a simple matter of self-defense. Not only did they believe that they themselves, rather than the Jews, were the real, albeit indirect, objects of organized Jew-hate, but they were extremely reluctant to furnish the anti-Semites with material that could have been used to confirm right-wing charges that the SPD was a "servant of the Jews." Thus they repeatedly protested that the Party fought

[10] Mierendorff, *Arisches Kaisertum oder Judenrepublik?* (Berlin, n.d.), 14. Mierendorff was non-Jewish.
[11] *Antisemitismus und Sozialdemokratie* (n.p., [1920]), 14, 15.

anti-Semitism not because it appeared to be directed at the Jews but rather because it was a tool of the reactionaries.[12] A 1920 SPD pamphlet explained the Party's position: "It fights against anti-Semitism not in order to shelter the Jews, in whose ranks it *numbers as many enemies as friends*, but rather in order to protect the German people from political and social reversion into long dead medieval conditions." [13] Similarly, SPD editor and Reichstag leader Wilhelm Sollmann, addressing a Berlin Jewish group in 1927, was careful to indicate that he warred against Judeophobia not out of special affection for Jews but out of "hatred for the vulgar ideology of anti-Semitism, which destroys reason." [14] Such professions did not, however, prevent German Socialists from repeatedly defending Jews.

The SPD's "plot theory" of anti-Semitism corresponded closely to the traditional Party views formulated during the Stoecker episode forty years before, and it was not easily set aside. However, a few Social Democrats challenged it with an interpretation that placed emphasis on the psychological crisis of the bourgeoisie in a time of economic instability. According to this explanation, large portions of the middle class were being ground between the two millstones of big business and the proletariat. Finding themselves the victims of intolerable economic pressures, the bourgeoisie looked around for devils and fixed upon the Jews. It was immaterial that no convincing evidence against the Jews was to be had; it was a purely irrational reaction. Rather than assuming that the well-financed activities of a small group of political reactionaries were responsible for the efflorescence of anti-Jewish feeling, this psychological analysis proposed that the right-wing parties simply were taking advantage of a verdict the bourgeoisie had already reached for itself.

Such was the conclusion reached in 1919 by Fritz Spiegel-

---

[12] *Was muss das schaffende Volk*, 8.
[13] *Antisemitismus und Sozialdemokratie*, 18. Emphasis in the original.
[14] *Vorwaerts*, January 28, 1927. Sollmann was non-Jewish.

berg, who applied his analysis specifically to farmers and the petty bourgeoisie.[15] A year later Jewish Social Democrat Ernst Hamburger agreed; noting that the newly proletarianized elements of the middle classes were psychologically unequipped to embrace Social Democratic thinking, he concluded that anti-Semitism served them as a kind of pseudosocialism in which the Jewish capitalists replaced the capitalist system as the cause of their trouble. Hamburger suggested that Jewish support for Germany's new government and the postwar influx of job-seeking intellectuals into the SPD confirmed bourgeois suspicions that Jews were at root responsible for their personal tragedies. In view of the irrational basis of anti-Semitism, said Hamburger, it was senseless to believe that Jew-baiting was the work of radical agitators alone, requiring nothing more than counteragitation. However, he offered no better solution of his own.[16] In 1924 Ernst von Aster pictured anti-Semites as the willing prisoners of a "devil theory" of history that was shielded by an impregnable complex of defense mechanisms:

> Anti-Semitism is the indispensable counterpart of our hero-worship. Whoever believes in the dear God—who as a *deus ex machina* will intervene in the fifth act and with one blow set everything right and splended—also believes in the devil, and in particular: whoever believes in God in human form believes also in the devil in human form. . . . God and devil, German (or, if you prefer, Aryan) and Jew. . . . That Germany, which was and can be proud of the thoroughness of its scientific work, is the country in which racial theories have found their most credulous adherents, even in the ranks of the supposedly cultivated, is a sign of a state of mind that has lost sight of reality and that will cling to its illusions at any price.[17]

15 *Ibid.*, August 15, 1919.
16 Hamburger, "Antisemitismus und Sozialdemokratie," *Sozialistische Monatshefte*, XXVI (1920), 393–401.
17 Aster, "Nationale Romantik," *Die Gesellschaft*, I (1924), 237, 238.

Although differing in their views of the origins and nature of the postwar wave of anti-Semitism, German Social Democrats were generally agreed by 1920 that Judeophobia had become a formidable weapon in the right-wing arsenal and were united in the conviction that anti-Jewish propaganda demanded forceful and consistent counteraction from the SPD. Most regarded it as basically a matter of self-defense. "First the Jews will lose equal rights, then the women, then the workers, then the Socialists." [18] For some, this obligation took on connotations of national pride. "*Anti-Semitism is a foreign body in the true German spirit and blood.* If we do not reject it, then Germany will debase itself to the level of one of the backward states of the East." [19] A very few other Social Democrats were willing to join Bavarian SPD leader Erhard Auer in acknowledging a purely moral obligation to fight such prejudice. "If we do not eliminate feelings of hatred and revenge, how shall we prepare the soil in which humanity, charity, decency, and morality can grow?" he asked a Munich SPD rally in 1920. He went on to call "all men of good will to hard and passionate work" against anti-Semitism. "We want to work together in ardent love for mankind; in spite of all barriers and all disturbances we will build a home in which every citizen with a sense of social solidarity can feel at home. . . . we want to transform racial consciousness into national solidarity and exhalt whatever will set the basis for a sound world citizenship." [20]

Whatever their reasons, German Socialists almost without exception supported Fritz Spiegelberg's militant 1919 verdict on anti-Semitism: "Every decent person must be shocked by these impulses. Our greatest wish is that the authors of these

[18] Buesing, "Duerfen wir Antisemiten sein?," 3.

[19] *Antisemitismus und Sozialdemokratie*, 17. Emphasis in the original.

[20] Auer, *Sozialdemokratie und Antisemitismus. Rede des Abgeordneten E. Auer, ehemaliger Minister des Innern, am 15. Dezember, 1920 im grossen Saale des Muenchener Kindl-Kellers* (Munich, n.d.), 14, 15. Auer was non-Jewish.

hideous crimes be brought to justice." [21] Indeed, the doctrin-
aire Marxist contention that only complete socialization could
effectively counteract Judeophobia rarely appeared during the
postwar decade. In 1920 Bruno Sommer adjudged the Jewish
question as essentially "a question of property mixed up with
religion"; with the disappearance of property in the means of
production only religion would be left, he wrote, and that, too,
would soon die away, taking the remnants of anti-Semitism
with it.[22] But most German Socialists no longer regarded Judeophobia as an immature form of anticapitalist revolt that would
ultimately assist the SPD by radicalizing the petite bourgeoisie.
Instead they perceived in it a clear and present danger to the
lives of their party and the state. Typical of their opinions was
the advice offered in 1922 by Philipp Scheidemann on the front
page of *Vorwaerts*: "The enemy is on the right and his weapons
are anti-Semitism, slander, the revolver, and prussic acid. . . .
Now this shameless agitation against particular persons or
races must be brought to an end. The anti-Semitic venom that
has been squirted for years by unprincipled youths can be
rendered harmless only by means of an energetic educational
campaign." [23]

Increased SPD interest in the Jewish problem in the postwar
years was reflected, among other ways, in the frequency with
which items dealing with anti-Semitism or Jewish matters appeared in *Vorwaerts*. From 1919 to 1928 a total of 605 such
news items appeared on its pages, or roughly 1 item for every
10½ issues of the newspaper. In contrast, during the years 1906
to 1914, only 114 news items that touched directly on Jews or
Judeophobia had appeared in the SPD central organ, or about
1 item for every 24 issues.[24] The SPD's principal theoretical

---

[21] *Vorwaerts*, August 15, 1919.
[22] Sommer, "Religioese Taeuschungen," *Die neue Zeit*, XXXIX (1920), 74.
[23] *Vorwaerts*, July 12, 1922.
[24] Throughout the Weimar period *Vorwaerts* appeared twice daily—morning and evening—Tuesday through Saturday, and once each on Sunday and

journal *Die neue Zeit* and its post-1923 successor *Die Gesell-schaft* together presented 23 articles partially or wholly devoted to the Jewish question between 1919 and 1928; during the same period the independent, right-wing Socialist journal *Sozialistische Monatshefte* published 41 such articles.[25] In addition, those years produced large numbers of SPD speeches, pamphlets, and brochures aimed at the same target.

Social Democrats of Jewish backgrounds accounted for a disproportionate share of SPD comment on anti-Semitism. Figures must necessarily be rough, but it is likely that they were responsible for at least a quarter of the total. Two Jewish Socialists, Ernst Hamburger and Eduard Bernstein, were among the critics of Judeophobia, and the editorial staff of *Vorwaerts* —on the pages of which most denunciations of anti-Semitism were unsigned—included many journalists of Jewish descent.[26] Among non-Jewish Socialists who were outspoken opponents of anti-Semitism were Philipp Scheidemann, Artur Crispien, and Erhard Auer.

In implementing their stated determination to combat anti-Semitism, a program of education to inoculate Germans against anti-Jewish notions seemed especially meritorious to the Socialists. Imbued with faith in man's ability and desire to find rational solutions to his problems, and certain that their own *Weltanschauung* provided a completely logical analysis of society, they placed much emphasis on purely intellectual arguments against Judeophobia. Striking at the heart of anti-Semitic ideology, Socialist spokesmen employed forceful appeals to reason to refute the contention that Jews as a race were differ-

---

Monday. During the prewar years it had appeared daily, except Mondays. Beginning in 1928 the evening edition of the SPD central organ was named *Der Abend*.

[25] The greater number of articles in the *Sozialistische Monatshefte* is explained by the greater interest taken by the journal in Zionism and by its publication of many short articles having essentially the character of news reports.

[26] See Chap. 1, pages 18–19.

ent from and inferior to the "Aryan" race. The most prominent Socialist intellectual, Karl Kautsky, had rejected the idea that race had anything to do with Jewish "racial characteristics" in his 1914 *Rasse und Judentum* (*Race and Jewry*), which he revised for a second edition in 1921. Closely following the orthodox Marxist line, Kautsky argued that Jews possessed such "unique" characteristics as cliquishness and a propensity to choose capitalistic occupations because of historical influences over which they had had little control during their nearly two thousand years in Germany. He felt that the most important of these influences, persecution at the hands of non-Jews, would expire upon the victory of socialism and thus permit the Jews to "dissolve, unite with their environment, and disappear." [27] Other Social Democrats agreed, accepting a purely environmental explanation for what were regarded as Jewish characteristics, while insisting that these did not make for fundamental differences between Jews and gentiles.[28] In 1923 *Vorwaerts* called attention to two studies of Jewish and non-Jewish school children; both studies showed that there were no appreciable dissimilarities in the children's abilities.[29] Later a Socialist pamphlet affirmed that differences in morals and intelligence levels between the various races were not as great as those between individuals within the same race.[30]

Above all, the Socialists made it clear that they did not accept the existence of a superior "Aryan" or "Nordic" race. They accused those who did of peddling "arbitrary, fantastic inventions." [31] Among those who were so criticized was Oswald

[27] Kautsky, *Rasse und Judentum*, 71–73.
[28] Alfred Beyer, review of Hans Fehlinger, *Rassenhygiene: Beitraege zur Entartungsfrage*, in *Die neue Zeit*, XXXVIII (1920), 590–91.
[29] *Vorwaerts*, March 15, 1923.
[30] *Was muss das schaffende Volk*, 15.
[31] Hans Heinrich, "Die Bedeutung des Unbewussten in historischen Materialismus," *Die Gesellschaft*, IV (1927), 352. See also Max Hodann, review of Fritz Kern, *Stammbaum und Artbild der Deutschen und ihrer Verwandten*, in *Sozialistische Monatshefte*, XXXIV (1928), 531; Max Hodann, review of

Spengler.[32] Also Hans F. K. Guenther, high priest of "scientific" racism and author of the widely read *Rassenkunde des deutschen Volkes* (*Ethnology of the German People*) conceded that Germans were by and large the products of racial interbreeding but insisted that a policy of careful selective breeding could maximize the "Nordic" component while minimizing less desirable elements. He believed the "Nordic" race possessed easily discernible physical characteristics. In 1927 Guenther drew the wrath of Socialist Hugo Iltis, who observed that, in view of the racist's own admission that at least ten races had been amalgamating in Germany for thousands of years, distinct racial traits could not possibly have persisted. Insisting that physical and mental characteristics are determined by geography, economy, culture, and education, Iltis concluded that Guenther had succumbed to "racial fantasies" for which the Socialist position was a healthy antidote: "If we love our race and our people, surely we must not therefore hate and despise others. We have and demand respect for all who bear the countenance of man. The day will come when the race-hatred and racial arrogance of our day will be regarded in the same way we now regard witchcraft and cannibalism—the lamentable remains of bygone barbarism." [33] Left-wing poet Arno Holz stated the Socialist case much more lightly:

> Don't let yourself be duped by hypocrites
> Who babble in dens of cunning;
> I know Christians who are Jews,

Walter Scheidt, *Rassenunterschiede des Blutes*, in *Sozialistische Monatshefte*, XXXIV (1928).

[32] Siegfried Marck, "Oswald Spenglers zweiter Band," *Die neue Zeit*, XL (1922), 437–43; Karl Schroeder, "Geschichtsmetaphysik: Ein Nachwort zu Oswald Spenglers 'Untergang des Abendlandes,' " *Die Gesellschaft*, III (1926), 542.

[33] Iltis, "Rassenwissenschaft und Rassenwahn," *Die Gesellschaft*, IV (1927), 113–14. Iltis, an Austrian Social Democrat, frequently drew praise from German Socialists for his attacks on racism. See Chap. 5, pages 136–38.

> I know Jews who are Christians.
> Whether their nose is straight or bent,
> The main thing is—they're individuals! [34]

The Socialists were equally unwilling to believe that men of supposedly superior race could be identified by their physical appearance. Speaking before a huge SPD rally against anti-Semitism in Munich on December 15, 1920, Erhard Auer noted that by *voelkisch* standards Kant, Goethe, Beethoven, Luther, and Schiller could not qualify as superior Germans because they did not fit the mold. He took special pleasure in adding Bavaria's dictatorial, far-right Premier Gustav von Kahr to the list of rejects.[35] Two years later a certain Professor Maurenbrecher also attacked *voelkisch* standards when he spoke to a smaller SPD meeting in Munich about the absurdity of assuming the persistence of racial purity in South Germany; that region, he said, had been inhabited by fifteen or twenty ethnic groups since before the Roman occupation and had been invaded repeatedly by foreign armies.[36] Taking a somewhat different approach, *Vorwaerts* printed an article by an anonymous Jew who claimed to have blond hair and who described recent conversations he had had with three anti-Semites who did not know he was a Jew. The first, under close questioning, confessed in a whisper that she was of Polish descent; the second, a young student wearing a swastika, was unaware that his great-grandfather had been a French soldier in the army of Napoleon I; the

---

[34] *Vorwaerts*, August 5, 1927. It will be noted that much has been lost in translation:

> Von Schwaetzern aus verschmitzten Buden
> Lass dich nicht heuchlings ueberlisten;
> Ich kenne Christen, das sind Juden,
> Ich kenne Juden, die sind Christen.
> Ob Nase grade oder krumm,
> Hauptsache — Individibum!

[35] Auer, *Sozialdemokratie und Antisemitismus*, 7.
[36] NSDAP Hauptarchiv, fol. 1898, no. 86.

third, the most outspoken of the lot, had recently married a part-Japanese woman.[37]

The Social Democrats were as ready to applaud and publicize the findings of scientists they regarded as objective on racial matters as they were to castigate those they considered biased. They made use of the book *Voelker, Rassen, Sprachen* (*Peoples, Races, and Languages*) by Felix von Luschan, the director of Berlin's Anthropological Museum, in which it was concluded that all of humanity belongs to a single race, that differences between ethnic groups are environmentally determined, and that while all ethnic groups have inferior individuals there is no "inferior race" as such.[38] Erhard Auer, in the speech alluded to above, referred his audience to *Das Rassenproblem* (*The Racial Problem*) by Ignaz Zollschan, whose studies of student groups had refuted racist claims about "Nordic" and Jewish physical and mental qualities.[39] Carlo Mierendorff cited the findings of von Luschan, R. Hartmann, and Max Mueller in support of his contention that an "Aryan" race does not exist and that the term properly refers only to a family of languages.[40]

The Socialists also turned their educational campaign against the doubts repeatedly cast on the patriotism of German Jews. A favorite right-wing argument was that large numbers of Jews had avoided military duty during the war and that, when forced to serve, they either had displayed consistent cowardice or simply had allowed themselves to be captured. As Hermann Mueller observed, "the only thing missing was the accusation that the Jews who fell in the World War had only played dead."[41] The Socialists, on the contrary, noted that many Jews had volunteered for military service and insisted that German

37 *Vorwaerts*, July 24, 1922.
38 *Ibid.*, February 8, 1923; *Was muss das schaffende Volk*, 15.
39 Auer, *Sozialdemokratie und Antisemitismus*, 7.
40 Mierendorff, *Arisches Kaisertum oder Judenrepublik?* 9.
41 Mueller-Franken, *Die November Revolution*, 108.

Jews in general had served their country willingly and faithfully in spite of the "martyrdom" they experienced in the Imperial Army, where they were "despised, teased, and abused, and every superior officer took pains to convince them of the inferiority of their persons." *Vorwaerts* indignantly disputed the figures of certain anti-Jewish "home-front heroes" which showed that only 14 percent of the Jews had served their country. It indicated that more than 20 percent of German Jews had seen military service during the war, of whom 21 percent had volunteered and 80 percent had fought in the front lines. *Vorwaerts* pointed out that the Iron Cross, first-class, had been awarded to 896 Jewish soldiers, and that 2,000 Jews had served as officers.[42]

An SPD pamphlet called attention to the twelve thousand Jews who had given their lives during the war. It admitted that this amounted to only 1.5 percent of the total Jewish population in Germany as opposed to an overall loss of 2 percent of the entire population, but the pamphlet made a strong case for attributing the disparity to historical and environmental influences. Since most German Jews emanated from the urban bourgeoisie, they were, on the average, better educated and hence better equipped to occupy noncombatant positions, while at the same time they were less likely to be physically fit than other recruits. Consequently, it was argued, a somewhat greater percentage of Jews was assigned to positions behind the front lines; "to insult the Jewish war-dead because of this statistically tiny difference could be accomplished only by the brutality and vileness of a depraved anti-Semitism." [43] Later another SPD brochure cited figures showing substantial Jewish participation in the wartime armed forces and quoted General

[42] *Vorwaerts*, August 15, 1919; January 3, 1920.
[43] *Antisemitismus und Sozialdemokratie*, 6. See also *Vorwaerts*, June 20, 1922; *Der Abend*, August 14, 1928.

Berthold von Deimling's testimony that the Jews in his command had fought as bravely as other Germans.[44]

In 1924 the Social Democrats delightedly told the story of Munich Judeophobe Dietrich Eckart, who had offered a thousand marks to any Jewish family that could prove it had furnished three sons to the fighting front for a period of three weeks, only to have Rabbi Freund of Hanover submit evidence for more than fifty such families; Eckhart paid up only after being sued. They also noted that among the soldiers from Bremen's Jewish community alone, five had won the Iron Cross, first class.[45] Ludwig Frank, Jewish SPD leader who had died as a volunteer in the early weeks of the war, was frequently recalled in emotive language as a symbol of both Jewish and Socialist patriotism.[46] *Vorwaerts* strongly protested when Minister of the Interior Karl Jarres balked at giving permission for the Jewish veterans of Berlin to hold memorial services for their fallen comrades in a Jewish cemetery on the tenth anniversary of the outbreak of the war. It raged that in the ten years since 1914 Germany was "fortunate to have arrived in Martin Luther's era. Long live progress and German 'culture.' " When an official change of mind permitted the services to take place after all, they included an honor guard from the *Reichsbanner*.[47]

The SPD also reacted to allegations that Jews had instigated the World War and then had extracted enormous profits from it. The Socialists submitted that Jews could not possibly have started the war, because "there was not one single Jew in the entire General Staff, the diplomatic corps, or any of the high decision making bodies; all of these areas were scrupulously

[44] *Was muss das schaffende Volk*, 4–5.
[45] *Ibid.*
[46] See especially Wally Zepler, "Sozialistische Bewegung," *Sozialistische Monatshefte*, XXX (1924), 715; Noske, *Erlebtes aus Aufstieg und Niedergang*, 44.
[47] *Vorwaerts*, July 31, 1924; August 4, 1924. For its part, the *Reichsbanner* also agitated against charges of Jewish shirking in the war. See *Das Reichsbanner*, July 15, 1924. NSDAP Hauptarchiv, fol. 1907.

kept racially pure, 'Aryan,' German *voelkisch*, and were watched anxiously to be sure that no unauthorized person should be admitted." [48] The Socialists acknowledged that there had been a disproportionately large number of Jewish war profiteers because of the traditional position of the Jews in the economy. But they insisted that Jews formed a small portion of the businessmen and industrialists who had profiteered whenever possible. The Social Democrats pointed out that in the key munitions and heavy-machinery industries not a single Jew had participated in the enormous profit taking. Finally, answering accusations that Jews had made unfair profits through their control of banking facilities, the SPD rejoined that the days of the decisive influence of such men as the Rothschilds and Oppenheims had ended thirty years before and that joint-stock companies and cartels had rendered capital completely impersonal. [49]

The closely related charge that Jews had caused the 1918 collapse by administering a "stab in the back" to the German front was equally anathema to the Socialists. They attacked the notion by pointing out that the German General Staff itself lost its nerve in October, 1918, after having squeezed the last possible sacrifice from the common people while leaving war profiteers like Thyssen and Stinnes untouched. [50] They accused the military leaders of perpetuating the myth of a Jewish *Dolchstoss* in "an organized attempt to deceive the people. . . . Ten years ago they saw white mice everywhere; today they see Israelites everywhere." [51] General Erich Ludendorff, the most prominent proponent of the "stab in the back" legend before 1923, was accused of disseminating "childish fables." *Vorwaerts* ridiculed the third volume of Ludendorff's wartime

---

[48] *Vorwaerts*, August 15, 1919.
[49] *Antisemitismus und Sozialdemokratie*, 6, 7.
[50] *Was muss das schaffende Volk*, 2, 3; see also *Vorwaerts*, August 24, 1926.
[51] *Der Abend*, November 8, 1928.

memoirs as an "Egyptian book of dreams" for its conclusion that "international Jewry" had willed German defeat in 1918. *Vorwaerts* contended that the author was simply trying to blot out his own responsibility for the catastrophy. Socialist Hans Wesemann noted that Ludendorff had blamed the Jews for every conceivable wartime misfortune with the exception of the greatest one—German militarism itself. Resolved to correct the oversight, Wesemann satirically told of visiting the Berlin Armory, where he had seen a banner captured by a Jewish war hero, Fusilier Cohn, in the 1864 Danish War, and he commented bitterly: "This Fusilier Cohn won the War of 1864 with unheard-of heroic deeds and in doing so laid the foundations of Prussian militarism. We can thank this Fusilier Cohn for the other wars and for the lost World War. This Fusilier Cohn, as the agent of Jewry, seduced the harmless German people first to militarism and then abandoned them to the vengeance of the Entente. He has thrown all of world history into confusion; whatever happens, Fusilier Cohn is to blame." [52]

Vorwaerts sought to disprove the myth of an international Jewish conspiracy against Germany by reporting right-wing denunciations in France against the leader of French socialism, Léon Blum, after he had attacked his government's decision to invade the Ruhr. "Our *voelkisch* racial anti-Semites are invited to indicate what they think of the Blum case," the newspaper stated. "Here is a Frenchman who had the courage to appeal to human rights, democratic justice, and the right to self-determination in favor of the German people who have been mistreated by his own fellow citizens. And although the great Ludendorff teaches that the Jews are a secret society dedicated to the destruction of Germany, this Frenchman is . . . a Jew." [53]

When racists exploited unstable economic and political con-

[52] *Vorwaerts*, February 23, 1922; August 2, 1922; February 17, 1923; November 18, 1921.

[53] *Ibid.*, January 19, 1923. See also *ibid.*, January 12, 1923.

ditions to excite Germans against the republic, the Social Democrats met and refuted their allegations that the Jews were at the bottom of all the nation's calamities. In a 1922 SPD pamphlet Paul Kampffmeyer asked rhetorically, "Who is guilty for want and misery?" and answered emphatically that it was the capitalist system and not the Jews.

> Unscrupulous demagogy refers with a loud and hoarse voice to "Jewish capital." Capitalism is neither Jewish and circumcised nor Christian and baptised, it is endowed with neither Semitic nor Aryan physical characteristics; it is a singularly impersonal arrangement of the modern economy which quite automatically produces on the one hand exploiting, profitbreeding owners of the means of production and credit, and on the other exploited wage earners deprived of all opportunities for independent labor. *You workers must not let yourselves be taken in by the tunes of the anti-Semitic Pied Piper, who promises to free you from the capitalistic, Jewish profiteer, but who does not want to attack exploitive capital in general and merely wants to replace Cohn and Levi with Stinnes and Mannesmann.*[54]

A year later Kampffmeyer attacked the *voelkisch* contention that Jews represented a spirit of parasitism, materialism, and gross selfishness, while at the same time refuting the accusation that Jews ran the SPD.[55]

Early in 1924 the Party's regional organization in Hanover published a booklet supplying propaganda against anti-Semitism for SPD speakers and functionaries; it stressed the economic roots of the Jewish question and provided Party-approved arguments to quash accusations of Jewish responsibility for Germany's economic troubles. The complaint that "Jews never

---

[54] Kampffmeyer, *Wer ist schuld an Not und Elend?* (Berlin, 1922), 3, 4. Emphasis in the original. Kampffmeyer, a leading Party editor and journalist, was a non-Jew.
[55] Kampffmeyer, *Juedischer Marxismus* (Berlin, 1923), 3–8.

work" was countered with evidence showing that the Old Testament and the Talmud demand work, that most Eastern European Jews were industrial workers and artisans, and that tens of thousands of German Jews also held such occupations. In giving the lie to the charge that Jews controlled the world economy for exploitive purposes, the booklet listed the eleven richest men in the world; among them, it noted, were the anti-Semite Henry Ford and the German reactionary industrialist Hugo Stinnes, but not a single Jew. On the list of the nine richest men in Germany was only one Jew, the Frankfurt banker Baron Maximilian von Goldschmidt-Rothschild. The SPD brochure also tried to refute the accusation that the Hebrew religion had spawned an exploitive antisocial spirit among its adherents. It demonstrated that the ancient Israelites had practiced agrarian communism and that the Hebrew scriptures demanded social welfare measures among believers and their extension by Jews to needy gentiles. Finally, racist criticism of "Jewish usury" was answered with the reminder that medieval rulers had compelled Jews to deal in monetary transactions. If it were wrong to accept interest, commented the booklet, Germany's largely anti-Semitic class of great landholders would have to be expropriated, and, indeed, the whole economic structure would have to be altered.[56]

The SPD also turned its educational efforts against the *voelkisch* charge that the overwhelming majority of Jews belonged to the most destructive and parasitical elements of the capitalist class. In doing so it called attention to Jewish scientists, artists, medical doctors, professors, philosophers, and politicians—men like Heinrich Heine, August Wassermann, Hugo Preuss, and Baruch Spinoza—who had made invaluable contributions to society.[57] *Vorwaerts* reflected on the death in 1925 of Hugo

[56] *Was muss das schaffende Volk*, 8–12. For another example of Social Democratic insistence that "socialism" was rooted in the Jewish religion, see Paul Pflueger, *Der Sozialismus der israelitischen Propheten* (Berlin, n.d.), 1–18.
[57] *Was muss das schaffende Volk*, 6.

Preuss: "Unfortunately, to be a Jew in Germany is to be considered inferior by a certain portion of the population. Preuss felt that often and deeply, and for this very reason he considered it fortunate to be able to serve his people as he did." [58] Erhard Auer mentioned in 1920 that there were well over forty thousand Jewish ordinary workers in Germany and took that as proof that Jews were both fit and willing to undertake manual labor.[59] Carlo Mierendorff pointed out that the masses of Jews in Eastern Europe and North Africa were exploited and penniless,[60] while *Vorwaerts* greeted a report of the successful participation of Jews in Russian agriculture as an effective contradiction to slurs that Jews were incapable of productive work.[61] Socialists also rejected allegations that Jews alone took excessive profits during the war and the subsequent crises of the republic.[62] They attributed the postwar inflation to the policies of Wilhelm Cuno's cabinet, in which, they were careful to point out, there was neither a Jew nor a Socialist.[63]

The Social Democrats were also sensitive to charges that Jews controlled influential positions for their own purposes. In 1922, for example, the *Deutsche Zeitung* alleged that Jews and Socialists dominated Berlin's hospitals and medical profession; *Vorwaerts* answered with a series of articles proving that both groups made up minorities in both the leadership and the rank and file of local doctors.[64] When Tuebingen Professor Adolf Basler pointed to the concentration of Jewish intellectuals in law and medicine, Socialist Robert Fuchs replied that those were the only professions open to Jews before very recent

[58] *Vorwaerts*, October 13, 1925.
[59] Auer, *Sozialdemokratie und Antisemitismus*, 12.
[60] Mierendorff, *Arisches Kaisertum oder Judenrepublik?* 11.
[61] *Vorwaerts*, February 2, 1927.
[62] Auer, *Sozialdemokratie und Antisemitismus*, 13–14; Mierendorff, *Arisches Kaisertum oder Judenrepublik?* 12.
[63] *Vorwaerts*, June 30, 1924.
[64] *Ibid.*, July 11, September 28, and October 11, 1922.

times.[65] A *voelkisch* complaint that the new German republic was overwhelmingly Jewish and served Jewish ends prompted *Vorwaerts* to inquire sarcastically about what the other 99 percent of the population was doing when the "Jewish" Spartacists were attacking the "Jewish" government. Adolf Hoffmann's annoyed reaction to the rash of indictments of the republic's "Jewish government" was a detailed, factual essay showing that of 135 cabinet posts filled from 1919 to 1924, only 6 had been occupied by Jews.[66]

Not even the most farfetched contentions of the lunatic fringe of the *voelkisch* movement escaped SPD refutation. In August, 1919, *Vorwaerts* reacted with levity to the "illogical nonsense" of one Dr. Hoffmann, the author of an anti-Jewish pamphlet that had portrayed Marxism as the vanguard of a Jewish-Bolshevist plot that would leave every patriotic German dead by Whitsuntide. "Now Whitsuntide has come and gone and we are all still alive; hopefully Dr. Hoffmann has also escaped being eaten up by a Jewish Bolshevik." Later, when the anti-Jewish *Reichsbote* shrieked that Jews had induced the Reichstag Commission on Causes of the Collapse to hold sessions on the Day of Repentance as a deliberate affront to Christians, *Vorwaerts* calmly noted that the protest really had little to do with religion since it was just another case in which "Jew-baiting and violence" were brought together "to foment discontent against the Commission of Inquiry and the Republic." [67] Imputations that the Talmud contained the blueprint of a Jewish conspiracy against the Christian world were traced to falsifications of and misleading quotations from the Hebrew

---

[65] Fuchs, review of Basler, *Einfuehrung in die Rassen- und Gesellschafts-Psysiologie*, in *Die Gesellschaft*, III (1926), 383–86.

[66] *Vorwaerts*, March 19, 1919. For similar cases, see issues of March 13 and September 2, 1919. Hoffmann's reaction published in *ibid.*, November 23, 1924.

[67] *Ibid.*, August 5, November 21, 1919.

holy book. The Socialists characterized the Talmud as being a combination of "instructions for religious ceremonies, a great deal of sophistry, but also moral teachings of the noblest kind, although mixed with explosions of hatred against the oppressors of Jewry, as against the intolerance of orthodox Christianity." Moreover, they maintained that the great majority of West European Jews knew little of the Talmud, which was used primarily in Eastern Europe and the Orient.[68]

German Socialists did not exclude information about racist books from their policy of educating their countrymen about anti-Semitic fallacies. One such book, *Die grosse Taeuschung* (*The Great Deception*) by Friedrich Delitzsch, polemicised against the Old Testament as a collection of myths and inaccurate Hebrew history that had been foisted on Christians by the nefarious Israelites. In reviewing the book, one Social Democrat agreed with some of Delitzsch's criticisms but rejected the strongly anti-Semitic tone of the book, concluding that the criticisms were valid only insofar as they were applied equally to all religions and holy writ.[69] A second Socialist attacked Delitzsch for ignoring the development of Judaism since the writing of the Old Testament and of dispensing raw emotionalism to stir up Judeophobia.[70] An even more scurrilous volume was Artur Dinter's popular novel *Die Suende wider das Blut* (*Sin Against the Blood*), which told of the horrible results of the defilement of a German woman's racial purity by a rich Jew. In 1921 *Vorwaerts* reported with satisfaction that even many *voelkisch* spokesmen found the novel too extreme, and it quoted one right-wing judgment that it constituted a "sin against the spirit of Teutonism." [71] Franz von Wendrin's *Die*

---

[68] *Antisemitismus und Sozialdemokratie*, 10, 11.

[69] Sommer, "Religioese Taeuschungen," 69–74.

[70] Herbert Kuehnert, review of Delitzsch, *Die grosse Taeuschung*, in *Sozialistische Monatshefte*, XXVIII (1922), 1031.

[71] *Vorwaerts*, August 4, 1921; see also *ibid.*, May 5, 1922, February 25, 1923, October 6, 1924.

Entdeckung des Paradies (*The Discovery of Paradise*) located the Garden of Eden in Germany and maintained that animal-like Jews had forced Germans to flee from their homeland, after which the latter were responsible for Chinese and Egyptian civilizations at their peaks. The thesis neither deserved nor received Socialist criticism, but it did prompt one Social Democrat to reject Wendrin's specific characterizations of Jews as materialistic and inferior beings, pointing to the enormous usury problems of "Judenrein" in ancient Greece and Rome and the fact that Jews had been the first permanently to take the step from paganism to monotheism.[72] And Hans F. K. Guenther's *Kleine Rassenkunde Europas* (*Short Ethnology of Europe*) did not escape the terse verdict: "Party-political ardor does not produce scientific conclusions." [73] In 1928 Max Hodann found Guenther's attempt to link artistic achievements with race highly prejudiced and therefore "unreliable." Accusing Guenther of ethnocentrism, Hodann marshaled authoritative evidence showing that every culture had its own concept of what is aesthetically pleasing.[74] In an associated review he flayed the author of a book about racial physical features for having ignored experiments showing that a uniformly tiny percentage of all groups of German citizens, including Jews, possessed "Nordic" physical attributes.[75]

The Socialists similarly did their part to expose as a fraud the notorious *Protocols of the Elders of Zion*. This book, a collection of lectures supposedly delivered in secret by the leaders of international Jewry outlining their plans to subvert and dominate the world, was proved a forgery in 1921 when a London

---

[72] O. L., review of Wendrin, *Die Entdeckung des Paradies*, in *Vorwaerts*, July 13, 1924, p. 17.

[73] Hans Haustein, "Menschenrasse," *Sozialistische Monatshefte*, XXXI (1925), 508.

[74] Hodann, review of Guenther, *Rasse und Stil*, in *Sozialistische Monatshefte*, XXXIV (1928), 530; see also K. Lewin, review of Friedrich Hertz, *Hans Guenther als Rassenforscher*, in *Vorwaerts*, February 15, 1931, p. 20.

[75] Hodann, review of Kern, *Stammbaum und Artbild*, 531.

Times correspondent discovered it had been plagiarized from an obscure satire on Napoleon III, reclothed for Russian consumption, and distributed by the Tsar's secret police after 1897.[76] Many extreme anti-Semites continued to take the *Protocols* seriously, however, and the German Socialists found it necessary to relate the origins of the "gross falsifications" and to denounce them as the "intellectual roots of the Rathenau murder." [77] In 1924 they warned that the racist bible had been reprinted under a different title, *The Zionist Protocols*, labeling the latter "old lies in new clothes." [78] Socialist Hermann Schuetzinger agreed that the volume was "an anonymous libel fashioned from the grossest falsifications." [79] The death in 1926 of Captain Mueller von Hausen, the man who had translated the *Protocols* into German, prompted *Vorwaerts* to note that the degree of irresponsibility of the various racist groups could be measured by the extent to which they depended on the "ridiculous fabrications." On a lighter note, it mockingly lamented that Bismarck had never been able to read the *Protocols*, for if he had, he might never have engaged a Jewish doctor and a Jewish attorney or valued the works of Heine and friends like Disraeli. Because he did, Bismarck was doomed to be dethroned as a *voelkisch* idol, *Vorwaerts* sarcastically suggested.[80]

Having perceived in anti-Semitism a reactionary device to divert attention from the failures of capitalism, to attack the republic, and to rehabilitate the political right, German Socialists worked hard to refute the main points of anti-Jewish ideology. In particular, they attacked racial doctrines and allegations that

---

[76] On the *Protocols*, see Norman Cohn, *Warrant for Genocide: The Myth of the Jewish World-Conspiracy and "The Protocols of the Elders of Zion"* (New York, 1966); James Parkes, *Antisemitism* (Chicago, 1963), 45–56.

[77] *Was muss das schaffende Volk*, 7. For information on Rathenau's assassination, see Chap. 3, pages 74–76.

[78] *Vorwaerts*, May 23, 1924.

[79] Schuetzinger, "Deutschvoelkische Agitation," *Sozialistische Monatshefte*, XXX (1924), 704.

[80] *Vorwaerts*, August 22 and 28, 1926.

Jews were unpatriotic. They also struck out at imputations that Jewish capitalists were conspicously responsible for Germany's economic distress—imputations that must have been prime sources of whatever anti-Semitism existed among SPD members. These formulations constituted the intellectual basis for direct Socialist attacks on the proponents of racism and for the defense of persecuted Jews.

Chapter III

The SPD Combats Anti-Semitism
as a Threat to the Republic
1918-1928

The conviction that anti-Semitism was an effective right-wing tool to undermine support for the Weimar Republic produced SPD determination to denounce Judeophobia. This determination never brought about a concerted Socialist campaign against Jew-baiting, but it did lead to frequent attacks on anti-Jewish organizations and activities, as well as appeals to Germans to shun these groups. Although the Social Democrats gave their sharpest opposition to anti-Semitism in the unstable months of 1918–19 and 1922–23, they ridiculed and assailed Judeophobia throughout the period 1919–28.

Important aspects of the Socialist efforts to combat anti-Semitism were the exposure, denunciation, and ridicule of anti-Jewish organizations, their leaders, and their tactics. In 1919 the SPD identified the *Deutschnationale Volkspartei* (German National People's Party—DNVP) as the only major German party that openly espoused anti-Semitism. In September, when this party was considering whether to exclude Jews from its ranks, *Vorwaerts* followed developments intently, observing scornfully that if the DNVP admitted them it would have "to call a partial halt to its elegant stimulation of pogroms and the like. But if they are excluded, it will lose a share of what every national idealist may not do without. Perhaps the Conservatives will ... propose a plebiscite over this important question—with Jews excluded, naturally." The Nationalists soon decided to bar Jews from their party and adopted a resolution denouncing "the ascendancy of Jewry" in the government and public life, a move that the Socialists accepted as proof that the DNVP had "swung entirely into the camp of inflammatory anti-Semitism." [1] They professed to be unworried that anti-Semitic appeals might help the Nationalists at the polls: "The Conservative leaders forget that the German voters are not illiterates and that they have forgotten neither the war years nor the pre-war period." Before the Kapp putsch the Socialists returned to the matter only long enough for a hearty laugh over the accusation, made in a radically anti-Semitic book, *Judas Schuldbuch (Judah's Book of Crimes)*, that DNVP leader Karl Helfferich was a Jew, a special handicap in view of Helfferich's Reichstag candidacy in Pomerania, the "anti-Semitic El Dorado." [2]

In 1920 *Vorwaerts* called attention to Nationalist cooperation with the extremist German *Voelkisch* Party and concluded that the influence of the rabidly anti-Jewish wing of the DNVP was on the increase. The impression was reinforced when a speaker at that party's 1920 convention in Hanover remarked, "If Siegfried is to be victorious, Judah must perish!"; this led the Socialist organ to call the gathering a "pogrom convention." The resignation of a large group of radical racists from the DNVP in 1922 spared the party from some leftist criticism, but it did not prevent *Vorwaerts* from reminding its readers of the party's policy of excluding Jews. When a Nationalist organ

---

[1] *Vorwaerts*, September 3, October 14, 1919. The denunciation of Jewish influences in Germany became Article 11 of the DNVP's program of October, 1920, "Grundsaetze der Deutschnationalen Volkspartei," which is reproduced in Wolfgang Treue (ed.), *Deutsche Parteiprogramme, 1861–1956* (Goettingen, 1956), 112. See also Walter H. Kaufmann, *Monarchism in the Weimar Republic* (New York, 1953), 66, 67.

[2] *Vorwaerts*, December 1, 1919; March 10, 1920.

complained that the Socialists would not cooperate with that party for even small tasks, the Socialist daily recalled the DNVP's "vulgar, rowdy anti-Semitism," which was one of the factors that prevented the SPD from approaching the Nationalists even "with a gas mask." [3] The DNVP's decision two years later to revive appeals to anti-Semitic prejudice impelled the Socialists once again to identify Judeophobia as the Nationalists' "principal means of propaganda against the Republic and democracy." [4] Carlo Mierendorff went so far as to allege that the DNVP set the policies of smaller *voelkisch* groups and gave financial support to their publications.[5]

While gleefully aware that such extreme *voelkisch* organizations regularly smeared the DNVP as "Judaized," most Socialists either assumed with Mierendorff that the slurs were made with Nationalist approval or concluded that such venom was to be expected from quarreling vipers. They never regarded the smear campaign as a possible cause of the DNVP's vacillation on the Jewish question, which they attributed entirely to opportunism. In 1921 *Vorwaerts* laid emphasis on the irony of an appeal for campaign contributions made by DNVP chairman Oskar Hergt to a wealthy Jew, and in 1925 it commented on a report that Jewish firms had been urged to advertise in a DNVP newspaper: "A true German can not tolerate Jews, but he will gladly take their money." The Socialist organ underlined the Nationalists' toleration of Jews among their functionaries and candidates, and it took particular delight in reprinting racist charges that Nationalist leader Count Kuno vonWestarp had both Jewish relatives and a Jewish fiancée. It also dredged up one of Westarp's old election speeches from 1908 in which he had recognized and defended equal rights for Jews, a far cry

[3] *Ibid.*, September 15, October 27, 1920; May 17, 1923; and January 22, 1923.

[4] Erich Kuttner and Franz Kluhs, *Die politischen Parteien in Deutschland* (Berlin, [ca. 1924]), 5; see also *Handbuch fuer sozialdemokratische Waehler* (Berlin, 1924), 167.

[5] Mierendorff, *Arisches Kaisertum oder Judenrepublik?* 8.

from his 1924 position. Late in 1924 *Vorwaerts* noted that Thuringian poet Ernst Pueschel was about to be read out of the DNVP for dissenting from the party's Judeophobia; recalling that, two years before, the Nationalists had been willing to take a stand against organized hatred of Jews, the newspaper concluded that anti-Semitism was for them simply "a matter of expediency." [6]

Among anti-Semitic parties of lesser importance in the period 1918–28, the *Nationalsozialistische Deutsche Arbeiterpartei* (National Socialist German Workers' Party—NSDAP) earned the most frequent Socialist condemnation. Formed in Munich in 1919 by Anton Drexler, the NSDAP (or Nazi Party) soon fell under the domination of Adolf Hitler, who molded it into the most energetic *voelkisch* organization in southern Germany. At the same time Gregor and Otto Strasser spread nazism to the industrial cities of the north. In 1921 the National Socialists formed their own private army of *Sturmabteilungen* (Storm Divisions—SA), and four years later they created the elite *Schutz Staffel* (Defense Corps—SS). While the Nazis subscribed to the entire gamut of anti-Jewish ideology, they placed special emphasis on what they called the Jews' "ultra-materialistic" and therefore "un-German" nature. They also harped on a supposed "Jewish plot" to dominate the workers with Marxism and thus enslave the world. In November, 1923, the National Socialists allied with General Erich Ludendorff to make their first bid for power in the abortive beer hall putsch. They subsequently survived the years of prosperity that followed to take advantage of the depression and gain power by "legal" means.

The Social Democrats took little notice of the NSDAP before 1922. In January of that year *Vorwaerts* attacked "Hittmann [*sic*]" and his henchmen as "the chief instigators of the

[6] *Vorwaerts*, January 5, March 20, 1923; February 5, 1921; October 20, 1925; April 12 and 16, June 21, July 15, 1924; March 16, December 28, 1924.

Bavarian anti-Semitic movement" and the leading Nazi newspaper, the *Voelkischer Beobachter*, as "the worst anti-Semitic
scandal-sheet." [7] By March, 1923, a Socialist spokesman placed
the National Socialists at the head of a list of the most dangerous
voelkisch organizations.[8] In January, 1923, *Vorwaerts* had
urged the suppression in Prussia of the "Greater German
Workers' Party," the North German affiliate of the Munich-
based Nazi Party.[9] But beyond a few negative glances at Nazi
racism, Berlin Socialists took much less notice of the Hitler
movement than did their comrades in Bavaria. It was in the
NSDAP stronghold of Munich that the Socialists gave their
most spirited resistance to Nazi anti-Semitism. A 1922 procla-
mation signed by the leaders of the SPD and the Socialist labor
unions in Munich sounded the alarm against an impending Nazi
putsch and warned of the "endlessly foul, endlessly stupid Jew-
baiting" spread by the Hitler party. The declaration admonished: "Among the members of all races and religions there are
men who are respectable and improper, noble and ignoble, hard-
working and parasitic." [10] Erhard Auer, in the words of his assistant Carl Landauer, did much to give Bavarian Socialism "an
unambiguous attitude against anti-Semitism." [11] In December,
1922, Auer, in a public speech, called for the kind of national
unity that would permit strong action against "secret societies,
race-hatred, and incendiary and murderous propaganda." [12]

The Munich of the inflationary crisis also provided the first
example of close cooperation between the SPD and the *Centralverein deutscher Staatsbuerger juedischen Glaubens* (Central Association of German Citizens of the Jewish Faith—CV),

[7] *Ibid.*, January 13 and 31, 1922.
[8] H. Mueller-Brandenburg, "Die deutschvoelkische Bewegung," *Die neue
Zeit*, XLI (1923), 438–42.
[9] *Vorwaerts*, January 9, 1923.
[10] NSDAP Hauptarchiv, fol. 1894.
[11] Landauer, "Erinnerungen an die Muenchener Sozialdemokratie," in Hans
Lamm (ed.), *Von Juden in Muenchen: Ein Gedenkbuch* (Munich, 1958), 312.
[12] *Muenchener Post*, January 14, 1923, NSDAP Hauptarchiv, fol. 1897.

the most prominent secular organization of German Jews. Following the assassination of Rathenau, the Munich Socialists braced themselves for a right-wing putsch by forming Security Detachments. In the event of a Nazi uprising, these paramilitary groups would attempt to keep the republican flag flying at the headquarters of the Socialist trade unions and the SPD's *Muenchener Post* building until outside relief could break the rebellion. Since the SPD lacked funds to finance the defense organizations, Socialist leader Carl Landauer arranged with the CV's managing director Ludwig Hollaender for secret contributions from the Jewish organization. Unfortunately for the SPD, one of its members was arrested while carrying a letter with details of the arrangement. The police revealed its contents to the Nazis, who used the information to create a scandal about a conspiracy between "Jewish capital and Social Democratic bosses." The Security Detachments were disarmed by the Munich police in September, 1923, just weeks before the abortive Hitler putsch during which the Nazis thoroughly ransacked the *Muenchener Post* building.[13]

The Socialists continued their surveillance of the Hitler movement after the Munich putsch. Although most Socialists tended to underestimate or ignore distinctions between various groups of anti-Semites, Paul Kampffmeyer acknowledged basic differences between DNVP and Nazi Judeophobia, giving grudging credit to the former party for having refused "entirely to concur with the gross nonsense of National Socialist racial policy." Noting that experts had found Nazi racist ideology "highly nebulous," he himself characterized it as "insane," the "senseless fury of political fanatics."[14] After the Nazis held demonstrations in Weimar in August, 1924, a cartoon in *Vorwaerts* showed Goethe stepping down from the famous

---

[13] Landauer, "Erinnerungen an die Muenchener Sozialdemokratie," 312–17.
[14] Kampffmeyer, *Der Nationalsozialismus und seine Goenner* (Berlin, 1924), 17.

monument he shares with Schiller before the Weimar National Theater with the comment that, in view of his dark hair, black eyes, and the fact that he had been born in the "Jewish city" of Frankfurt am Main, he thought it best to leave town for a few days just to be safe. The Socialists also paid attention to Nazi outrages against Jews, censuring nineteen youthful Hitlerites arrested for anti-Semitic violence in Berlin in 1927 and savagely mocking their protests of innocence. That the SPD did not yet regard the NSDAP as a major threat is apparent from a suggestion made to the Reichstag Justice Committee in 1927 by left-wing Social Democrat Kurt Rosenfeld that the speaking ban on Hitler be lifted on the grounds that the Nazi menace to the state had been overestimated. *Vorwaerts* jovially agreed: "It would please us if Hitler ... were allowed to rave against the Jews, as he loves to do!" [15]

Other small *voelkisch* groups received SPD attention from 1918 to 1928. Among the most active in the early years of the republic was the *Ausschuss fuer Volkserklaerung* (Committee for the Education of the People), which in May, 1919, warmed up the old ritual-murder legend in a public declaration that Jews had murdered at least a hundred Berlin children (in the satirical words of *Vorwaerts*, "processing them into sausages"). To the committee's admonitions to "destroy and kill all who rise up against the divine order," however, the Socialist organ remarked: "It is high time that a stop were put to their organization's activities. These incitements to violence from the right surpass everything that has been written or spoken on the Spartacist side." Shortly thereafter the Socialists urged the Ministry of Military Affairs to cut off the flow of anti-Semitic materials being distributed by the committee to officers and men in the army and navy. In February of the next year *Vorwaerts* contemptuously denounced one of the committee's leaders, a certain Wolff-Harnier, who had publicly deprecated the toler

15 *Vorwaerts*, August 22, 1924; June 29, January 14, 1927.

ant philosophy of Baruch Spinoza and distributed pamphlets in which Jews ostensibly confessed to having sold gentile women into slavery and to having advocated the widespread practice of abortion in order to encourage non-Jews to commit racial suicide.[16] Other racist organizations came in for similar SPD censure. Early in 1919 the Party's Berlin newspaper warned parents of an outwardly neutral but actually reactionary and anti-Semitic youth club that was recruiting members in local secondary schools. *Vorwaerts* pointed to the secrecy with which the *Deutschvoelkischer Schutz- und Trutzbund* (German *Voelkisch* League for Offense and Defense) surrounded itself as being evidence of the league's fear of public reaction to its outrageous deeds rather than as a necessary security measure against Jewish conspirators, as the league itself explained. Later *Vorwaerts* rebuked the league after its members manhandled people who had disagreed with the anti-Semitic bombast of a speaker at one of its meetings. The Socialist daily was similarly incensed when police prohibited Social Democrats from refuting an anti-Jewish harangue at another of this group's rallies. Occasionally the Socialists merely made light of the racist groups, as they did in 1920 when they labelled the formation by Theodor Fritsch of the "German Socialist Party" a premature April-fools joke." More typically they thundered against the Jew-haters, as they did in 1919 when the Pan-German League's *Deutsche Zeitung* ended a tirade against the practice of making Jews army officers with a plaintive, "Must it really be?" "Yes, it must be," answered *Vorwaerts*. "It must be that even the corruptors and contaminators of the people from the camp of the *Deutsche Zeitung* . . . will recognize the Jews as fellow countrymen possessing equal rights." [17]

[16] *Ibid.*, May 7, 1919. (For a similar case, see issue of February 1, 1920.) See also *ibid.*, July 12, 1919; February 7, 1920.
[17] *Ibid.*, January 17, November 29, 1919; April 9, June 30, 1921; February 19, 1920; May 25, 1919.

In October, 1922, the DNVP's most intransigent racists—Reinhold Wulle, Albrecht von Graefe-Goldebee, and Wilhelm Henning—lost out in an internal party struggle, seceded from the party, and the following December founded the *Deutschvoelkische Freiheitspartei* (German *Voelkisch* Freedom Party).[18] In January, 1923, *Vorwaerts* stigmatized the contents of an anti-Jewish pamphlet distributed by the Freedom Party as "racist nonsense." [19] Even earlier, in October, 1922, Prussian Minister of the Interior Carl Severing (SPD) had warned the Prussian Parliament of the danger presented by one of the Party's predecessors, the German Freedom League. *Vorwaerts* applauded Severing's suggestion that it be kept under close surveillance throughout the Reich.[20] Later, when Wulle wailed that his party could not get a fair hearing before the courts of the republic, the Socialist organ accepted it as proof that he would "not shrink before the most imbecilic fictions" in casting suspicion upon a judicial decision not yet handed down. Richard Kunze's German Social Party and the *Stahlhelm* came in for similar treatment.[21]

Socialists took real pleasure in taunting the *voelkisch* organizations for their difficulties in keeping Jews out of their midst and for accusations they threw at each other of Jewish domination. They twitted the racist *Deutscher Herold* (German Herald) for requiring written certification of ethnic background for membership, urging it instead to require blood samples for greater accuracy. When a Judeophobe "proved" that Christ was an "Aryan," *Vorwaerts* observed laughingly that the discovery made it necessary for every racist to trace his family tree back two thousand years to prove his racial purity.

---

[18] Lewis Hertzman, *DNVP, Right-Wing Opposition in the Weimar Republic, 1918–1924* (Lincoln, Neb., 1963), 137–58.

[19] *Vorwaerts*, January 4, 1923.

[20] *Sitzungsberichte des preussischen Landtags*, 177th Sess. (1922), IX, 12751–52; *Vorwaerts*, October 21, 1922.

[21] *Vorwaerts*, April 27, 1923; October 10, 1921; April 14, 1924.

Reinhold Wulle's frantic efforts to defend himself against a charge that his grandmother was Jewish sent *Vorwaerts* into ecstasies, and when similar charges were made against other racists, it recalled his case with the taunt, "Wulle, Wulle, think of your Grandmama!" [22] In 1926, shortly after the DNVP had decided that only "Aryans" could sit as party representatives in parliamentary bodies, *Vorwaerts* published a cartoon showing Jewish SPD Reichstag Deputy Julius Moses, a practicing medical doctor, giving blood tests to all the Nationalist representatives "for Semitic bacteria." [23] The Socialists sometimes added fuel to the controversies with their own allegations that various *voelkisch* personalities were ethnically Jewish, as they did in 1923 in the case of Bavarian Judeophobe Johannes Munk. A similar charge against Hanau racist Dr. Freisler-Kassel resulted in a legal suit and a fine for the author of the charge, Socialist attorney Stephan Kann.[24]

German Socialists dealt out ridicule and derision to the anti-Semites. When in 1921 the German Austrian Alpine League of mountain climbers decided to exclude Jews, *Vorwaerts* sneered: "The workers long ago . . . formed their own tourist organizations, which naturally have nothing to do with such rubbish. The mountains have a religion of their own." [25] Where name-calling was concerned, the Socialists more than held their own. Anti-Semitic leaders were branded "murderers," "clowns," and "Jew-eaters"; their newspapers were called "smut-sheets," and their songs were labelled "gutter hymns." Because of the anti-Semitic posture of the Nationalist *Kreuz-*

---

[22] *Ibid.*, September 29, 1921 (see also issue of January 31, 1920); August 7, 1923; March 21, 1924; see also issues of February 13, 1921, January 19, March 29, 1924.

[23] *Ibid.*, March 30, 1926. It is perhaps no accident that the newspaper's *ad hoc* word "Semikokken" bears a rather close resemblance to "Streptokokken."

[24] *Ibid.*, March 25, 1923; November 7, 1925.

[25] *Ibid.*, August 18, 1921; Hans Bauer, "Der judenfreie Alpenverein," *ibid.*, February 26, 1925, p. 2.

zeitung, the Socialists in 1924 revived the name given it in 1849—*Galgenzeitung (Gallows Press)*.[26]

The Social Democrats also ridiculed anti-Semites for opinions that were contrary to elementary knowledge or that displayed gross inconsistency. An essay by Social Democrat-turned-racist Max Maurenbrecher in his *Deutsche Zeitung*, about Gotthold Lessing's great contributions to the development of the German spirit and literature, induced them to remind him of Lessing's poetic drama *Nathan the Wise*, a plea for religious liberty and a satire on anti-Semitism. A *voelkisch* description of Karl Marx as a "Jewish millionaire" received the derision it deserved, and disagreements between different racists over whether Columbus was a Jew or whether Goethe had displayed Jewish traits aroused Socialist impatience and scoffing.[27] When in 1925 the racists in the Reichstag voted in favor of a bill appropriating 1,200,000 marks for the "cultural activities" of Christian churches and Jewish synagogues, *Vorwaerts* lampooned them for contributing to the further Judaization of Germany.[28]

While the SPD regarded the political right as the principal source of anti-Semitism in the period 1918–28, beginning in 1923 it also felt itself obliged to give attention to what it considered Judeophobia from a new and unexpected source, the German Communist Party. In that year the KPD inaugurated a policy of "national Bolshevism," an attempted "rapproachement between German nationalism and Russian Communism" based on their common antipathy to Western culture and capitalism.[29] It included at least one effort to appeal to *voelkisch* Judeophobia and harness it to the KPD's broader struggle

[26] *Vorwaerts*, July 27, September 3, 1920; December 14, 1922; June 27, 1923; January 24, 1924; February 6, 1926; June 22, 1927; April 29, 1924.

[27] *Ibid.*, May 17, 1921; November 20, December 25, 1924; December 15, 1926; Walter Koch, "Geschichte," *Sozialistische Monatshefte*, XXVIII (1922), 371.

[28] *Vorwaerts*, June 17, 1925.

[29] Klemens von Klemperer, *Germany's New Conservatism: Its History and Dilemma in the Twentieth Century* (Princeton, 1957), 139. For a generally

against capitalism. In the summer of 1923, Communist leader Ruth Fischer—who was herself of Jewish background—addressed a KPD-sponsored meeting of University of Berlin students at which she seemed to endorse their anti-Semitism while trying to turn it against capitalism: "You cry out against Jewish capital, gentlemen? Whoever condemns Jewish capital, gentlemen, is already engaged in the class struggle even if he doesn't realize it. You are against Jewish capital and want to eliminate the stock-manipulators. Rightly so. Trample the Jewish capitalists under foot, hang them from the street-lamps, stamp them out!" In reporting the incident, *Vorwaerts* conceded that Fischer had urged her audience to consider the pernicious activities of non-Jewish capitalists as well, but it castigated her for using a demagogic ploy to attract racist elements to her party and called her an anti-Semite.[30] The following day *Vorwaerts* printed a poem, "The New Anti-Semites," calling attention to the fact that Fischer and other KPD leaders were Jews:

> "Hep-hep, hi-ho, and Out with the Jews!"
> Is that Hitler marching to a pogrom?
> The very street begins to shake,
> And many burghers sneak away fearfully,
>   But, look—the Communists!
>
> "Hep-hep!" In front the editors
> of *The Red Banner*. Sobelsohn

---

excellent discussion of this and a subsequent attempt by the KPD to realize such a rapprochement, see *ibid.*, 139–50.

30 *Vorwaerts*, August 22, 1923. The judgment that Fischer's outburst was motivated by anti-Semitic intentions—a conclusion that is shared by Ossip K. Flechtheim and Klemens von Klemperer—is probably not justified. On the other hand, Fischer's own attempts to explain away the incident do not succeed in freeing her from the entirely justified charge of demagogy. Flechtheim, *Die Kommunistische Partei Deutschlands in der Weimarer Republik* (Offenbach on the Main, 1948), 294; Klemperer, *Germany's New Conservatism*, 145–46; Ruth Fischer, *Stalin and German Communism: A Study in the Origins of the State Party* (Cambridge, Mass., 1948), 283.

(Karl Radek) leads the great throng,
Arm in arm with Reventlow!
   And then comes Werner Scholem.

Scholem carries a huge sign:
"Hang the kosher profiteers!"
He is heard to say contentedly:
"Don't I look just like an Aryan?"
   And then comes Ruth Fischer.

Her hair a peroxide-blond,
Ruth Fischer marches right along,
For she, full of courage and craft,
Rallied the *voelkisch* students.
   And then comes—Knueppel Kunze.

Friend Kunze looks quite pleased,
And smirks: "Here I'm right at home.
With Radek, Scholem, and Katz I'm
United in jolly new Jew-hate."
   Crash! There goes the first window . . . .[31]

In 1924 *Vorwaerts* railed against the KPD's organ in Halle, *Klassenkampf*, for dwelling on the aims of Jewish capitalists so much that the racist press in central Germany reprinted from it.[32] During the Reichstag election campaign of that year the Socialists continued to criticize this temporary Communist flirtation with anti-Semitism.[33] The Communists occasionally hurled similar accusations at the SPD; in 1928 the KPD roared that a *Der Abend* caricature of a Communist clearly was meant to appeal to "the worst anti-Semitic instincts," [34] an accusation that had no basis in fact.[35]

The DVP, a right-of-center bourgeois party that never

---

[31] *Vorwaerts*, August 23, 1923. The poem is a very free adaptation of *Die Musik kommt* by the nineteenth-century lyric poet Detlev von Liliencron.
[32] *Ibid.*, August 14, 1924; December 29, 1926.
[33] See page 85.
[34] *Die rote Fahne*, August 3, 1928. See also *Neue Zeitung* (Munich), January 22, 1932, NSDAP Hauptarchiv, fol. 1904, no. C–98.
[35] *Der Abend*, August 2, 1928. The cartoon satirized a KPD attempt to bribe

openly espoused anti-Semitism, came under Socialist fire for harboring a racist wing and for occasionally appealing to anti-Jewish prejudices. As early as 1920 the SPD accused it of joining the DNVP in blaming the Jews for the loss of the war.[36] Three years later Toni Sender warned her SPD comrades against forming a "great coalition" cabinet with the DVP because of the latter's intimate ties with prominent industrialists who helped finance "Hitler's anti-Semitic hate-propaganda."[37] Just before the Reichstag election held in December, 1924, *Vorwaerts* reported that a journalist of the *Berliner Tageblatt* (whose editor, Theodor Wolff, was a Jew) had been thrown out of a DVP election rally by swastika-wearing *Stahlhelm* members who abused him with anti-Semitic insults. The Socialist organ concluded that Gustav Stresemann's party had virtually embraced Judeophobia, which *Vorwaerts* took as a sign of the DVP's deterioration. Soon thereafter it sharply criticized the DVP's central organ *Die Zeit* for its racist opposition to the appointment of a Jew as principal of a Berlin secondary school. In 1927 *Vorwaerts* lashed out at "Dr. Stresemann's *Taegliche Rundschau*" for "cheerfully reprinting" an untrue *voelkisch* assertion that Socialist leader Otto Braun had accepted four million marks from Jewish sources to be used for agitation among farm workers when Braun was Prussian Minister of Agriculture in 1920.[38] On one occasion, when *Die Zeit* alleged that Jews of Eastern European origin were a major source of financial support for the *Reichsbanner*, *Vorwaerts* reproached

---

members of the Socialist Workers Youth Movement to act as informers for monthly payments of fifty marks. Over the inscription "Let the little children come unto me!" it caricatured a sinister-looking "Communist educator of youth" with a crooked nose, but it was in no way anti-Semitic.

[36] *Vorwaerts*, January 7, 1920.

[37] Sender, *Grosse Koalition?* (Frankfurt on the Main, 1923), 9; see also *Vorwaerts*, November 8, 1923.

[38] *Vorwaerts*, December 21, 1924; January 16, 1925; January 15, October 8, 1927. At that time the DNVP was a part of Wilhelm Marx's fourth coalition cabinet, in which Stresemann served as Foreign Minister. The *Taegliche Rundschau* had earlier transferred its sympathies from the DVP to the DNVP.

the DVP for opportunistically cultivating anti-Semitism whenever the tactic promised to work to its advantage.[39]

The SPD often subjected individual anti-Semitic leaders to contempt. That Ludendorff and his associates in the *Tannenbergbund* regarded themselves as the only remaining unpolluted Germans prompted the Socialists to urge him and his "three dozen Germans" to leave the land of Jews, Papists, and Free Masons in favor of some isolated South Sea island.[40] In a systematic critique of Ludendorff's opinions, Socialist Hermann Schuetzinger concluded that the old general simply had found reality unbearable and had withdrawn from it.[41] Other Socialists mocked him as "a man who is persecuted by the Jews everywhere," as "Elder of Zion Ludendorff," and as one of Germany's "spiritual giants."[42] A 1927 *Vorwaerts* cartoon pictured Ludendorff posturing beside his second wife, Matilde, who, dressed in Teutonic finery, was giving a lecture: "The sum of 1, 9, 1, and 4 is 15. The number 15 signifies Jehova. Hence all-Judah unleashed the World War in 1914. The next year with the sum of 15 is 1932." The sum of Erich and Matilda, remarked *Vorwaerts*, was zero. When the old war hero criticized the monument erected in 1927 to commemorate his victory at Tannenberg, saying it was covered with symbols showing it had been designed by Jews and Free Masons, the Socialist organ merrily repeated his ramblings. A cartoon pictured him assailed by Stars of David, numbers adding up to fifteen, and ghostly Jews; the caption read: "Help! Help! The psychiatrist!"[43]

[39] *Vorwaerts*, January 3, 1925.

[40] *Ibid.*, October 20, 1926.

[41] Schuetzinger, "Der Fall Ludendorff," *Sozialistische Monatshefte*, XXX (1924), 691–98.

[42] *Muenchener Post*, November 17, 1924, NSDAP Hauptarchiv, fol. 1811, no. 15.

[43] *Vorwaerts*, March 8, May 4, 1925; April 1, September 28, October 8 and 16, 1927; January 8, 1928.

Psychiatric disturbances were also attributed to DNVP leader Count Ernst zu Reventlow in 1925 after a speech in which he had called the League of Nations a "Jewish institution" controlled by Zionists and the Social Democrats "prisoners of Jewish capital." *Vorwaerts* also poured shame on him for an essay justifying past executions of Jews convicted of the ritual-slaughter of gentiles.[44] Richard Kunze, who loudly complained that Jews had avoided their obligations to the Fatherland in the war, was exposed by the Socialists as being himself a malingerer who never fired a shot in battle and who deserted his post as guard at a military prison in the first moments of the November revolution.[45] Nor were the Social Democrats above scandalmongering; in 1924 the *Muenchener Post* printed evidence of an extramarital liaison between Karl Spiller, a *voelkisch* deputy in the Thuringian Parliament, and a Jewish woman.[46]

The type of person attracted by anti-Semitic arguments was treated with similar disdain. In 1920 *Vorwaerts* described the "gluttony" that ran rampant at the exclusively "Aryan" spa on the North Sea island of Borkum. Noting that many Germans still lacked basic necessities, it praised the refusal of Bremen's Socialist longshoremen to load supplies destined for people who had "no scruples about depriving infants of their milk—with swastikas and the chanting of the Borkumlied," the "anti-Semitic national hymn." Later the Socialist organ reported the founding of a racist chess league with the observation that its members were probably afraid that their Jewish opponents could play a better game; it suggested that they prove the superiority of their "Aryan" spirit by playing against such Jewish chess masters as Emanuel Lasker, Akiba Rubinstein, Siegbert Tarrasch, and Jacques Mieses. Rank-and-file *voelkisch* activists

44 *Ibid.*, April 2, 1925; November 23, 1924.
45 *Was muss das schaffende Volk*, 6.
46 *Muenchener Post*, August 4, 1924, NSDAP Hauptarchiv, fol. 1465, no. 7.

were castigated for having surrendered to "the lowest instincts and the blackest traditions of the dark medieval past." [47]

> Someone stands on the corner and shouts as regularly as a clock striking the hour: "Down with the Jeeeeews!" "The Jeeeeewish Danger!" "The *Deutsche Wochenblatt!*" There you will find them all: the faces of impeccably respectable pimps and swindlers, hussies wearing cheap ... makeup and perfume, even students with popping eyes and the characteristics of Ludendorff, and above all heroic adolescents ... ! For amusement they jingle their swastikas and golden arm and foot chainlets. The call goes out with burning ecstasy—"Down with —— the Jews!" ... One of them laughs: "Friend, that was splendid! Again yesterday we made hash of one of the curs! And was he surprised, the Jew-boy! And shriek! I nearly died laughing. It's so true: Grab the Jews and hit 'em hard." [48]

In 1925 Otto Hoersing told a *Reichsbanner* rally that Judeophobes were "political criminals" and asked: "Is it not a pity that people with Christian views are not ashamed of their anti-Semitism in spite of the Biblical admonition that all men are created in the image of God?" [49]

Not content with exposing and ridiculing their racist enemies, the Socialists occasionally challenged them in direct confrontation. The *Schutz-und Trutzbund* had to cancel a 1920 anti-Jewish rally in Augsburg after both Majority and Independent Social Democrats threatened to break it up and sent nearly five hundred demonstrators to the racists' meeting hall. [50] The leader of the *voelkisch* "German Social Party," Richard Kunze, was popularly known as "Knueppel Kunze" because his con-

---

[47] *Vorwaerts*, September 2 and 9, 1920; February 1, 1922; April 13, 1924.
[48] *Ibid.*, October 8, 1922.
[49] NSDAP Hauptarchiv, fol. 1902, no. C–10.
[50] Secret reports of State Security Division, Augsburg, to Bavarian Ministry of the Interior, March 29, April 12, 1920, Acten des Bayerischen Staats- Ministeriums des Innern, fol. 66255, nos. 174–76, 188.

stant companion was a rubber truncheon he called "Heda," which he insolently referred to as his instrument for settling intellectual arguments. In 1923 he scheduled two meetings in the Upper Silesian city of Goerlitz. Before Kunze arrived, members of the Goerlitz Jewish community asked local SPD leader Otto Buchwitz to answer the racist's inevitable anti-Jewish harangue, to which he readily agreed. After Kunze had finished his first speech, Buchwitz answered him at length and, backed by a large group of Socialists he had brought with him, refused to forego a discussion period. But Kunze wanted to clear the hall for his second meeting. When one of the Socialists shouted, "How's Heda, Kunze?" he pulled out his truncheon, only to be disarmed by Buchwitz and his comrades, delivered to the waiting police, and ushered directly to the train station, never to return to Goerlitz.[51] A similar fate awaited one of Kunze's assistants, a certain Mertz, at a meeting he addressed in Frankfurt on the Oder during March of the same year. The local Socialists were there in force; their leader, Wilhelm Krueger, answered Mertz's inflammatory, anti-Semitic speech with a stinging rebuttal and brought the meeting to an end by leading cheers for the republic and the SPD. The less violent tactic of boycott was proposed in 1928 by *Vorwaerts*, which exposed the open denial of jobs to Jews by the Civil Servants' Cooperative, suggesting that many of its members who had joined without being aware of its attitude toward Jews would want to "open their eyes to the true nature of the association."[52]

Socialist spokesmen also called upon Germans to shun Judeophobia. During the unsettled months after the end of the war, the SPD addressed a number of appeals directly to the people, warning them of the anti-Semitic menace and calling for their cooperation against it. The first of these originated in the lead-

---

[51] Otto Buchwitz, *Fuenfzig Jahre Funktionaer der deutschen Arbeiterbewegung* ([East] Berlin, 1949), 109–11.
[52] *Vorwaerts*, March 13, 1923; November 2, 1928.

ing organ of the Workers and Soldiers of the Revolution, the *Vollzugsrat* of Berlin, in December, 1918; its author, Max Cohen-Reuss, was a Majority Socialist representative of the soldiers' councils. In its original form it said, in part:

> Of late, large numbers of anonymous pamphlets have been distributed that quite openly incite anti-Semitism. The pamphlets have not been ineffective. As *Vorwaerts* reported on December 11, repeatedly Jews and " ' Christians,' who because of the way they look are insufficiently protected against suspicions that they are Jews," have been physically attacked. If this shameless pamphleteering continues we will have to reckon with the possibility of experiencing the disgrace of anti-Jewish pogroms in Germany itself. The Executive Council of the Workers' and Soldiers' Councils feels itself obliged to turn against reactionary anti-Semitic actions in the sharpest possible manner. . . . The Executive Council appeals to the sound intelligence of the German people and is convinced that in their overwhelming majority they will oppose anti-Semitic, reactionary agitation and will not tolerate the persecution of Jews in any form whatever.[53]

Following an unnecessarily long debate over whether or not to include the names of specific SPD and USPD leaders who had been made special targets of anti-Jewish agitation, the motion was carried without change. Members of both parties spoke in its behalf, and it was published in *Vorwaerts* on December 14.

Similar in nature was the appeal of May 14, 1919, by the Office of the Berlin Chief of Police warning Berliners of the "dark elements" that were spreading hatred against Jews and foreigners in the German capital. "We struggle against the vicious policies of imperialism, not against individuals who are themselves guiltless. Those who promote racial hatred commit an injustice and most seriously sin against the interests of their

[53] Mueller-Franken, *Die November Revolution*, 108–10.

own people." [54] At about the same time a brochure signed by the twenty-two women of the SPD delegation in the Weimar National Assembly appealed to "German women and girls" to combat anti-Semitism as a degenerating influence in German politics that must inevitably lead "from political struggle to bloody racial war. We dare not put up with this. *We must make common cause against it!*" (Emphasis in the original.) Insisting that the Jews were neither better nor worse than other portions of the German population, the SPD ladies explained that the leaders of the DNVP promoted racial antagonisms solely because they wanted "to blot out the traces of their guilt" for war and defeat and thereby return to the seats of power. The authors reminded German women that right-wing success would also mean an end to women's rights as promised by the new government and closed by urging support for the SPD, which they represented as the intransigent enemy of social, political, and racial oppression. [55]

Similar appeals were made by Social Democrats during the equally dark months of 1922–23. An "Appeal to the Party" from the SPD Central Committee on July 13, 1923, demanded discipline and unity so that "the criminal activities of the Fascists and Jew-baiters and the reactionary plots against the Republic and democracy" might be "fought with vigor and enthusiasm." [56] In order to raise money to protect the republic and German Jewry from their opponents on the right and left, the SPD appealed for contributions to its "Emergency Fund for the Protection of the Republic." [57] One such request warned of an imminent right-wing putsch that would include pogroms against the Jews, who were being used as scapegoats for prob-

[54] *Vorwaerts*, May 15, 1919.
[55] Archiv des Vorstandes der Sozialdemokratischen Partei Deutschlands, Bonn, hereinafter cited as SPD Archiv, Flugblaetter, fol. IV (1918–33).
[56] *Vorwaerts*, July 13, 1923.
[57] I have not been able to determine how this fund was used.

lems caused by the rightists themselves. Another complained of "anti-Semitic incitements to murder" whose authors remained unpunished and secure. A third, published just after the Hitler-Ludendorff putsch and outbreaks of violence against Jews in Berlin in November, 1923, gave as an important purpose of the fund the suppression of "anti-Semitic outrages." [58]

In addition to urging Germans to eschew anti-Semitism, the SPD proved itself ready to take the offensive against perpetrators of anti-Jewish outrages. Among the first of these crimes was the most tragic—the assassination of Bavarian USPD leader Kurt Eisner on February 21, 1919, by a young, radically reactionary student, Count Anton von Arco-Valley. Although it acknowledged that Eisner's race was not the primary cause of his murder, *Vorwaerts* cast much of the blame on elements of the "bourgeois press" that had agitated against Eisner as a "Galician Jew." A few days later it reprinted part of an article from the far-right *Deutsche Tageszeitung* suggesting that the name "Eisner-Kosmanowski" be placed on the radical leader's grave and observing that one of the few notable deeds in Eisner's life had been his participation in the burial of his mother in a Jewish cemetery. Under the headline "Disgusting!" *Vorwaerts* labeled the author of the insults a "looter of corpses." Subsequently, however, the Socialist organ was able to take a good deal of pleasure in *voelkisch* embarrassment over the discovery that Count Arco himself was a half-Jew.[59]

The murder three years later of Walther Rathenau drew a similar response from the Social Democrats. For Germans seeking a scapegoat for the problems of mid-1922, Rathenau—a Jew, an outspoken republican, and Germany's moderate Foreign Minister—was a perfect target. For months before that fateful summer, right-wing hoodlums had revelled in reciting an inflammatory poem that ended with the lines:

[58] *Vorwaerts*, November 26, December 17 and 24, 1922; November 13, 1923.
[59] *Ibid.*, February 21 and 22, 1919; January 21, 1920.

Shoot down Walther Rathenau,
The dirty, God-damned Jewish sow! [60]

On June 24, 1922, three youthful, rabidly nationalistic students, members of Captain Hermann Ehrhardt's "Organization Council," assassinated Rathenau as he was being driven from his home in Grunewald to his ministry.[61]

Aware that on the day preceding the assassination Nationalist leader Karl Helfferich had delivered an abusive tirade against Rathenau in the Reichstag, most Socialists were convinced that he bore at least a part of the moral guilt for the assassination. Their reaction was typified by the helpless fury of the aged Eduard Bernstein, who greeted Helfferich's next appearance in the chamber with the cry, "Murderer!" They noted that the anti-Semitic groups from which the students came had been so impressed with Helfferich's speech they had sent him a floral bouquet decorated with the black, white, and red colors of Imperial Germany. Many Social Democrats erroneously assumed that the Nationalist leader had known of the assassination plot and had given it his approval.[62] "Helfferich incites—Erzberger is murdered. Helfferich incites—Rathenau is murdered," commented *Vorwaerts*.[63] On the afternoon of the assassination hundreds of thousands of Socialist workers demonstrated against it by spontaneously marching in quiet

[60] Eduard Fuchs, *Die Juden in der Karikatur: Ein Beitrag zur Kulturgeschichte* (Munich, 1921), 284. *Vorwaerts* reacted to the poem with scorn: "Schiller's *Tell* and Kleist's *Hermannsschlacht* turn pale beside this *voelkisch* poetry." But the newspaper soon felt obliged to defend itself against Communist and Nationalist charges that the Socialists themselves had made up the lines to discredit the political right. See *Vorwaerts*, June 26 and October 1, 1921.

[61] For details of the assassination, see Robert G. L. Waite, *Vanguard of Nazism: The Free Corps Movement in Postwar Germany, 1918–1923* (Cambridge, Mass., 1952), 219–20.

[62] Paul Loebe, *Der Weg war lang* (Berlin, 1954), 102–104.

[63] *Vorwaerts*, June 24, 1922. Matthias Erzberger, a leading member of the Center Party, had been killed on August 26, 1921, by members of the same "Organization Council."

determination through middle- and upper-class sections of Berlin. Three days later, as President Friedrich Ebert (SPD) delivered Rathenau's funeral oration, more than a million workers demonstrated in Berlin against the assassins, while other huge meetings were held under Socialist auspices in other principal cities of the Reich.[64]

The trial of the one assassin apprehended alive, Ernst Werner Techow, revealed to the Socialists that he and his companions had assimilated fantastic hallucinations. They believed Rathenau was a "creeping Bolshevist" and one of the three hundred "Wise Men of Zion" who were determined to spread the ideas of Lenin in Germany and bring the entire world under Jewish control. Techow's naive sincerity convinced Socialist leader Julius Leber that the real malefactors were the Jew-haters who had poisoned the assassins' minds.[65] *Vorwaerts* agreed. In addition to numbering Helfferich among those guilty, the newspaper reproduced and excoriated anti-Semitic attacks made against the slain minister before the assassination by Alfred Roth, a leader of the League for Offense and Defense, and by DNVP Reichstag deputy Wilhelm Henning, who had called Rathenau a "tool of Jewish Bolshevism." Philipp Scheidemann agreed that organized anti-Semitism was at the root of the outrage and linked it with other incidents in which the political right had formented anti-Jewish agitation against the republic. Unwilling to exonerate the students of all guilt, however, the Socialists complained that the total of thirty-three years in jail sentences meted out to everyone convicted of involvement in the crime was far too weak a punishment for such an atrocity. Until the advent of the Third Reich the Social Democrats kept Rathenau's memory alive with yearly graveside memorial services to commemorate his martyrdom, notwithstanding the fact

[64] Count Harry Kessler, *Walther Rathenau: His Life and Work* (New York, 1930), 357–60.

[65] Leber, *Ein Mann geht seinen Weg: Schriften, Reden und Briefe von Julius Leber* (Berlin, 1952), 134–35.

that he had been one of Germany's richest capitalists. Two years after the assassination *Vorwaerts* reacted with disgust to a racist contention that the Jews themselves had shot Rathenau as a prorepublican propaganda stunt.[66]

German Socialists reacted vigorously to anti-Jewish riots that took place in Berlin on November 6, 1923. Crowds of Berliners, angered by inflation, unemployment, and governmental instability, let themselves be led by racist agitators into the city's Jewish quarter for speeches and demonstrations that ended with the plundering of Jewish shops and the manhandling of the owners. Only with difficulty was the situation kept from getting completely out of hand. The SPD reacted quickly. The next morning *Vorwaerts* printed a resolution signed by the leaders of the Berlin Socialist trade unions:

> Workers, contemplate the men who incite you to acts of violence. German racist agitators have stirred up the misguided masses to pogroms. The great assault on Berlin's Jewish quarter is being prepared carefully and with cool calculation by German racist demagogues for the purpose of intensifying the confused political conditions in Germany to the point of catastrophe and to make the masses useful to the dark aims of Fascism. The German-racist leaders do not want merely to agitate against Jews; at the same time they want these excesses to act as proof that only a dictatorship of the right can guarantee public peace in Germany.
>
> Workers! Comrades! Pillaging the Jews will not root out capitalistic exploitation. If Kohn can no longer profiteer today, tomorrow Stinnes and Thyssen will profiteer just that much more. The Jewish as well as the Christian exploiter, the black as well as the white Jew will fall only when capitalism falls. Only fundamental intervention in the exploitive capitalistic economy can save the German people.[67]

[66] *Vorwaerts,* June 26 and 27, July 12, October 15, 1922; June 25, 1924.
[67] *Ibid.,* November 7, 1923.

Soon thereafter SPD chairman Artur Crispien blamed both the KPD and the *voelkisch* parties for the anti-Semitic incidents. "Berlin has been befouled. *A disgrace for a nation that considers itself civilized.*" (His emphasis.) Crispien reiterated the SPD's "plot theory" of Judeophobia and pictured the capitalists as rubbing their hands with glee because their agents had sidetracked the masses. He emphasized the need to trample the capitalist system under foot rather than Jews, individual capitalists, or any other group. He took pains to show that tradesmen and salesmen had their necessary function in the economy, and said that anyone wanting to avoid them should join a consumers' cooperative. In conclusion he warned that anti-Semitism could not bring socialism but, on the contrary, would aid only the reactionaries.[68]

The SPD also responded with no less than twelve protest meetings,[69] the most important of which was addressed by Karl Hildebrand, a member of the Reichstag and of the Party's Central Committee. Hildebrand, too, reiterated the Party's "plot theory." He maintained that the right wing used anti-Semitism both as a smoke screen and as a cause of chaotic conditions from which it hoped the people would seek salvation in a reactionary revolution. He ended by flailing the Berlin police for failing to protect Jews energetically enough, urging his listeners to double their efforts against anti-Semitism and for the republic. The essence of Hildebrand's arguments was repeated a few days later by one "Comrade Pastor Franke," who addressed the "German League for Human Rights" on the subject "The National and Cultural Disgrace of Jew-baiting." SPD Reichstag member Adolf Hoffman also spoke against anti-Semitism before an open Party meeting on Berlin's west side; at the end, a resolution was unanimously adopted declaring war

---

68 *Ibid.*, November 8, 1923. Crispien was a non-Jew.
69 Friedrich Stampfer, *Die vierzehn Jahre der ersten deutsche Republik* (Karlsbad, 1936), 337.

on organized animosity toward Jews, "which distracts the attention of the people from those responsible for their misfortunes and their distress." [70]

The Social Democrats believed that the events of 1923 had brought the republic close to collapse, and they were determined to meet any attempt to overthrow it with force of their own. They realized that the *Reichswehr* could not be trusted and that the *Stahlhelm* and the Nazi SA presented constant threats to German democracy. Late in 1923, at the initiative of Otto Wels, the Socialists laid plans for the creation of a nonpartisan, paramilitary organization to defend the republic. The organization, which came into being on February 22, 1924, was called the "*Reichsbanner* Black-Red-Gold" (after the republican flag) and was placed under the leadership of Otto Hoersing, the SPD *Oberpraesident* of the province of Saxony.[71] Although Democrats and Centrists were welcomed into its ranks, the membership of the *Reichsbanner* was from the beginning overwhelmingly Social Democratic, and most important decisions were made for the organization by the SPD Central Committee.[72] Its first appeal for members took issue with anti-Semitism:

Thousands of young men have been formed into armed storm companies under the leadership of men . . . who shamelessly misuse the ideas of Fatherland and nation in order to hide their

[70] *Vorwaerts*, November 14 and 22, December 5, 1923.

[71] Friedrich Otto Hoersing, a non-Jew, remained as chief of the *Reichsbanner* until January, 1932, when he quarreled with the SPD leadership over national economic policies and left both it and the *Reichsbanner* to found his own Social Republican Party. He was succeeded by Karl Hoeltermann, also a non-Jew. Hoersing died in 1937 in a Berlin Jewish hospital, where he had asked to be taken to spend his last days. Arnold Paucker, *Der juedische Abwehrkampf gegen Antisemitismus und Nationalsozialismus in den letzten Jahren der Weimarer Republik* (Hamburg, 1968), 270; Franz Osterroth, *Biographisches Lexikon des Sozialismus* (Hanover, 1960), I, 138–40.

[72] Karl Rohe, *Das Reichsbanner Schwartz Rot Gold: Ein Beitrag zur Geschichte und Struktur der politischen Kampfverbaende zur Zeit der Weimarer Republik* (Duesseldorf, 1966), 266–67, 314–24, 337–39.

own guilt and secret aims behind disgraceful Jew-baiting. *We Republicans will never forget that Jewish soldiers fought and bled shoulder to shoulder with Catholics, Protestants, and free-thinkers.* The number of dead and badly wounded Jewish soldiers proves this. This imbecilic anti-Semitism, which has even poisoned the minds of children, not only makes Germany ridiculous in the eyes of the world but is also dangerous to both our domestic and foreign affairs.[73]

The appeal was superbly effective; within a year the *Reichsbanner* boasted more than three million members. A militantly republican weapon had been added to the Socialist arsenal, and its opposition to anti-Semitism was unmistakable.

Less obtrusive anti-Jewish incidents also occupied Socialist attention during the years 1918–28. The physicist Albert Einstein had to cancel a series of lectures in February, 1920, because students repeatedly interrupted him with shouted anti-Semitic slogans. The Socialists commented: "Professor Einstein is one of the few Germans whose names are today regarded with unlimited and uncontested respect. If a band of green youths believes that the only way to defend German esteem is to abuse this man with anti-Semitic filthiness, the state of mind of these 'saviors of Germany' is really disagreeable." [74] When, in the same year, anti-Semites in Munich physically attacked Dr. Magnus Hirschfeld and broke up a meeting he was addressing on the subject of venereal diseases, the local SPD organ labelled it a "shrieking infamy against civilization [*weithinschreiende Kulturschande*] for our city of art and science" and assailed Munich law officers for failing to make a single arrest in the case.[75] Socialist deputy Alwin Saenger carried this attack into the Bavarian Parliament, holding the state government "co-

73 *Vorwaerts*, March 7, 1924. Emphasis in the original.
74 *Ibid.*, February 13, 1920.
75 *Muenchener Post*, October 5 and 7, 1920. See also *Vorwaerts*, October 5, 1920; February 5, 1922.

responsible" for the beating because its "criminal neglect" had permitted anti-Semitic groups to thrive in Bavaria.[76] In a similar case, on Christmas Day, 1925, aged Jewish philosopher Gregorius Itelsohn was brutally beaten by racists and inflicted with wounds from which he subsequently died. " 'Peace on earth and good will to all men'—as the *voelkisch* perceive it," commented *Vorwaerts*. On a more personal note, the Socialist organ indignantly related that SPD Reichstag Deputy Kurt Rosenfeld was forced to endure anti-Semitic abuse from a group of racists he encountered while travelling on a train. It was as disdainful over a report from the United States that Jews in Massena, New York, were accused of the ritual-murder of a child who, it was later found, had merely lost her way in the forest.[77]

Vorwaerts expressed outrage over large numbers of anti-Jewish postcards sent to Berlin addresses from Czechoslovakia in 1919. These contained highly unflattering caricatures of Jews together with biblical quotations that appeared to justify pogroms against them. "Must we admit such filth?" inquired the SPD organ. An anti-Jewish demonstration on the Kurfuerstendamm in 1921 led the Socialist daily to demand that the police take measures to prevent such scenes from getting out of hand, while shortly thereafter it turned its wrath on the Kahr regime in Bavaria for making a point of ignoring the dangers presented by such demonstrations. On one occasion, when a Jew used a gun to protect himself from a racist mob and wounded two attackers, *Vorwaerts* regarded him as a hero and acclaimed his vindication in a court of law. Reporting in 1924 one of the earliest examples of the desecration by racists of

---

[76] *Verhandlungen des Bayerischen Landtags: Stenographische Berichte*, 12th Sess., 1920, I, 384. Saenger later broadened his attack on state and municipal authorities in Bavaria and Munich to what he described as their failure generally to give adequate protection to Jews or control Judeophobes. *Ibid.*, 58th Sess., 1921, II, 841; 60th Sess., 1921, III, 227–28, 230.

[77] *Vorwaerts*, December 29, 1925; May 9, 1926; October 9, 1924; November 2, 1928; New York *Times*, October 3, 1928.

Jewish cemeteries, *Vorwaerts* spoke of "frankly unbelievable vandalism." It was equally outraged two years later when the *voelkisch* Breslau newspaper *Schlesische Volksstimme* tried to arouse pogrom sentiments by linking the suicide of a Jewish worker with the sex-murders of two small children and implying that ritual-slaughter was involved.[78]

Unwilling to lay blame for anti-Jewish violence at any door but that of these professional Jew-haters, *Vorwaerts* told of a worker who returned from the war with a mental disorder, failed to find employment, and after reading anti-Semitic pamphlets tried to blackmail two wealthy Jews for forty thousand marks. The newspaper assigned guilt solely to the authors of the "pogrom pamphlets," lamenting that their "victim" had to spend a year in prison while they went unmolested. Similarly, it reported an attack by Jews (in which two were seriously wounded) upon anti-Semitic demonstraters on Berlin's fashionable Kurfuerstendamm with open sympathy for the attackers. The Socialists urged the Berlin police to prevent a repetition of such occurrences by suppressing all anti-Jewish demonstrations.[79]

The Social Democratic Minister-President of Prussia, Paul Hirsch, speaking before the Prussian Constituent Assembly on November 15, 1919, excoriated the political right for injecting the "spirit of inquisition and witch-burning" into relations between Jews and non-Jews, a development that he especially deplored because of its unwholesome influence on the minds of the young. Although he singled out the DNVP for special condemnation, Hirsch indicted the entire anti-Jewish movement: "What is most essential is that almost the whole of the right-wing press, with its incessant and extremely malicious polemics against the Jews, engenders with absolute security an atmos-

[78] *Vorwaerts*, June 30, 1919; February 28, 1921 (see also issues of January 29, 1919, October 14, 1920); *ibid.*, August 9, 1921; December 30, 1920; July 30, 1924; June 15, July 6, 1926.
[79] *Ibid.*, July 15, August 14 and 16, 1919.

phere that is so sultry that even without outside inducement the situation must one day explode of itself, discharging the diligently collected dynamite." As he made these remarks, Hirsch was frequently interrupted by shouts and catcalls from the right. At one point the din grew so loud he was unable to continue, but after the chairman had restored a semblance of order he was able to conclude his speech to the cheers of his fellow Majority Socialists.[80] The speech was given prominent coverage in *Vorwaerts* and was reprinted in pamphlet form for distribution by the SPD.[81]

In making these statements, Hirsch could as easily have represented the USPD as the SPD, so nearly identical were the positions of the two parties on the subject of anti-Semitism.[82] Yet neither of them seemed quite convinced that the other was completely free from Judeophobia. In January, 1920, for example, Jewish SPD leader Ernst Heilmann delivered a public speech on the topic "Democracy or Soviet Dictatorship?" He was repeatedly interrupted by cries of "Mass murderer!" "Traitor to the workers!" and "Out with the Jew Itzig!" *Vorwaerts* identified the perpetrators as "Independents," apparently referring to USPD members. Conversely, on July 26, 1919, USPD leader Hugo Haase called the attention of the Weimar National Assembly to the rise of anti-Jewish agitation and asserted that the Majority Socialists, who then headed the national government, had failed to take adequate countermeasures. Haase was particularly annoyed over the distribution of anti-Semitic materials in the military services.[83]

---

[80] *Sitzungsberichte der verfassunggebenden preussischen Landesversammlung*, 82nd Sess., 1919, V, 6507–508.

[81] *Vorwaerts*, November 16, 1919. Paul Hirsch, *Fuer Republik und Demokratie!* (Berlin, 1919), 1–16. See also Paul Hirsch, *Der Weg der Sozialdemokratie zur Macht in Preussen* (Berlin, 1929), 243–44.

[82] For the position of the USPD, see the resolution adopted unanimously at the meeting of its party congress on December 6, 1919. *Protokoll ueber die Verhandlungen des ausserordentlichen Parteitages in Leipzig vom 30. November bis 6. Dezember 1919* (Berlin, n.d.), 455.

[83] *Vorwaerts*, January 17, 1920; July 27, 1919. See also page 90.

The SPD employed propaganda to combat anti-Semitism in the various national, state, and local elections held between 1919 and 1928. The campaign for the Reichstag election held on June 6, 1920, produced an SPD pamphlet that repeated the Party's view that anti-Semitism was "only a sly appeal to stupidity," while placing the SPD firmly behind equal rights for Jews: "To it an honorable Jewish man is of no less value than a Christian, and the Christian swindler is no better than the Jewish." [84] Richard Fischer called attention to the right wing's use of anti-Jewish slogans in the campaign, while *Vorwaerts* roasted the DNVP for spreading a scurrilous poem implying that Jews were steadily increasing their domination over the whole government: "In the interest of Germany it is to be regretted that one of the parties should carry on its election campaign on such a low level that the medieval and thoroughly Russian spirit of Jew-baiting should be paraded before the eyes of the world." The Socialist daily also blasted DVP election propaganda that referred to such prominent leftist "Jews" as Karl Radek, Eduard Bernstein, and Karl Kautsky as men of "an alien race." *Vorwaerts* wondered if such agitation had the approval of party chairman Stresemann, who had married a woman of that "alien race." [85] Counteracting similar propaganda during the 1921 election campaign, Erna Buesing wrote: "The Jews are not foreigners; on the contrary, we have in our Fatherland 540,000 Germans of the Jewish faith. Naturally every enlightened person should regard religion as his very own private affair." [86] Also during that campaign, *Vorwaerts* underlined quarrels between different *voelkisch* groups that were marked by accusations of Jewish takeover, which, the newspaper pointed out, was the same charge levelled at republicans. [87]

Both right-wing and left-wing anti-Semitism was made a

[84] SPD Archiv, Flugblaetter, fol. II, (1918–33).
[85] *Vorwaerts*, May 30, 14, and 25, 1920; Kautsky was not a Jew.
[86] Buesing, "Duerfen wir Antisemiten sein?" 3.
[87] *Vorwaerts*, February 13 and 16, 1921.

target of Socialist reproach in the campaign for the first Reichstag election in 1924. Artur Crispien pointed to Ludendorff as a "racist champion of capitalistic reaction" and a key salesman in the capitalist scheme to undermine support for the SPD with anti-Semitic appeals. *Vorwaerts* delightedly revealed that one of Ludendorff's forefathers had married a Jewish woman.[88] It also blasted Albrecht von Graefe-Goldebee for having declared the DNVP willing to accept contributions from Jewish sources under some circumstances.[89] Ruth Fischer's "anti-Jewish" outburst of the previous year was reproduced and the KPD castigated for "attempting familiarity with the Fascists."[90] A special item in *Vorwaerts* on the eve of the election repeated the usual "plot theory" of Judeophobia and took pains to disprove stories that Jews had gained control of the government with facts showing the contrary.[91]

During the second 1924 Reichstag election campaign, *Vorwaerts* described the speeches delivered by Reinhold Wulle: "One takes his dictionary and places before each word the prefix 'Jew.'" Count Westarp was made to look quixotic for his posturings against Jews, France, and free trade. On the eve and morning of election day, *Vorwaerts* again printed special denunciations of anti-Semites and their outrageous tactics. Electioneering for Berlin municipal offices in 1925 produced the usual SPD denunciation of the DNVP's anti-Semitism as well as Socialist attacks on the DVP for injecting Jew-hatred into one of its campaign pamphlets. On the day before the election *Vorwaerts* condemned the DVP for allying with the "black-

---

[88] *Ibid.*, April 17, 25, and 29, 1924. The SPD practically ignored Ludendorff when he ran for president in 1925. The only criticism of his hatred for Jews appeared in *ibid.*, March 28, 1925.

[89] *Ibid.*, April 30, 1924. Although Graefe had left the DNVP in 1922 with his racist colleagues, he retained close ties with the Party and for all practical purposes continued to be regarded as a member. George L. Mosse, *The Crisis of German Ideology*, 231.

[90] *Handbuch fuer sozialdemokratische Waehler*, 178.

[91] *Vorwaerts*, May 3, 1924.

white-red anti-Semitic" bloc of the DNVP and two small *voelkisch* parties in an election in Upper Silesia.[92]

More stable conditions in 1928 seemed to call for less Socialist electioneering against anti-Semitism in the Reichstag election campaign of that year. Noting that the DNVP used the slogan "We Hold Fast to God's Word" on its election posters, *Vorwaerts* wondered how it reconciled its "tedious, insipid anti-Semitism" with the command to "Love thy neighbor as thyself." It asked Germans to reject "un-Christian anti-Semitic agitation" by repudiating the Nationalists on election day.[93] An anonymous Socialist spoofed the DNVP and the splinter parties that competed with it by portraying a mythical gathering of all their leaders as one long debate over how much Jewish blood the various rivals had inherited.[94]

SPD publicists displayed continuing concern over the persistence of anti-Jewish and antirepublican sentiments in the judiciary, the army, the administrative bureaucracy, and the schools—all of which had been inherited largely intact from the old regime. German jurists aroused SPD ire when they handed down clearly anti-Semitic judgments. In 1922 a Berlin judge declined to convict the leaders of a demonstration against Jews because he felt anti-Semitic insults were a harmless outlet for feelings that would otherwise erupt in violence. *Vorwaerts* rejected the explanation and urged the Ministry of Justice to take action against the judge. Later the interpolation of anti-Jewish remarks into a mild judgment against an anti-Semite led the Socialist daily to deplore "the unparalleled decay of our modern justice. A state that tolerates that kind of spirit in its administration of justice removes itself from the ranks of civilized states." A case involving use of the slogan "Down with the Jewish Republic!" by the Young German Order was

[92] *Ibid.*, November 16, December 6 and 7, 1924; October 18, 22, and 24, 1925.
[93] *Ibid.*, May 15, 1928.
[94] "Der Buergerblock bei der Wahlvorbereitung," *Jungsozialistische Blaetter*, VII (1928), 100–101.

thrown out of court in 1926 because the judges agreed that the prominent participation of Jews in founding the republic and "the exorbitant power and excessive influence" of Jews in the state gave the charge some validity; *Vorwaerts* raged that the decision could have come from the pen of Wulle, Hitler, or Julius Streicher, the most violent of the Nazi Judeophobes. After a Jewish farmer in East Prussia was assaulted while attending a meeting of local agriculturalists, his legal suit against the attackers resulted in a trivial fine levied against the defendant and the judicial comment that the Jew really had no business at a Christian gathering. The decision reminded *Vorwaerts* of an old Russian story: a stone thrown at a Jew broke a window when the intended target ducked; naturally the Jew had to pay for the damage, for had he not ducked, the window would not have been smashed.[95]

In a speech delivered at a Party rally in Berlin on February 14, 1928, Ernst Heilmann complained that altogether too many trials involving Jews or anti-Jewish actions ended in unfair verdicts. Incredulous laughter from his audience met his story of a Pole who called a Berlin Jew a "German pig"; brought to trial, the Pole was acquitted when the judge decided that no Jew could be insulted by the name because none was really a German. Heilmann was even more outraged over an unnamed judge who excused anti-Semitic acts on the grounds that they represented the efforts of the best and most respected citizens to return Germany to a leading position in Europe.[96]

German Social Democrats often found sentences assigned to anti-Semites unnecessarily mild. In 1924 a Judeophobe who had asserted that the renaissance masks which decorated the Rathenau mansion in Berlin had been fashioned after the heads of decapitated kings was found innocent of slander because, the judge said, he had expressed his "conviction" in

[95] *Vorwaerts*, June 20, 1922; April 19, 1924; June 25, 1926; February 9, 1927.
[96] Heilmann, *Die Sozialdemokratie in Preussen* (Berlin, 1928), 23.

the absence of information to the contrary. *Vorwaerts* found the decision "simply incomprehensible. . . . What will the judge say if a Communist expresses the 'conviction' that Hindenburg has stolen silver spoons?" It poured similar contempt on another acquittal of an anti-Semite whose actions the court held to have been motivated by "passionate love for his Fatherland." An insignificant fine assessed to a Judeophobe in 1925 led the Socialist organ to remark that the decision invited every anti-Semite with extra pocket money to indulge his prejudices cheaply. Repeated judicial refusals to ban singing of the anti-Jewish "Borkumlied," said *Vorwaerts*, gave "tacit approval to violent interference in the freedoms of Jewish fellow citizens." As ready to cheer as to complain, the Socialist organ on three occasions endorsed gratifyingly stiff penalties dealt out to Jew-haters.[97]

In 1922 SPD deputies Erich Kuttner and Ernst Heilmann excoriated the Prussian Minister of Justice Hugo am Zehnhoff in the General Committee of the Prussian Parliament for tolerating lenient judicial attitudes toward anti-Semitism.[98] Kuttner was especially indignant because the desecration of Jewish cemeteries and the use of inflammatory anti-Jewish slogans often went entirely unpunished; he subsequently repeated his objections before the entire parliament.[99] The Socialists applauded when later that year the Ministry of Justice issued an order that Jews were to be regarded as a "class" under the terms of a law prohibiting the incitement of class antago-

[97] *Vorwaerts*, March 19, 1924 (see also issue of September 10, 1922); March 26, 1924 (for similar cases, see issues of June 11, 1921; August 30, 1922; July 7, 1927); March 19, 1925 (see also issues of May 27, 1924; July 7, 1927); May 15, 1925 (see also issues of July 5 and 22, 1924; December 7, 1926); October 24, 1922; July 22, 1924; March 25, 1927.

[98] *Preussischer Landtag: Stenographische Berichte des Hauptausschusses*, 120th Sess., 1922, XX, 12–17; 121st Sess., 1922, XX, 20–22; *Vorwaerts*, April 25, 1922.

[99] *Sitzungsberichte des preussischen Landtags*, 140th Sess., 1922, VII, 9951–63; *Vorwaerts*, May 21, 1922.

nisms. Rejecting a *voelkisch* claim that the order made Jews a privileged group, they insisted it was a duty to protect Jews from excesses.[100] That the measure was insufficient to provide such protection became apparent only too quickly. Four years later the right-wing Socialist leader Wolfgang Heine felt obliged to flay the "boundless racial hatred" that still marked many legal judgments involving Jews and their opponents.[101]

In one prominent case having anti-Semitic overtones, German Socialists took an active part in averting a miscarriage of justice. In 1926 a Jewish manufacturer in Magdeburg, Rudolf Haas, was accused of murdering his accountant out of fear that the employee might betray allegedly dishonest business dealings. The local criminal inspector, an anti-Semite, remained convinced of Haas's guilt even after the body of the accountant was found in the cellar of a home occupied by an unemployed Nazi. Attempts by the *Oberpraesident* of the province of Saxony, Otto Hoersing, to replace the criminal inspector with another from Berlin were blocked by the chief justice of the state court, who was also no friend of the Jews. Hoersing would not be put off. He enlisted the aid of Prussian Minister of the Interior Severing, and together they withstood a torrent of right-wing abuse to replace the anti-Semitic inspector with two investigators from Berlin. In a short time evidence was uncovered proving the unemployed Nazi was the murderer. Without Hoersing's determination and Severing's cooperation, Haas might have fallen victim to the anti-Jewish prejudices of the Magdeburg court.[102] The Social Democrats in the Prussian Parliament successfully demanded disciplinary proceedings against the justice who had blocked Hoersing's first attempts to secure a further investigation into the charges against

[100] *Vorwaerts*, October 26, 1922.
[101] Heine, "Die Beamten der Republik," *Sozialistische Monatshefte*, XXXII (1926), 612. Heine was non-Jewish.
[102] Heinz Braun, *Am Justizmord vorbei: Der Fall Koelling-Haas* (Magdeburg, 1928), 5–271.

Haas.[103] To their disgust, the proceedings resulted only in a mild fine for the justice.[104]

The persistence of Judeophobia in the officers' corps of the armed forces was another source of disturbance to German Socialists. The republic's first *Reichswehr* Minister, Socialist Gustav Noske, was less than successful in dealing with the problem. In 1919 he replied to criticisms from USPD leader Hugo Haase about the distribution of anti-Semitic materials in the military services. Noske readily agreed that anti-Jewish agitation had become "extremely dangerous" but declared that it was as difficult to trace the anti-Semitic leaflets to their sources as it was to uncover the origins of Spartacist papers. Still, he promised to do everything possible to minimize the racist threat and to "condemn most decisively and take steps against every anti-Semitic move among the troops." [105]

Not all Majority Socialists felt Noske was doing enough to counteract anti-Semitism. A few days after his speech, *Vorwaerts* acidly replied: "Perhaps it will interest him to learn that anti-Semitic propaganda has already entered the army and is cultivated there by certain officers who abuse their authority." Then it reported the case of an infantry captain who encouraged the dissemination of *voelkisch* literature and opinions in his command; every protest against the officer, said the SPD newspaper, had been met with flat refusal to investigate the matter. A few months later it complained that the official publication of the Third Army Brigade had alleged that "Jews and their sympathizers" dominated the Reichstag Commission on Causes of the Collapse; *Vorwaerts* appealed to the Reichswehr Minister to stop the publication of this "obviously subversive" periodical.[106]

---

[103] *Jahrbuch der deutschen Sozialdemokratie fuer das Jahr 1927* (Berlin, 1928), 246–47.
[104] *Der Abend*, April 24, 1928; January 15 and 22, 1929; *Vorwaerts*, January 25, 1929.
[105] *Vorwaerts*, July 27, 1919.
[106] *Ibid.*, July 31, 1919; January 1, 1920.

When Noske was removed from office immediately following the Kapp putsch the Socialists demonstrated less forbearance toward the army, demanding, for example, that swastikas be removed from helmets and implying that proletarian wrath would fall on the soldiers unless the racist symbols were eliminated. *Vorwaerts* also insisted that Noske's successor, Otto Gessler, suppress the distribution of anti-Jewish leaflets by Free Corps' members. In May, 1920, the Socialist organ dealt at length with the virulence of anti-Semitism in the army and with reports that gangs of soldiers had smeared swastikas on a synagogue and on Jewish homes in Duisburg. "Cleanse the army of this reactionary anti-Semitic fellowship!" the newspaper demanded. Later it complained of anti-Semitic songfests led by soldiers in the amusement arcade at the spa of Swinemuende. The Reichswehr Minister himself came in for Socialist criticism in 1924 for refusing to declare the anti-Jewish *Stahlhelm* off limits to army officers and men.[107]

German Socialists also expressed concern over anti-Semitism in the administrative bureaucracy. In 1920 they complained of an undersecretary in the Bavarian Ministry of Labor who had alleged that Jewish civil servants were in league with the head of the Communist International, Gregory Zinoviev, to foment a Bolshevik revolution in Germany. An outraged *Vorwaerts* demanded the removal of a Berlin bureaucrat whose delighted reaction to news of Rathenau's assassination was: "There'll be Jew-brains for dinner today, ladies—Rathenau was just shot in Grunewald!" When a young civil servant was dismissed for reporting that a superior in his department was distributing anti-Jewish propaganda, *Vorwaerts* complained that this "unbelievable state of affairs" would have to be altered by the Prussian government. It reacted in much the same way to a refusal by Prussian state welfare officials to aid a Jewish veteran with foot problems because, they said, flat feet were a Jewish

---

[107] *Ibid.*, March 24, April 6, May 27, August 17, 1920; July 6, 1923; April 19, 1924; see also issue of February 6, 1928.

"racial characteristic." [108] In 1924 racists forced the Jewish president of the Thuringian State Bank to resign, and others in the Bavarian Parliament demanded and got an investigation into the number of Jews in the state civil service. Social Democrats protested against both efforts to eliminate Jews from the bureaucracy.[109] On the other hand, they praised the *Regierungspraesident* of Potsdam for making a Bergholz innkeeper remove a sign that read: "Jews, agents, peddlers, and musicians are forbidden to enter my property." [110]

Sensitive to Judeophobia in all levels of German academic life, the SPD criticized the toleration of anti-Semitic teachers and the exclusion of Jews from positions as educators. In 1920 *Vorwaerts* denounced a Berlin elementary school teacher for making anti-Jewish statements in class, thereby stimulating an investigation that led to disciplinary action against him. Later it lashed out at Prussian Minister of Education Otto Boelitz for his reluctance to place Jews in administrative positions in the educational system. The Socialists also expressed annoyance over the anti-Jewish lectures of a Jena Professor of Zoology, Dr. Ludwig Plate,[111] and they excoriated the DVP Minister of Education in Thuringia, Dr. Richard Leutheusser, for doing nothing about them.[112] The racial doctrines disseminated by Plate and other extremist educators were denounced as "animalistic breeding doctrines" that could have no ennobling influence on German youth.[113]

Anti-Semitic student groups found no sympathy in *Vorwaerts*. In 1919 it reported with disgust the enthusiastic recep-

[108] *Ibid.*, November 13, 1920; July 8, August 30, 1922; October 14, 1926. See also "Aus der Sozialpolitik: Heilstaette oder Bethaus?" *Gewerkschafts-Zeitung*, XXXVIII (1928), 90–91.
[109] *Vorwaerts*, April 15, July 26, September 26, October 1, 1924.
[110] *Der Abend*, December 11, 1928.
[111] *Vorwaerts*, October 28, 1920; February 2, 1921; September 18, 1924; July 31, 1927.
[112] *Jahrbuch...1927*, p. 288.
[113] *Vorwaerts*, June 15, 1921.

tion that Berlin University students gave an anti-Jewish lecture. Two years later the newspaper told of a Jewish student at the University of Giessen who was insulted by racist students and who made the mistake of answering in kind, for which he was attacked by the mob; in the ensuing trial the Jew was convicted of provoking the attack while the racists went free—all of which left a sardonic *Vorwaerts* wondering which to admire more, "the valor of the anti-Semites or the judicial impartiality of the court." Efforts by anti-Jewish students in Munich to block the appointment of a new Jewish professor at the university prompted the Socialist organ to remind the Bavarian Ministry of Education that the racist demands were unconstitutional and must be rejected.[114] Finding the situation unimproved in 1927, the Socialists still spoke of the "exasperating spirit of anti-Semitism" among right-wing students,[115] but they took heart in a decision by the Prussian government to require student organizations to sever all ties with officially anti-Jewish Austrian student groups on pain of losing state authorization and financial support.[116]

In opposing restrictions on the admission and rights of Jewish students, the Socialists again appealed to the provisions of the Weimar Constitution guaranteeing equal rights to all citizens. In 1919 *Vorwaerts* criticized the student government at the University of Hanover for restricting suffrage to "students of German descent." The *Kreuzzeitung*'s proposal for a *numerus clausus* for Jewish students, which it defended as a service to Christianity, caused *Vorwaerts* to fume: "What a symbol of the prostitution of genuine Christian teachings by the pogrom-lusting apostles of international 'Christian' reaction!" In 1920 the Socialist daily demanded the withdrawal of a Berlin Tech-

---

[114] *Ibid.*, May 11, 1919; May 12, 1921 (see also issues of August 2, 1922, and May 10, 1923); June 7, 1923.
[115] Heinz Krueger, "Der Kampf in der Studentenschaft," *ibid.*, July 14, 1927; see also issues of September 19 and 22, 1928.
[116] *Vorwaerts*, September 28, 1927.

nical University application form that inquired deeply into the applicant's ethnic background, remarking that it might prove useful to one of the *voelkisch* groups but could not be tolerated in a public school. Later the newspaper thundered against the exclusion of Jews from the officially recognized Foreign Students' Organization of the University of Berlin as "a flagrant violation of the spirit of the constitution." [117]

From 1918 to 1928 Social Democratic commentators opposed the postwar wave of anti-Jewish agitation as part of a reactionary conspiracy to thrust the blame for war, defeat, revolution, and inflation on a racial scapegoat and to mobilize the masses against the Weimar Republic and its principal supporter, the SPD. They therefore regarded attacks on Jews as indirect, but nonetheless dangerous, attacks on themselves, and they repeatedly attacked racist associations, condemned anti-Semitic excesses, and ridiculed *voelkisch* absurdities. In doing so they did not ignore anti-Semitism's regrettable effects on the lives of the Jews and its corrupting influences on German society as a whole.

[117] *Ibid.*, October 30, 1919; October 2, 1920 (see also issue of November 17, 1925); December 15, 1920; January 17, 1927.

Chapter IV

The SPD and the Jews
1918-1928

SPD attacks on anti-Semitism emphasized the necessity of defending the republic rather than the need to protect Jews per se. Socialist comments for or against Jews—with the notable exception of matters concerning Eastern European Jewish refugees— were uncommon during the years 1918–28. However, notwithstanding the presence of some individual anti-Semites in the Party, the majority of Socialist spokesmen who commented on Jews as a group did so in a complimentary and sympathetic way.

German Socialists extended both help and sympathy to the *Ostjuden* (Jewish refugees who had come to Germany from Eastern Europe). Of all the Jews in postwar Germany, these suffered the hardest lot. Before 1914 nearly ninety thousand of them had taken refuge in Germany from Russian pogroms. During and after the war they were joined by seventy thousand more, some of whom were enlisted by the wartime German military government in Poland as workers for war industries, others of whom sought refuge in Germany from the anti-Semitism of the Tsarist and White Russian armies or from communism.[1] Their presence in Germany after the armistice

[1] S. Adler-Rudel, *Ostjuden in Deutschland 1880–1940* (Tuebingen, 1959), 60.

aggravated the already acute problems of housing and unemployment and proved a boon to racist propagandists, who frequently tried to obscure the distinctions between the newcomers and German Jews.

German Socialists attempted to stem the tide of resentment that arose against the *Ostjuden* by calling attention to the conditions under which the refugees had come to Germany and asserting that they would leave at the first opportunity. In 1920 *Vorwaerts* replied to DNVP criticisms of the *Ostjuden* by recalling General Ludendorff's 1914 appeal to the Jews of the conquered Russian territories that they collaborate with the occupiers and regard Germans as their deliverers from Russian Judeophobia.[2] In 1924 the Socialists noted that during the war *Ostjuden* had been deported to Germany or enticed there as contracted laborers by the very people who after the war became their chief detractors.[3] Rejecting the *voelkisch* accusation that the newcomers intended to plunder the German economy, *Vorwaerts* maintained that the refugees merely thought of Germany as a way station on their voyage to America or Palestine. It demanded that Social Democrats help the refugees adjust to their temporary home, assist them in finding jobs, and under no circumstances support demands that they be returned to the east, where persecution and death awaited them.[4] In 1922 the newspaper responded to a racist rally against the *Ostjuden* by observing that nearly half of them had already left Germany and that the rest would soon follow. As late as 1928 Jakob Leschtschinski compassionately described the fate of the remaining Jewish refugees in Berlin, telling of doctors reduced

[2] *Vorwaerts*, July 30, 1920. Four years later it reprinted the entire appeal and drew from it a similar moral. *Ibid.*, October 10, 1924.

[3] *Was muss das schaffende Volk*, 6–7.

[4] *Vorwaerts*, October 8, 1920; see also Alfred Marcus, "Die Ostjuedische Durchwanderung," *Sozialistische Monatshefte*, XXVII (1921), 342–44; *Vorwaerts*, October 22, 1921.

to hawking dry goods, engineers to selling flashlights, and journalists to operating candy stands.[5]

Social Democrats also shielded *Ostjuden* from unjustified accusations and physical harassment. Answering DNVP charges that the uprooted Jews were responsible for Berlin's acute postwar housing shortage, *Vorwaerts* contrasted their overcrowded living conditions with the twelve-room homes occupied by Russian emigre nobles. In April, 1920, the Party organ fumed over the mass arrests and internment of Jewish refugees by army units in Wuensdorf,[6] while the Bavarian Government's subsequent efforts to expel all *Ostjuden* prompted Erhard Auer's public condemnation.[7] In the Bavarian parliament Socialist Deputy Alwin Saenger excoriated the state government for these expulsions, citing several pitiful cases in which alien Jewish families with sick children or much-decorated war heroes were ruthlessly uprooted from well-established homes.[8] The following August, *Vorwaerts* censured the actions of German security police in Upper Silesia who had herded eight hundred Jewish refugees back across the Polish border, and it demanded a government investigation of the matter.[9] When in 1922 the *Regierungspraesident* of the Duesseldorf area began numerous expulsion proceedings against *Ostjuden*, his efforts were blocked by Jews of that region who turned for help to Heinrich Limbertz of Essen, a leader of the local Miners' Union and a Socialist deputy in the Prussian parliament.[10] Limbertz brought the matter before the parliament on June 17. He firmly denied contentions that the *Ostjuden* harbored criminals, political radicals, and freeloaders and insisted that they had proved

5 *Vorwaerts*, May 7, 1922; April 24, 1928.
6 *Ibid.*, January 31, 1920; April 1, 1920. See also page 100 of this chapter.
7 Auer, *Sozialdemokratie und Antisemitismus*, 11.
8 *Verhandlungen des Bayerischen Landtags*, 10th Sess., 1920, I, 267–71.
9 *Vorwaerts*, August 19, 1920. Apparently no such investigation was held.
10 Adler-Rudel, *Ostjuden in Deutschland*, 91–93.

to be honest workers and loyal union members. Replying to Limbertz's plea that the expulsions be halted, Minister of the Interior Carl Severing stated that he had already taken steps to do so and that no attempts to expel Jewish refugees would be tolerated.[11]

Later that year the DNVP introduced a motion in the Prussian parliament to expel all the *Ostjuden* from Germany and prevent any more from coming in.[12] Severing attacked the proposal by citing statistics proving that Jews made up only a minority of refugees from the east. Warning against anti-Semitic excesses, he recited Lessing's words in *Nathan the Wise:* "We first come into the world not as Christians and not as Jews and not as Moslems, but rather as human beings." Speaking for the SPD delegation, Oscar Cohn answered the DNVP's vilifications of *Ostjuden* by recounting the conditions of their entry and contending that without their labor the weapons for Germany's last-ditch 1918 offensive would not have been available. He castigated the Nationalists for ignoring humane considerations and forgetting that German protests of abuses against German minorities in bordering territories would lose their moral justification if Jewish refugees in Germany were treated badly. Cohn begged Germans to have empathy with the *Ostjuden,* and he ended on a prophetic note: "What the Jews experience of forced migration and suffering in wars and after wars could also one day be German destiny." [13]

German Socialists praised and cooperated with Jewish organizations that helped Jewish refugees. In 1921 and 1922 the Socialist trade unions supplied information that was published by the *Arbeiterfuersorgeamt der juedischen Organisationen*

---

[11] *Sitzungsberichte des preussischen Landtags,* 149th Sess., 1922, VIII, 10762–66; *Vorwaerts,* June 18, 1922.

[12] *Sammlung der Drucksachen den preussischen Landtags,* 1922, V, 3357–58, no. 2932.

[13] *Sitzungsberichte des preussischen Landtags,* 188th Sess., 1922, X, 13556–610; *Vorwaerts,* November 30, 1922.

Deutschlands (Workers' Welfare Office of Jewish Organizations in Germany) showing that the *Ostjuden* made willing workers, did not aggravate the problem of unemployment, and did not justify complaints that they were clannish or dirty.[14] At that time, too, one Socialist trade union official in Essen went so far as to request union funds to aid the local *Arbeiterfuersorgeamt*, though without success.[15] Socialist Alfred Marcus showered praise on the Jewish organization for its efforts to find employment for *Ostjuden*.[16] SPD member Paul Nathan was a leader of the *Hilfsverein der deutschen Juden* (Relief Association of German Jews) until his death in 1927.[17] When he was subjected in 1926 to an anti-Semitic press campaign that smeared him as an agent of the *Ostjuden*, Nathan rejoined that he felt it was his duty as dictated by "the principles of humanitarianism without discrimination as to Christians or Jews or any others" to help all who were unjustly persecuted.[18]

Most Social Democrats in official positions proved themselves sensitive to the plight of the Jewish refugees. Wolfgang Heine,[19] Prussian Minister of the Interior in 1919, was feared by German Jews who remembered that as a student he had been an anti-Semite, but their fears vanished when they read his ordinance of November 1, 1919, which set down conditions for the *Ostjuden*. It permitted their expulsion only in cases in which

---

14 Nachlass Bernstein, fol. B–68.

15 Reiter to ADGB Central, Berlin, August 24, 1921; Alban Welker to ADGB District Committee, Essen, August 27, 1921, ADGB Akten, fol. NB–211.

16 Marcus, "Produktive Ostjudenfuersorge," *Sozialistische Monatshefte*, XXVII (1921), 707–11.

17 For information about Nathan's services to that organization, consult Ernst Feder, "Paul Nathan, the Man and his Work," *Leo Baeck Institute Year Book III* (London, 1958), 60–80.

18 *Vorwaerts*, January 13, 1926.

19 For allegations that Heine attacked Alexander Helphand in anti-Semitic terms at the SPD's 1901 Party Congress, see Z. A. B. Zeman and W. B. Scharlau, *The Merchant of Revolution: The Life of Alexander Israel Helphand (Parvus), 1867–1924* (London, 1965), 46–47; Silberner, *Sozialisten zur Judenfrage*, 201.

they broke the law or remained perpetually unemployed. Those against whom expulsion proceedings were begun could be defended by the *Arbeiterfuersorgeamt*, and if their offense was unemployment, that organization was to be given an opportunity to find them work. It also limited the number of foreign workers in any one plant to ten and released all who had been arrested or prepared for expulsion unless in accordance with the new regulations.[20]

The only known exception to this friendly attitude came on March 27, 1920, when Berlin's Socialist Chief of Police, Eugen Ernst, directed a raid on the Jewish quarter of the capital, ostensibly in search of smugglers and Bolshevik agents. About one thousand *Ostjuden* were arrested, of whom three hundred were detained at a concentration camp at Wuensdorf, near Zossen. Eventually all those arrested were released. After three days *Vorwaerts* firmly condemned the incident but tried to shift blame to the army.[21] Among SPD spokesmen, only Jewish Social Democrat Ernst Hamburger denounced the police chief's action in the *Sozialistische Monatshefte* as "a concession to anti-Semitism." But Hamburger subsequently became personally acquainted with Ernst after the latter was transferred to Breslau, and the Social Democrat now believes the former police chief was not a true anti-Semite but rather was incompetent and too easily influenced by his reactionary subordinates.[22]

In November, 1920, Prussia's Braun-Severing Cabinet announced that after February, 1921, unemployed *Ostjuden* would be subject to compulsory internment in special camps.[23] The decision was made against Social Democratic wishes, and

[20] Adler-Rudel, *Ostjuden in Deutschland*, 66, 158–61.
[21] *Vorwaerts*, April 1, 1920. See also page 97 of this chapter.
[22] Hamburger, "Antisemitismus und Sozialdemokratie," 400; Hamburger, personal letter, May 18, 1967. A. Joseph Berlau's contention that the raid proved there was an "SPD campaign against the Eastern Jews" is a gross exaggeration. A. Joseph Berlau, *The German Social Democratic Party, 1914–1921* (New York, 1949), 345–47.
[23] Adler-Rudel, *Ostjuden in Deutschland*, 115.

not all SPD members were willing to accept it. The Duisburg district committee of the *Allgemeiner Deutscher Gewerkschaftsbund* (General German Trade Union Federation— ADGB) complained to Severing that anti-Semitic civil servants were certain to regard the order as a signal to mistreat all Jewish refugees. It insisted that the *Ostjuden* had caused no unemployment in the Rhineland (where most of them had gone to live) and wanted to know why Jewish refugees were being singled out for special treatment when Dutch and Italian workers were present in much greater numbers.[24] In another letter to the ADGB Central in Berlin, the Duisburg committee commented: "We want to express our astonishment that a union man like Severing could have given his name to an ordinance of such antisocial spirit."[25]

After Severing's replacement in April, 1921, by Alexander Domenicus of the DDP, conditions in the internment camps were permitted to deteriorate. In July, SPD Reichstag Deputy Mathilde Wurm investigated and publicly condemned the camps as "a cultural disgrace."[26] Socialist Alfred Berger, who was active in the *Arbeiterfuersorgeamt*, worked hard to arrange a meeting of ADGB officials with the SPD and USPD deputies in the Prussian parliament and leaders of the Jewish organization to consider means of alleviating camp conditions. Berger enlisted the support of at least one local union leader in Bochum.[27] On July 5, Alban Welker of the ADGB's central committee invited Isaak Kornfeld of the Berlin *Arbeiterfuersorgeamt* to help him make arrangements for such a meeting.[28] Whether or not one actually took place is not apparent, but on

24 Helbig to Carl Severing, February 14, 1921, ADGB Akten, fol. NB–211.

25 Kleiters [?] to ADGB Central, Berlin, February 14, 1921, ADGB Akten, fol. NB–211.

26 Adler-Rudel, *Ostjuden in Deutschland*, 116–18.

27 G. Wissmann (of the Miners' Union in Bochum) to ADGB Central, Berlin, June 30, 1921, ADGB Akten, fol. NB–211.

28 Welker to Kornfeld, July 5, 1921, ADGB Akten, fol. NB–211.

July 14, Ernst Heilmann arose in the Prussian parliament to excoriate the subhuman conditions that were being tolerated for the interned refugees and to complain that the camps did nothing to solve the problems presented by the presence of *Ostjuden* in Germany. Oscar Cohn of the USPD forcefully endorsed Heilmann's speech the following day.[29] With Severing's return to his old post the following November the camps were reformed and gradually eliminated, being abolished altogether in December, 1923.[30]

Although ready to offer temporary hospitality to the *Ostjuden*, most Social Democrats were unwilling to let them stay on permanently, feeling that Germany's unemployment and racial problems rendered naturalization undesirable. In 1920 Erhard Auer stated flatly that under existing conditions the newcomers could not be welcomed as permanent residents.[31] The next year Theodor Mueller repeated a widespread Socialist opinion when he wrote: "Every immigrant from the East causes the migration of a well qualified German worker to the West." [32] SPD Reichstag Deputy Gustav Hoch called for changes in the policies of the Bureau of Migration to expedite the emigration of *Ostjuden*.[33] Carl Severing looked to the League of Nations to find new homes for the refugees in underdeveloped parts of the world, but in 1922 he also requested Germany's Foreign Minister, Dr. Frederic Hans von Rosenberg, to enter into talks with Russian and Ukrainian representatives to arrange for the return to their former homes of as many *Ostjuden* as volunteered.[34] Severing later called upon the

---

[29] *Sitzungsberichte des preussischen Landtags,* 40th Sess., 1921, II, 2747–49; 41st Sess., *ibid.,* 2867–72.

[30] Adler-Rudel, *Ostjuden in Deutschland,* 118–19.

[31] Auer, *Sozialdemokratie und Antisemitismus,* 11.

[32] Mueller, "Die Einwanderung der Ostjuden," *Die neue Zeit,* XXXIX (1921), 330. For a similar statement see Mueller-Brandenburg, "Die deutschvoelkische Bewegung," 440.

[33] *Vorwaerts,* January 16, 1921.

[34] Severing to von Rosenberg, December 27, 1922, in Nachlass Bernstein, fol. B–68.

League to make it possible for Jewish refugees to resettle in Palestine.[35]

The *Ostjuden* problem encouraged sympathy for Zionism among German Social Democrats. Most of them regarded Palestine as an ideal home for Jewish refugees, although they never suggested that Zionism had anything to offer German Jews. The most enthusiastic SPD supporters of Zionism—including Eduard Bernstein, Rudolf Breitscheid, Oscar Cohn, and Paul Loebe—looked to Palestine as a laboratory for socialism. They were joined by most of their fellow Socialists in admiration for the growth of cooperative agriculture and socialist unions there.[36] From 1919 to 1928 *Vorwaerts* published no fewer than fourteen lengthy articles about the construction of socialism by the resettled refugees.[37] Prewar Socialist antipathy for Zionism did not, however, disappear entirely. In 1920 Bruno Sommer found it unfair and illegal for Jews to snatch Palestine from the Arabs: "With the same right that European Jews today demand back Palestine from the resisting Arabs, the Franks of France could reclaim all the Germanic regions that they settled before their mass migration." [38] Paul Nathan, a firm friend of the *Ostjuden*, was sceptical of Palestine's ability to absorb many refugees and advised Jewish refugees who could not gain admittance to South Africa or North America to return to Eastern Europe.[39]

The relationship of leading Social Democrats with three prominent Jewish refugees who ran afoul of the law in Germany exposed the SPD to a violent anti-Semitic campaign of

[35] *Vorwaerts*, January 5, 1923.

[36] *Ibid.*, August 19, 1925; May 4, 1922; January 20, 1925; February 1, 1921; Artur Holitscher, "Eine juedische Arbeitsarmee in Palaestina," *ibid.*, June 8, 1922, p. 2; see also *ibid.*, November 24, 1925; April 20, 1926.

[37] See, for example, Philipp Paneth, "Juedische Kolonisation in Palaestina," *Vorwaerts*, January 20, 1924, pp. 4–5; Felix Fechenbach, "Konstruktiver Sozialismus," *ibid.*, April 30, 1926, pp. 1–2; Miriam Schnabel-Hoeflich, "Hebraeisches Arbeitertheater in Palaestina," *ibid.*, February 4, 1927, p. 13.

[38] Sommer, "Religioese Taeuschungen," 71.

[39] *Vorwaerts*, January 22, 1926.

defamation and no end of embarrassment during and after 1925. This resulted from the so-called "Barmat Affair." The brothers Julius, Salomon, and Henri Barmat had originally moved from Russia to Holland, where during the war they had arranged food deliveries to Germany and established contacts with the SPD through friends they had made among Dutch Social Democrats. Using these contacts, the brothers ultimately moved to Berlin, where the inflation enabled them to build an industrial empire based on borrowed and depreciating money, much of it obtained from the Prussian State Bank. In Germany they cultivated friendships within several political parties, including the SPD, and Julius Barmat served as a contact between German Socialists and their counterparts in Belgium and Great Britain. However, none of the brothers actually joined the SPD. Suddenly, on the eve of the new year, 1925, the office of the state prosecutor in Berlin ordered the brothers arrested and their assets frozen. They were charged with having incurred debts under false pretenses, but in their court trial, which did not end until 1928, Julius Barmat alone was convicted of having bribed public officials. The names of two leading Socialists, Gustav Bauer and Ernst Heilmann, were dragged through the trial. Bauer, a leader of the ADGB and a Reichstag deputy, had been employed by the Barmats for work involving the use of his political contacts, and Heilmann had served on the board of directors of the Barmat concern. Neither was implicated in dishonest behavior, but Heilmann, a close personal friend of Julius Barmat, unwisely remained loyal to him in the face of public opinion.[40]

From the day the scandal broke until after the establishment of the Third Reich, the right wing held up the Barmat Affair as evidence of SPD corruption.[41] In vain the Party's Central Com-

[40] Landauer, *European Socialism*, I, 1005–1007; *Vorwaerts*, January 1 and 2, 1925; March 31, 1928.
[41] See, for example, *Voelkischer Beobachter*, April 7, 1925; March 31, April 1 and 2, 1928.

mittee declared that neither it nor any individual Social Democrat had used his influence to profit the Barmats or anyone else.[42] In January, 1925, Rudolf Breitscheid and Hermann Mueller, both gentiles, defended the SPD and the Barmats in the Reichstag. Breitscheid maintained that the importance of the affair was being exaggerated because the Barmats were *Ostjuden*. Enumerating the long list of prewar scandals involving nobles and conservatives, he sarcastically suggested that they all must have been Jews. Mueller answered Nazi shouts of *"Ostjude!"* by asserting that a man's origins were irrelevant. He recalled that the Socialist *Ostjude* Alexander Helphand had won German citizenship during the reign of Wilhelm II, which, he noted, at that time was "harder to get than the iron cross, first class." [43] But the accusations never stopped. As Carl Landauer has observed, "at least the greater part of the middle class wanted to be convinced that the republic and the Social Democrats were rotten and consequently gave scandalmongers their chance." [44] It is also worth noting that the affair stimulated resentment within the SPD against placeseekers like the Barmats who had worked with or entered the Party after the war, and that this resentment occasionally took on anti-Semitic overtones.[45]

The Socialist struggle against anti-Semitism supplemented and sometimes joined hands with a similar program carried on by the *Centralverein*. Officially a nonpartisan organization, the CV had a membership which was overwhelmingly bourgeois and supported the DDP, although a significant minority was Social Democratic. Two Socialists, Oscar Cohn and E. Behrend (a union leader from Beuthen), served on its executive com-

[42] "Die Barmathetze," *Sozialdemokratische Partei-Korrespondenz: Ergaenzungsband, 1923–1928*, pp. 213–15.
[43] Breitscheid and Mueller, *Gegen den Rechtskurs* (Berlin, 1925), 11–13.
[44] Landauer, *European Socialism*, I, 1007.
[45] Interview with Dr. Hans Hirschfeld, February 16, 1967.

mittee.[46] From 1919 to 1928 *Vorwaerts* published no fewer than seventeen speeches delivered to the Berlin local of the CV; in doing so it reiterated Socialist solidarity with Jews against Judeophobia. Sometimes Social Democrats were asked to address the Berlin CV. In 1920 Socialist Adolf Ritter, speaking as an official representative of his Party, assured the organization that the SPD would "never cease to combat reaction as it is embodied in anti-Semitism on the principle that all who bear the countenance of man are equal." Seven years later Wilhelm Sollmann received the group's prolongued applause when he repeated the SPD's pledge and spoke of the fight on bigotry towards Jews as part of a struggle to save German civilization.[47] CV support for SPD efforts in Bavaria has been discussed earlier. A letter from the CV to Dr. Felix Heimann of Magdeburg, revealed by a Nazi source in 1924, indicated that the CV also provided material aid to the *Reichsbanner*, a fact that spurred the Nazi campaign to smear the SPD as the servant of "Jewish capitalists." [48] German Socialists also gave approving notice to the meetings and propaganda of the *Verein zur Abwehr des Antisemitismus* (League to Combat Anti-Semitism) and to efforts against Judeophobia by the *Reichsbund juedischer Frontsoldaten* (National Association of Jewish Veterans).[49]

The SPD's militant stand against anti-Semitism betrayed an uncomfortable realization that Judeophobia had penetrated the ranks of the working-class movement itself. While the Socialists continued to look upon anti-Semitism as primarily a middle-class phenomenon, only Carlo Mierendorff made the bold as-

[46] Alfred Wiener, "The Centralverein deutscher Staatsbuerger juedischen Glaubens—Its Meaning and Activities" (unpublished typescript in the Wiener Library, London), 3, and Supplement II.

[47] *Vorwaerts*, November 21, 1921; January 17, November 25, 1924; January 28, 1920; January 28, 1927.

[48] *Die Nationalsozialist*, November 25, 1924, NSDAP Hauptarchiv, fol. 1906, no. A–34.

[49] *Vorwaerts*, March 20, 1924; August 28, 1926; April 24, 1924; January 6, 1926; September 16, 1927.

sertion that the entire proletariat had recognized the falseness of racist contentions. "*Voelkisch* bibles and ciphers have never made the heads of the workers dizzy. They coolly ask themselves, 'which are bigger, *voelkisch* phantasies or *voelkisch* mouths?' " [50] More typical was Erhard Auer's expression of alarm at the Bavarian Party Congress in October, 1918, over the increase in anti-Semitism in the SPD:

Letters have reached me from party comrades in various places in north and south Bavaria which lead me to conclude that even in our organizations the racial question has come up for debate and that a point of view is being accepted that, in my opinion, is incorrect. It is maintained that the majority of Jews systematically avoided dangerous and difficult military service and that, when under pressure they were placed in positions of military authority, they dealt with the soldiers in their command and the civilians with whom they were forced to do business in the most haughty and offensive manner. It is said, further, that while these in part robust people shirked their military service, women and girls had to be used in the field. Two letters maintain that the Israelites demanded consideration for their religious point of view while they paid no attention to the feelings of others, and that Israelite women acted in a frankly inflammatory manner by flaunting their garments. It is further contended that through hoarding they have become the wildest profiteers, and that this profiteering is intensified by the exchange of goods, which they carry on systematically and according to plan. In individual cities it has gone so far that lists have been made up and submitted to the authorities. Several such lists were sent to me with the request that I support and promote this action.[51]

Auer made it clear he did not support such actions and affirmed

[50] Mierendorff, *Arisches Kaisertum*, 8.
[51] Quoted in Alb. Grimpen, *Judentum und Sozialdemokratie* (Leipzig, 1919), 17.

that shirkers and profiteers could not be associated with a particular race.

Concern was also expressed by Karl Kautsky shortly after the armistice. Writing in the independent *Welt am Montag*, Kautsky cautioned that the nomadic wanderings of some workers threatened to lead them straight into the anti-Semitic camp.[52] Fritz Spiegelberg in 1919 affirmed that precisely this had happened, noting with dismay that the "highly developed commercial spirit" of the Jews and their "active, superior intelligence" had produced "obvious embitterment even among the proletariat" and, for some, the feeling that "capitalist" and "Jew" were interchangeable terms.[53] Late in 1920 Erhard Auer again warned that anti-Semitic intrusions into the SPD constituted an increasingly serious problem for the Party.[54]

Fears that anti-Semitism would surface in the SPD were confirmed shortly after the armistice in 1918. The sailor Otto Strobel, a Majority Socialist representative on the Berlin *Vollzugsrat*, and a certain Hall-Halsen published in the *Deutsche Tageszeitung* of December 13, 1918, an appeal to Germans to end Jewish domination of their government and to realize that most Jews were capitalists and therefore deadly enemies of Social Democracy. Strobel was quickly removed from all his official posts and from the SPD as well.[55]

Such intrusions were not confined to the Party's rank and file. A few Socialists who held positions of responsibility betrayed an aversion for Jews. One of the first to do so was August Winnig, who had occupied various positions in the Socialist trade unions since 1905. Winnig worked his way through the ranks of the German Builders' Union, becoming its vice-president in 1913. During the war he was an outspoken member of

[52] Anton Fendrich, *Der Judenhass und der Sozialismus* (Freiburg in Breisgau, 1920), 6.
[53] *Vorwaerts*, August 15, 1919.
[54] Auer, *Sozialdemokratie und Antisemitismus*, 31.
[55] Mueller-Franken, *Die November Revolution*, 97.

the "imperialist" wing of the SPD,[56] and in October, 1918, Prince Max von Baden sent him to the Baltic to establish good relations with the new Baltic governments. After the November revolution, President Ebert kept him on as Minister *Plenipotentiary* to the Baltic Provinces and *Oberpraesident* of the Province of East Prussia.[57] In July, 1919, Winnig wrote in the right-wing Socialist journal *Die Glocke* a bitter condemnation of Social Democrats who were reluctant to oppose a harsh peace treaty, among whom he included many "non-German members of our Party."

> We have a number of such men and women in leading positions in the party, and from the beginning we have extended to them the hospitality with which we accepted emigrants from the East. They have performed many good services for us as agitators and writers, and they may continue to do so. But they should—as their own interests demand—restrain themselves from giving their advice to the German nation on all matters that touch on national feelings when their foreign origins obstruct their understanding of the feelings of the German nation. They can . . . be a friend of the nation in whose culture they live, but they can never become so assimilated into the nation that they can supply competent interpretations of those national emotions which in the final analysis have their origin in the dark mysteries of the blood. We are fully capable of understanding the fact that our comrades of Jewish descent perceive their ideal in a nationless society of peoples, for they have been dealt a hard fate by nations that are firmly established. But they should not attempt the impossible by trying to talk [us] into such an idea . . . [because we are] a nation

---

[56] Edwyn Bevan, *German Social Democracy during the War* (London, 1918), 27.

[57] Winnig has left behind a number of autobiographical volumes. For the period before his October, 1918, appointment, see August Winnig, *Der weite Weg* (Hamburg, 1932); for the years 1918–22 consult Winnig, *Heimkehr* (Hamburg, 1935).

that could acknowledge it only by surrendering the last vestiges of dignity.[58]

A Jewish Social Democrat in Breslau, Georg Landsberg, quickly took exception to Winnig's complaint in a letter to *Die Glocke* in which he assailed the East Prussian governor for wanting Jews to think and act as second-class citizens. Winnig replied that he had meant nothing of the kind, and *Die Glocke* accepted his explanation and refused to print Landsberg's letter. Finally, at Landsberg's request, the protest letter was printed in *Vorwaerts* in October.[59] Winnig has recorded that his article aroused considerable opposition from fellow Socialists, among them Ernst Heilmann, who privately rebuked him and urged him to correct the anti-Semitic impression he had made with a public renunciation of Judeophobia, but Winnig refused. That December the East Prussian district executive committee of the SPD called Winnig to account for his violently nationalistic attitudes.[60] At that time *Vorwaerts* openly sympathized with him as a man who had done his best for Germany and the Party, and it expressed concern lest demands arise for similar actions against Noske, Wels, Scheidemann, and Ebert. In the end the district committee decided not to censor Winnig. Not until he openly sided with Kapp and Luettwitz a few months later did the Party expel him.[61] Thereafter, Winnig became increasingly antagonistic to the SPD, joining the far-right "Old Social Democratic Party" in 1927 and eventually throwing in his lot with the Hitler movement.[62] Interestingly, Winnig maintained cordial relations with some Social Democrats for a time after his expulsion. Gustav Noske, who held Winnig

---

[58] Winnig, "Glossen zur Ratifizierung," *Die Glocke*, V (1919), 500.
[59] *Vorwaerts*, October 2, 1919.
[60] Winnig, *Heimkehr*, 226–28.
[61] *Vorwaerts*, December 29, 1919; January 6, March 27, 1920.
[62] Winnig, *Das Reich als Republik 1918–1928* (Stuttgart and Berlin, 1929); Winnig, *Europa: Gedanken eines Deutschen* (Berlin, 1937).

in high regard and believed the Party should have readmitted him, retained friendly personal contacts with him during the early 1920's and would have worked on a publication edited by Winnig had time permitted.[63] Rudolf Wissell also remained on good terms with Winnig, and as late as September, 1932, the latter thanked Wissell for "comradely cooperation" in their work on arbitration boards.[64]

Why did the SPD fail to take official action against Winnig for his anti-Semitic outburst of 1919 immediately after it appeared? The most obvious reason was the Party's special sensitivity, in the wake of the Spartacist revolt, to challenges from the left; these made the SPD all too eager to preserve Party unity. Winnig's important office also tended to protect him from regular Party discipline. But it is also true that his attitudes did not fit the dominant Socialist conception of Judeophobia and probably were not universally accepted as anti-Semitic. In 1919 he was not yet a reactionary using anti-Jewish appeals to lead the workers down the garden path. He seemed rather to have expressed the suspicions of trade-union "realists" for the SPD's "Jewish intellectuals," suspicions Party leaders knew to be shared by many ordinary Socialists, but ones that they regarded more as a problem of intraparty rivalry than of anti-Semitism. Winnig's statement, together with others he made at that time, was surely embarrassing to the SPD leaders, but it did not seem to justify full-scale disciplinary proceedings at a time when the Party was under attack from all sides.

Several other more or less prominent Social Democrats publicly acknowledged their anti-Semitism after breaking with the Party in the early 1920's. Emil Kloth, who before 1919 had been president of the Book Binders' Union and an SPD representative

[63] Noske, *Erlebtes aus Aufstieg*, 182.
[64] Nachlass Rudolf Wissell, correspondence with Winnig, 1920–21, fol. III, nos. 2490–92, 2494; Winnig to Wissell, September 1, 1932, *ibid.*, fol. XVI, no. 11629.

on the Neukoelln borough council in Berlin, was expelled from the Party in October, 1919, for having written a rashly anti-union article in a nonsocialist newspaper. Subsequently he wrote two intensely anti-Socialist and anti-Semitic pamphlets.[65] By 1924 he had gone over entirely to the *voelkisch* opponents of the SPD.[66] Another Socialist renegade, Emil Unger-Winkelried, rose through union ranks to become a reporter for *Vorwaerts*, a position he held until he broke with the SPD immediately following the Kapp putsch. Allegedly he left because he was nauseated by Party corruption. Shortly before his departure Unger had condemned anti-Semitic attacks that had been made on Oscar Cohn, pouring contempt on those who evaluate a man "not according to his character and accomplishments but rather according to his derivation." [67] According to Erich Kuttner, Werner Peiser, editor of *Vorwaerts*, had repeatedly praised Unger before his desertion "as a fighter in the front rank against anti-Semitism" and had stressed the reporter's ethical aversion to Judeophobia; but this praise, continued Kuttner, "did not hinder him [Unger] from indulging in the sharpest anti-Semitism after his departure from the Party." [68] In 1920 Unger founded the anti-Marxist Reform Socialist Party, and four years later he joined with Winnig and Kloth to form the *Vereinigung nationalgesinnter Arbeiterfuehrer* (Union of Patriotic Labor Leaders), which was designed to facilitate cooperation between various "socialistic" *voelkisch* groups. Unger joined the NSDAP in 1932, and in 1934 he published a strongly anti-Jewish denunciation of the SPD.[69]

65 *Vorwaerts*, October 14 and 15, 1919; Kloth, *Einkehr: Betrachtungen eines Sozialdemokratischen Gewerkschaftlers ueber die Politik der deutschen Sozialdemokratie* (Munich, 1920); Kloth, *Sozialdemokratie und Judentum* (Munich, 1920).

66 *Vorwaerts*, April 14, 1925; Noske, *Erlebtes aus Aufstieg*, 277.

67 Emil Unger, "Politische Koepfe," *Die Glocke*, V (1920), 1500.

68 Kuttner to Otto Landsberg, December 15, 1924, Nachlass Wolfgang Heine, fol. XVIII, no. 448.

69 Unger-Winkelried, *Von Bebel zu Hitler*.

A number of lesser Social Democrats also openly embraced anti-Semitism. Christoph Weiss, a slater from Hinterhof (near Nuremberg), was an active member of the SPD and, after 1917, of the USPD, but by the end of 1920 he had abandoned Marxism and written an anti-Socialist, anti-Jewish pamphlet.[70] Walter Daedelow left the SPD to join the KPD, but by 1933 he had found his way to the Nazi Party and composed a vehemently anti-Semitic brochure based on the *Protocols of the Elders of Zion*.[71] Arno Franke, who until 1924 worked in the SPD press service, resigned from the Party in that year after expulsion proceedings had been started against him for publishing an anti-Semitic denunciation of Marxism under a pseudonym.[72] He promptly joined the Winnig-Kloth-Unger group of *voelkisch* "socialists." [73] Two prewar Social Democratic leaders of the *Freireligioese Bewegung* (Free Church Movement), Gottfried Traub and Max Maurenbrecher, broke with the SPD during the war. Traub subsequently joined the anti-Semitic wing of the DNVP and became a member of the party's central committee, while Maurenbrecher took over as editor-in-chief of the *voelkisch* organ of the Pan-German League, the *Deutsche Zeitung*.[74]

Men who broke with the SPD over the Jewish question or who manifested hatred for Jews after leaving the Party often left behind a plethora of material defending their actions. In contrast, almost nothing appeared in print about Judeophobes who remained within the Party, a fact which makes it difficult to assess the extent to which anti-Semitism infiltrated Socialist ranks. Emil Unger and August Winnig, the former writing

---

[70] Weiss, *Vom Juden-Sozialismus geheilt!* (Lorch, 1920).
[71] Daedelow, *Michel wach auf!* (Berlin, n.d.).
[72] *Vorwaerts*, January 24, March 6, 1924.
[73] Oskar Krueger, *Proletariat: Ein deutschen Arbeiter-Manifest* (Berlin, 1928), 29.
[74] George L. Mosse, "Die deutsche Rechte und die Juden," in Mosse and Paucker, *Entscheidungsjahr*, 214–15.

after the Nazi seizure of power, argued that anti-Jewish sentiments prevailed throughout the lower and middle ranks of the
Socialist proletariat, albeit under the surface.[75] Their testimony
must, however, be regarded with suspicion, for both felt obliged to show cause for their own long service to "the party of
the Jews," and both were eager to demonstrate that German
workers had followed Semitic leaders only in the absence of an
anti-Jewish, socialistic alternative.

The fact that only one anti-Semitic incident involving a
minor SPD functionary has come to light from a reliable source
suggests that the infiltration of Jew-hatred into the leadership
of the Party should not be overestimated. The incident in question involved Carl Landauer, who once, during the early
1920's, was the May Day speaker in Prien, a small town in the
Chiemgau of Upper Bavaria. Landauer has recounted his con-
versation with the chairman of the Social Democratic local in
the nearby village of Aschau, who approached him after his
talk and said:

> "Your talk was very good, and I wonder whether you could
> come to us in Aschau a couple of weeks from today to speak
> at a public meeting."
> "I am sorry," I said, "but I am not free on that day, but I
> will tell Nimmerfall"—the regional secretary—"to send you a
> speaker."
> "A pity," he answered, "that you cannot come, because I
> liked your speech, but if you can't, please tell Nimmerfall to
> send us somebody really good—but listen, tell him not to send
> us a Jew because that won't do with us in Aschau."
> Whereupon I said: "Now listen, I am a Jew myself."
> He looked at me and said: "If you can possibly make it, I
> would still want to have you—just don't tell anybody that you
> are a Jew." [76]

75 Unger-Wilkelried, *Von Bebel zu Hitler*; August Winnig, *Vom Proletariat zum Arbeitertum* (Hamburg, Berlin, Leipzig, 1930), 183–92.
76 Landauer, personal letter, May 24, 1966.

In addition to the few cases of direct anti-Semitism that appeared in the SPD between 1919 and 1928, indirect anti-Semitism, principally in the form of unfavorable comments on the activities of anti-republican and anti-Socialist Jews, occasionally found its way into the Party, as it had before 1914. It was mildly anti-Semitic in that it probably reinforced any anti-Jewish stereotypes that may have existed among Socialist workers; at the same time it was indirect in that it almost certainly had no anti-Semitic intent, expressing irritation over the actions of individual Jews rather than hatred for Jews as a group. In 1926 *Vorwaerts* lashed out at the leadership of Berlin's Jewish community for employing "delaying tactics" and manifesting "scandalous behavior" and "utterly reactionary attitudes" in salary negotiations with workers from the local Jewish cemetery. German Socialists were also annoyed over reports that Jewish capitalists had placed greed above all other considerations by contributing money to the DNVP, noting caustically that in addition to "racial anti-Semitism" and "gutter anti-Semitism" there was such a thing as "cash-box anti-Semitism." They were equally critical of the *Verband Nationaldeutscher Juden* (League of German Nationalist Jews), an organization of assimilationist Jews led by the reactionary Dr. Max Naumann. Naumann's close relations with the DNVP induced *Vorwaerts* to observe that only masochism or avarice could lead him and his compatriots to support an obviously anti-Jewish party. It also found irony in the league's supernationalism, noticing "something completely un-German in anti-Semitic racial hatred." A 1922 pamphlet entitled *Juedischer Antisemitismus und Arbeiterschaft* (*Jewish Anti-Semitism and the Working Class*) by Social Democrat Carl Eisfeld of Hagen attacked the Naumann group for giving aid and comfort to the anti-Semitic movement.[77] The Socialists clearly felt that all Jews

[77] *Vorwaerts*, September 28, 1926; February 5, July 7, 1921; December 10, 1921; March 1, 1922. I have not been able to obtain a copy of Eisfeld's pamphlet.

had a minimum obligation to support the republic. They therefore asked Jews to adopt "a more positive form of defense" against anti-Semitism than panic or irritation—namely, a "united front of all who are willing to work together for the reconstruction of Germany without regard to their personal interests." [78]

Such indirect anti-Semitism played a much smaller role in the SPD of 1919–28 than it had in the prewar Party, and it was further dwarfed by the amicable attitudes displayed toward German Jews by SPD spokesmen in their comments on Jewish affairs. Raphael Seligmann found the guiding educational and ethical principles for the development of democracy rooted in Judaism,[79] while Adolf Allwohn recognized the Hebrew faith as the source of "the religion concealed in Marxism" and as an "effective, creative factor in shaping the development of a new kingdom of God on earth." [80] The Socialists welcomed the establishment of a Jewish Theater in Berlin, reviewing its offerings with frequent approval and invariable courtesy. On one occasion they commented that it was a pleasure to see "a large, in part 'pure Germanic,' audience receiving enjoyment from really good Jewish art." [81] Announcements for dozens of meetings of Socialist and non-Socialist Jewish organizations appeared in the pages of *Vorwaerts* in the period 1919–28.

The SPD's generally favorable attitudes toward Jews and its opposition to anti-Semitism rendered it vulnerable to allegations that it was a "party of the Jews," a charge to which it was highly sensitive. *Voelkisch* contentions that Jews ran the Party were swiftly refuted; as *Vorwaerts* commented on the eve of the

[78] *Vorwaerts*, November 28, 1919.

[79] Seligmann, "Die Pharisaeer," *Sozialistische Monatshefte*, XXX (1924), 576.

[80] Allwohn, "Die Botschaft vom Reich Gottes," *Sozialistische Monatshefte*, XXVIII (1922), 26.

[81] See, for example, *Vorwaerts*, June 23, 1921; July 27, 1927; September 3, 1921.

1921 elections to the Prussian parliament: "Christians are made into Jews, while Jews who do not belong to the Party become Party leaders; Jewish comrades who are active somewhere in the Party are named as 'leaders,' while some of the best known leaders of Social Democracy are left out." After listing thirteen non-Jewish Socialists, it sneered: "Naturally none of them can be a Social Democratic leader for none of them is a Jew." Answering the charge that Marxism was a Jewish philosophy, Paul Kampffmeyer pointed out that the first really scientific formulation of socialism was made by a non-Jew, Friedrich Engels (in his *The Situation of the Working Class in England in 1844*), while Marx himself had rooted his reasoning in the philosophies of Kant and Hegel, both non-Jews.[82]

The sensitivity of Social Democrats to charges that they showed favoritism to Jews sometimes made them reluctant to associate closely with Jews in ways that might seem to confirm the racist allegations. In 1927 Prussian Minister-President Otto Braun rejected Herbert Weichmann as his personal assistant because he did not want to "give new sustenance to the imbecilic anti-Semitic babble." But good civil servants were hard to come by at that time. When a non-Jew supplied by the Ministry of the Interior proved to be lacking in political acuity, Braun returned unenthusiastically to Weichmann, who quickly proved himself to be an enormous asset and became a close political advisor to the Minister-President.[83] In a similar case, Braun approved the appointment of Robert Weissmann as State Secretary in the Prussian Ministry of State thinking that he merely had a Jewish-sounding name. He later expressed satisfaction that the anti-Semites would not be able to exploit the appointment in the usual way, only to be informed by Hans Hirschfeld that Weissmann was ethnically Jewish even though

[82] *Ibid.*, February 19, 1921; September 11, 1924; Kampffmeyer, *Juedischer Marxismus*, 3–8.
[83] Braun, *Von Weimar zu Hitler* (Hamburg, 1949), 180–82.

his family had converted to Christianity. Braun was at first astounded and then amused by his error, but he did nothing to withdraw Weissmann's appointment. He subsequently reaffirmed his abhorrence for Judeophobia in unmistakable terms: "I have fought against this political pestilence all along . . . because it only assists in the deception of the politically immature masses and redounds to the dishonor of every civilized nation." [84]

While SPD uneasiness over accusations that it showed favoritism to Jews may have stimulated infrequent criticisms of Jewish capitalists, it never induced Party organs or spokesmen to employ direct anti-Semitic appeals. On the contrary, such intrusions of anti-Jewish opinions into the German Socialist movement as may have occurred usually remained covert and were rendered insignificant by Socialist hostility toward prejudice against the Jews. The most important potential weakness in the SPD's front against anti-Semitism was its reluctance to believe that most anti-Semites really hated Jews. Its often repeated "plot theory" that Judeophobia was primarily a reactionary weapon for agitating against the Weimar Republic and the political left seemed to minimize the possibility that *voelkisch* leaders seriously intended to follow through on their extreme demands—wholesale withdrawal of Jewish civil rights, expropriation of Jewish property, and expulsion of Jews from Germany—if given the opportunity.

The impression that anti-Semites were insincere was strengthened by the Socialist contention that DNVP agitation against Jews was motivated by opportunism,[85] and the impression was reinforced by imputations that other racists were inconsistent in their attitudes toward Jews. In 1920, for example, *Vorwaerts* told of an anti-Semite in Stargard, Prussia, who was

[84] Hirschfeld interview, February 16, 1967; Braun, *Von Weimar zu Hitler*, 182.
[85] See Chap. 3, pages 56–57.

ejected from a Jewish shop and, when confronted with copies of anti-Jewish essays he had written, stuttered pitifully that he had no choice since he had to make his living somehow. Later that year German monarchists, many of whom were anti-Semites, hired a Berlin firm of Jewish lawyers (Loewenfeld, Friedemann, and Pinthus) to represent Hohenzollern claims to the fortune Kaiser Wilhelm had left behind in 1918; *Vorwaerts* commented: "Swastika and Star of Zion tolerate each other beautifully as long as a third symbol—a golden calf—appears with them." In 1923 the newspaper pointed out that the Nazi *Voelkischer Beobachter* had denounced the Deutsche Bank as "the biggest Jewish bank in Germany," yet on another page in the same issue the Nazi paper urged its readers to send contributions to the Nazis' account in that bank. In a similar vein, *Vorwaerts* noted in 1925 that Austria's anti-Jewish Foreign Minister, Dr. Viktor Mataja, had secretly supplied government funds to the Jewish Biedermann Bank in an unsuccessful attempt to enrich himself. On another occasion the Socialist organ contended that even the most inveterate Judeophobes never attacked Jews who advocated conservative politics.[86]

All of these examples of *voelkisch* opportunism on the Jewish question contributed to an unmistakable impression that Jews were meant only as diversionary targets who in any final reckoning would have much less to fear from "anti-Semitism" than would the Socialists themselves. This attitude in no way diminished SPD opposition to Judeophobia, but it did divert its emphasis away from the real or potential plight of the Jews.

While a few individual Social Democrats embraced anti-Jewish opinions in the early years of the Weimar Republic, there is no evidence to indicate that many members followed their example. Infrequent Socialist criticisms of anti-republican Jews tended to perpetuate the stereotype of greedy, irrespon-

[86] *Vorwaerts*, January 2, November 24, 1920; October 22, 1927; August 22, 1923; December 24, 1925; April 29, 1922.

sible Jewish capitalists, but these criticisms were insignificant compared to the SPD's much more recurrent condemnations of all forms of Judeophobia. It could hardly be expected that the anti-Semitic feelings and propaganda that played such a great role in Germany at that time should have left the ranks of the Social Democrats entirely untouched. What is most remarkable is that, in spite of continual right-wing efforts to smear the SPD as an instrument of the Jews and the damaging connections between Jewish capitalists and Socialists highlighted by the Barmat scandal, German Social Democracy neither attempted to disassociate itself from the struggle against Judeophobia nor resorted to anti-Semitic demogoguery for its own benefit.

The SPD's interpretation of anti-Semitism as a tactic in the reactionary crusade against the republic possessed both strengths and weaknesses. Its great disadvantage was its underestimation of man's capacity to believe the preposterous and to perform the appalling. It gave the impression that anti-Semitic leaders and parties were insincere in their demands against Jews, thereby minimizing the prospect of long-term dangers for Jews. On the other hand, the SPD's "plot theory" offered ordinary Germans an easily understandable explanation of anti-Semitism, one that tied their own vital interests to the struggle against Judeophobia. As long as large sections of the proletariat remained as convinced that the SPD and the Weimar Republic represented their best interests as they did from 1919 to 1928, anti-Semitic parties could hardly hope to win a mass following among the industrial workers.

Chapter V

Socialist Explanations and Refutations of Anti-Semitism
1929-1933

The last five years of the Weimar Republic encompassed its zenith as well as its collapse. By 1928 Germany had regained its prewar prosperity and seemed well on the way to establishing stable internal political conditions. A majority of the German voters demonstrated their acceptance of the republic in the Reichstag election held on May 20, 1928, when 62 percent of them voted for prorepublican parties. Only slightly more than 27 percent voted for the parties that contained the republic's most outspoken enemies, the NSDAP, the KPD, and the DNVP. Then, beginning in 1929, the depression radicalized German politics by paralyzing the economy, creating an army of unemployed, and proletarianizing many members of the middle class. This was reflected in the last free Reichstag election, held on November 6, 1932, when nearly 59 percent of the German electorate cast its votes for the three major antirepublican parties, while just under 39 percent remained true to parties that supported the republic.

The principal beneficiary of this radicalization of German political life was the wildly anti-Semitic NSDAP. It won less than 3 percent of the votes in 1928, but in the Reichstag election held two years later it multiplied its electorate more than seven times, and in July, 1932, it replaced the SPD as Germany's largest party by winning 37 percent of the votes. The depression transformed the Nazis from a disturbing but relatively insignificant anti-Semitic party into the first successful anti-Jewish political mass movement in history. Since nazism was as anti-Semitic before 1929 as it was from 1930 to 1933, it would appear that its anti-Semitism was not the source of its mass support. Intensified economic problems, nationalism, and fears of bolshevism excited by the growth and vigor of the KPD seem to have been the primary sources of Nazi success, rather than Judeophobia per se.

Nazi anti-Semitism after 1929 presented a somewhat different problem to Social Democrats than the more diffused Judeophobia of the first years of the republic. The latter never managed to unify itself and seemed capable of producing only isolated outbursts of violence against Jews. Nazi anti-Semitism not only united the anti-Jewish forces but at the same time integrated them into a movement with a larger and much more dangerous *Weltanschauung*. Furthermore, the NSDAP challenged the SPD for leadership of the German workers.[1] Understandably, then, German Socialists felt that the most effective way to combat Judeophobia was to combat nazism and to do everything possible to prevent a Nazi takeover. The Socialists increased their efforts to confine the spread of anti-Semitism while making these efforts a part of their larger struggle against nazism.

German Social Democrats explained post-1928 Nazi anti-Semitism both as part of a reactionary plot against democracy and as a consequence of bourgeois psychological disturbances. Most Socialists persisted in defining it in terms of capitalistic diversionary measures and conspiracies against the republic. An anonymously authored 1930 SPD pamphlet accused the Nazis of deliberately attempting to make the Jews into scapegoats for

[1] Max H. Kele, "Nazi Appeals to the German Workers, 1926–1932" (M.A. thesis, Tulane University, 1963).

capitalism's failure to promote stable prosperity. Their anti-Semitism, it said, was a "shrewdly reasoned diversionary offensive for the benefit of big capital."[2] Georg Bauer warned his fellow union members that Nazi agitation against Jews was no different from any other aspect of Nazi propaganda in that its purpose was "to break up the unions and thereby enchain the worker to the dictation of his employer."[3] A 1931 Socialist pamphlet explained that the Nazis had mated terror and anti-Semitism in order to convince the bourgeoisie that "Jewish-democratic parliamentarianism" was untenable and that a Fascist dictatorship alone could eliminate Jewish influence and thus save Germany from Marxism and bolshevism.[4]

While maintaining their theory that Judeophobia was part of a reactionary conspiracy, as they had before 1929, the majority of Socialist writers gave new emphasis to psychological aspects of the animosity toward Jews. Suggesting that Nazi eagerness to deceive was matched by bourgeois willingness to be deceived, the writers used psychological explanations to account for the acceptance of anti-Semitism by increasing numbers of Germans. Indeed, after 1929 such explanations were advanced more frequently than was the crude "plot theory." After the great Hitlerite victory in the Reichstag election of September, 1930, Philipp Kuenkele commented with grudging admiration: "National Socialism knows how to camouflage uncomfortable facts and objections as intrigues of the Jews, and this it does with incredible dialectical demagogic polish. For example, during the embittered election campaign, whenever appeals from highly respected non-Jewish men and women appeared, justly indentifying anti-Semitism as an affront to civilization, National Socialism was able to sweep these actions aside

[2] *Die Nazi-Fibel: Eine Handvoll Naziluegen und Ihre Widerlegung* (Darmstadt, [1930]), 10.

[3] Bauer, "Zuerst Betriebsfunktionaere, dann nationalsozialistischer Gewerkschaften," *Gewerkschafts-Zeitung*, XLI (1931), 62.

[4] *SS Diktator* (Halle, 1931), 11–12.

merely by declaring that they were 'friendships bought with Jewish money.' " [5]

Hermann Heller, a Jewish professor of law at the University of Frankfurt and a leader in the Socialist Youth Movement, expressed a common Socialist opinion when he told delegates to a regional SPD convention in Hamburg in 1930 that the Nazis used anti-Semitism to appear anti-capitalist and thus managed to "play dexterously with existing racial instincts." [6] Another Socialist, one Dr. Sussheim of Nuremberg, found the essence of Judeophobia in middle-class neuroses, but, he added, "Capital puts up with the Nazi struggle against 'Jewish capital' because it knows that senseless anti-Semitism is an effective means of agitation for their hirelings, through which attention is diverted from the real causes and parties guilty of military defeat and economic and social want." [7] A year later a leading non-Jewish Socialist professor at the University of Jena, Anna Siemsen, took a similar position. She too explained Judeophobia as abnormal psychology but could not bring herself to apply the same terms to the men who controlled the Nazi Party from behind the scenes. "The rich bourgeoisie and the great landholders, who support and profit from German fascism, quite naturally see through to the untenability and absurdity of National Socialist ideology. But for them it is a convenient means of mass suggestion. . . . A small pogrom is always preferable to a large capital levy." [8] Jewish novelist Arnold Zweig, who stood close to the SPD, took a somewhat different tack. He

[5] Kuenkele, "Wahllehren des 14. September 1930," *Jungsozialistische Blaetter*, X (1931), 17.

[6] *Hamburger Echo*, June 14, 1930. Heller's contention was well founded. See Kele, "Nazi Appeals," 29–35, 59–60.

[7] Sussheim, "Die nationalsozialistische Seuche," *Das freie Wort: Sozialdemokratischen Diskussionsorgan*, II (February 9, 1930), 25. See also Sussheim, "Wirtschaftliche Interessen gegen Hetzphrasen," *ibid.*, II (August 17, 1930), 22–24.

[8] Anna Siemsen, "Dass jeder tuechtige Mann aus Tahiti stammt," *Jungsozialistische Blaetter*, X (1931), 44. See also August Siemsen, *Anna Siemsen: Leben und Werk* (Hamburg, 1951), 121.

traced anti-Semitism to bourgeois inability to accept the political downfall of the old regime and to the emotional problems aroused by the dethroning of established power. But he also accused "the old powers of the authoritarian state" of having begun as early as 1917 to try to shift the blame for every problem upon the Jews—a policy, he said, they had followed ever since.[9]

Socialists who advanced psychological interpretations of Judeophobia placed emphasis on middle-class inability to face realistically the demands and weaknesses of capitalist society in a time of economic stress. Frequently, but not invariably, this interpretation traced the roots of this neurosis directly to the depression, which had intensified competition between the owners of big and small businesses to the detriment of the latter, and had thus proletarianized great masses of the *Mittelstand*. It was argued by Rudolf Breitscheid in a speech before the SPD's 1931 Party Congress that these masses, intellectually and emotionally unprepared to evaluate their plight objectively or to accept Social Democratic solutions, found a scapegoat in their Jewish competitors.[10] In 1930 Walter Mannzen found in anti-Semitism an ideological superstructure for the class struggle between small enterprises and big industries, banks, and department stores, much as religion had supplied an emotionally satisfying ideology for the wars of the sixteenth and seventeenth centuries. Walter Pahl castigated the average bourgeois for reacting to increased competition with raw emotionalism rather than with reason and thereby "suppressing his insecurity through faith in a racial struggle." In Carlo Mierendorff's esti-

[9] Zweig, "Antisemitismus und der Vater Staat," *Die Fackel* (September 4, 1931), 5–6.

[10] This was Breitscheid's argument in his remarks on the topic "Victory over National Socialism," in *Protokoll: Sozialdemokratischer Parteitag in Leipzig 1931* (Berlin, 1931), 93–95. Similar convictions were expressed in Guenter Keiser, "Der Nationalsozialismus, eine reaktionaere Revolution," *Neue Blaetter fuer den Sozialismus*, II (1931), 270–77; *Der Abend*, February 10, 1932.

mation, the success of Nazi anti-Semitism lay in its "successful chemical bond between . . . individual economic interests and elementary feelings of hatred." [11] Jewish Social Democrat Ernst Fraenkel held that anxiety over competition for professional positions had become an important source of the anti-Jewish neurosis. "Students, white-collar employees, retailers cling to their bourgeois existence. They hate everyone who wants to take one of the limited positions that the bourgeois world has yet to dispose of." [12]

Socialists who attributed the spread of Nazi anti-Semitism to irrational bourgeois responses to economic depression often recognized elements of continuity with earlier movements against Jews. In 1932 Jens Grieter argued that Hitler and Stoecker had more in common than their first names because both depended upon the wrath of people who had been robbed of social security by capitalism but who remained unwilling or unable to grasp the economic causes of their fate.[13] Also in 1932 Wilhelm Sollmann agreed that, then as before, political anti-Semitism was "invariably bound up with the understandable longing of the declassed to regain their former economic and social positions." He added that both the Nazis and their predecessors found what they took for confirmation of their anti-Jewish attitudes in the fact that Jews often suffered less from economic shocks than did the masses of the people. The only difference Sollmann could find between the old and

[11] Mannzen, "Die sozialen Grundlagen des Nationalsozialismus," *Neue Blaetter fuer den Sozialismus*, I (1930), 371; Pahl, "Der Run zum National-sozialismus," *Sozialistische Monatshefte*, XXXVI (1930), 867; Mierendorff, "Gesicht und Charakter der nationalsozialistischen Bewegung," *Die Gesell-schaft*, VII (1930), 494. See also Mierendorff's "Ueberwindung des National-sozialismus," *Sozialistische Monatshefte*, XXXVII (1931), 224–29.

[12] Fraenkel, "Antifaschistische Aufklaerungsarbeit," *Sozialistische Bildung* (1930), 331.

[13] Grieter, "Die Juden sind Schuld," *Der Abend*, March 2, 1932, p. 5. See also Br——, "Die Rebellion des Kleinbuergertums," *Hamburger Echo*, December 22, 1931, pp. 1–2; *Leipziger Volkszeitung*, November 14, 1930; *Der Abend*, August 25, 1932.

the new anti-Semitism was the pseudoscientific facade which the Nazis had managed to give their racial prejudices.[14]

Socialist contentions that Jew-hate was rooted in middle-class frustrations over the decline of capitalism did not differ substantially from SPD explanations of pre-1914 anti-Semitism, although they were expressed in more sophisticated terms. Rudolf Breitscheid recalled in his 1931 Party Congress speech the traditional Socialist interpretation of Judeophobia as an immature form of anticapitalist revolt. The Nazis, he said, "attribute [economic instability] to the fateful influence of Jewry and have in anti-Semitism a new incitement for those members of the bourgeoisie who are groaning under bank capital and high rents. Anti-Semitism as the socialism of the fool reappears here in grandiose style." [15] Jens Grieter subsequently agreed, contending that the political right held the Jews "responsible for capitalism because it shrinks from criticism that goes to the root of the matter—to capitalism itself." [16] But the Socialists never suggested, as they had before 1914, that this immature revolt against capitalism would eventually aid the SPD by radicalizing the bourgeoisie. On the contrary, they recognized in anti-Semitism part of the Nazi threat to their very existence.

Not all German Socialists who traced Judeophobia to middle-class psychological disorders agreed that economic paralysis alone provided a satisfactory explanation. Alfred Braunthal found in the depression only one of many factors that had contributed to widespread dissatisfaction with the insecurity of modern existence and consequent bourgeois longing for a less complicated society. The bourgeoisie, he said, held Jews re-

---

[14] Wilhelm Sollmann, "Der politische Antisemitismus: Seine Grundlagen und seine Ausweglosigkeit," in Hermann Bahr and others (eds.), *Der Jud ist Schuld . . . ? Diskussionsbuch ueber die Judenfrage* (Basel, 1932), 267–70.

[15] *Protokoll . . . Leipzig 1931*, p. 93.

[16] *Der Abend*, February 10, 1932. See also *Leipziger Volkszeitung*, December 17, 1930.

sponsible for everything it disliked about the modern world, from mass production to modern architecture. "Middle-class anti-Semitism, which originated in the early capitalist era, corresponds in National Socialism to a vague, but utterly reactionary political and economic romanticism that toys with the notion of a return to the corporate state [*Staendestaat*] and artisanship of the Middle Ages." [17] Agreeing that antimodernism was the basis of much bourgeois Judeophobia, Arthur Rosenberg likened Nazi aversion for Jews with the "university anti-Semitism" of Heinrich von Treitschke and his followers in the 1880's. Treitschke, he said, had longed for a preindustrial society in which men worked out of interest and a sense of duty rather than to make money, and he had attacked the Jews because he saw in them the embodiment of materialism and liberalism. Rosenberg contended that significant elements of the German bourgeoisie, and especially professors, students, and intellectuals, became Nazis in order to combat such "Jewish inventions" as materialism, socialism, and democracy out of romantic longing to regain an innocent world.[18]

Other Social Democrats found the key to Nazi hatred for Jews in middle-class inferiority complexes. Erich Kuttner, who was himself of Jewish descent, traced bourgeois feelings of inadequacy to the events of 1918 and their consequences. The dissolution of the old hierarchy had ended the policy of granting privileges on the basis of birth and wealth to men of no particular talents. Too, Germany's loss in World War I, and her subsequent position as a black sheep among nations had shaken men and women who had come to identify personally with the fate of the nation. Both developments had robbed the middle

---

[17] *Jahrbuch ... 1930*, p. 431.
[18] Arthur Rosenberg, "Treitschke und die Juden: Zur Soziologie der deutschen akademischen Reaktion," *Die Gesellschaft*, VII (1930), 81–83. For a more recent statement of this thesis, see Stern, *The Politics of Cultural Despair*. Rosenberg, a professor of history at the University of Berlin and a non-Jew, had left the KPD to join the SPD in 1927.

class of the feelings of self-worth without which no one can live, and the depression had only made matters worse. As a result, the average bourgeois overcompensated with intense feelings of racial pride and racial hatred. The Jews, Kuttner argued, were ideally suited to be victims of this mass neurosis precisely because they were *not* inferior; because they were generally successful people, they seemed to confirm the Nazi "devil theory" of Jewish conspiracy and *moral* degeneracy. As proof that anti-Semitism proceeded from feelings of inferiority Kuttner pointed out that desecrations of Jewish cemeteries and mob attacks on Jews showed that anti-Semites consistently felt themselves inadequate to confront the objects of their hatred on equal terms. He concluded that the only way to deal with the problem was to enlighten those so afflicted about the true nature of their neurosis, contending that self-knowledge alone could bring healing.[19]

Friedrich Wendel, a prominent Socialist journalist, editor of the Party's humor magazine *Der Wahre Jacob*, and a gentile, argued that middle-class Jew-haters had turned the Jews into "scarecrows" possessing not only every conceivable vice, but also many of the virtues that the millions of bourgeois mediocrities lacked. An imaginary Nazi was made to confess: "I haven't the faintest understanding of complex economic matters and am incapable of thinking clearly and methodically—since Karl Marx was quite the opposite, Karl Marx was a disgusting Jew! I am a dunce—hence all intelligence and mental agility is suspiciously Jewish!"[20] A *Reichsbanner* pamphlet written by CV leader Alfred Hirschberg found in Nazi racial consciousness "not racial pride but rather fear of the greater ability of others, apprehension over competition in which one might be

---

[19] Erich Kuttner, *Pathologie des Rassenantisemitismus* (Berlin, 1930), 5–20, 31–32. For a similar argument, see *Freie Volkswacht*, July 14, 1931.
[20] Friedrich Wendel, "Adolf Hitler im Spiegel der Rassenlehre," *Der Abend*, August 8, 1930, p. 3. See also Hermann Wendel, "Hitlers Hepp Hepp," *Fraenkische Tagespost*, October 15, 1930, pp. 1–2.

left behind." In a 1932 manuscript Albert Suedekum, a Jew who had been Finance Minister in the first postwar Prussian government and then a professional journalist, accused the Nazi racists of overcoming their inferiority complexes with a variation on their Fuehrer's "big lie"—loud claims of racial superiority. Suedekum traced Hitler's aversion for Jews to the Fuehrer's own subconscious "suspicion of belonging to those who are racially inferior." [21]

Two uncommon, noneconomic-determinist, psychological interpretations of Nazi anti-Semitism were offered by Socialist academicians Bruno Altmann and Otto Jenssen. Altmann found the source of Germany's "national psychosis" in the change in social relationships between Jews and non-Jews during the preceding century. He likened the lot of German Jews to that of American Negroes, who, after emancipation, found themselves the objects of hatred by their former masters: "Anti-Semitism is the explosion of the former oppressors and scorners against those who once were degraded but who are now raised up." Jenssen offered a quite different explanation, detecting in Nazi racism elements of primitive clan-egoism that had their origins among nomadic warriors. He suggested that it served as an "ersatz religion" that was "tied up in many ways with primitive conceptions stored away in the subconscious." [22]

The Socialists found confirmation of their psychological explanations in Nazi anti-Semites who behaved abnormally. In 1930 Nathan Gurdus told of a sadistic Nazi physician at a Frankfurt am Main public clinic who goaded a seriously injured Jewish patient to stand and, in doing so, to fracture both his leg bones. After a *voelkisch* warning that "Jewish psycho-

---

[21] [Alfred Hirschberg], *Das wahre Gesicht des Nationalsozialismus* (Magdeburg, [1929]), 23; Albert Suedekum, *Die mit dem Minko*, in Nachlass Suedekum, fol. 160–a, nos. 13–20.

[22] Bruno Altmann, "Rassenfimmel und Rassenhass," *Sozialistische Bildung* (December, 1930), 364; Otto Jenssen, "Magie, Wirtschaft und Politik: Auch ein Beitrag zum Hitlerismus," *Die Gesellschaft*, IX (1932), 182.

analysis" would damage the "non-Jewish spirit," an anonymous Socialist concluded that the powers which the author of the warning feared already had "taken fatal hold on the brain of this 'Apollonian' genius." Otto Friedlaender found that the fundamental emotion that ran through Alfred Rosenberg's *Der Mythus des XX. Jahrhunderts* was "nothing other than distressing, hysterical and frankly grotesque race-anxiety." [23] When a Vienna professor brought a paranoid to class to demonstrate megalomania and persecution complex to his students, Nazis among them cheered the mental patient's demand that the Jews be expelled to solve the economic crisis. This led an anonymous Socialist to wonder how many "mad men" inhabited the ranks of the NSDAP. [24]

Although these attempts by German Socialists to account for Judeophobia with psychological insights produced a number of divergent interpretations, together they demonstrated SPD determination to provide a realistic explanation for the apparent popularity of anti-Semitic ideas in the last years of the Weimar Republic. The crudely economic-determinist "plot theory" was not dropped, but by itself it no longer dominated Social Democratic comment on the problem. Nor did all Socialists think it enough simply to attribute the intensification of anti-Semitism to the depression. In searching for racism's deeper causes, a number of them developed quite sophisticated analyses that made use of advanced social-psychological concepts. It would seem, therefore, that the contention that German socialism understood the irrational nature of Nazi appeals only imperfectly is an exaggeration, at least where anti-Semitism is concerned. [25]

---

[23] *Der Abend*, November 4, 1930; F. D., "Die Psychoanalyse — eine judisch-satanische Erfindung," *Sozialistische Bildung* (July, 1930), 222–23 (the adjective is Nietzsche's); Friedlaender, "Der Mythus des Herrn Rosenberg," *Sozialistische Bildung* (February, 1931), 53.

[24] A. S., "Irrsinn der Zeit," *Sozialistische Bildung* (November, 1932), 232.

[25] Erich Matthias, "Die Sozialdemokratische Partei Deutschlands," in Erich

The persistence among Social Democrats of the "plot theory" as a full or partial explanation of anti-Semitism in the last years of the Weimar Republic naturally helped to perpetuate the impression that the leaders of the anti-Jewish movement were insincere. German Socialists who were persuaded that anti-Semitic agitators had more important goals in mind than tormenting the Jews could hardly have been expected to regard anti-Semitism as a serious threat to the Jews. Moreover, the new popularity among Socialists of psychological explanations of Judeophobia may have fostered a feeling that there was no satisfactory way to combat such a mass neurosis. Anna Siemsen argued that rational arguments could never be effective against irrational fears and that it would be "completely incorrect" to suppose that members of the middle class could "be won over by showing them the stupidity of their beliefs." [26] An SPD brochure announcing a meeting of republicans in Rothuerben stated the view trenchantly; it discouraged anti-Nazis from attending an NSDAP meeting scheduled for the same evening because "in ten minutes speaking time you cannot refute the nonsense about Jews that has been dished out for several hours." [27] Both views—the conspiratorial and the psychological —helped induce the Socialists to confine their attacks on Nazi anti-Semitism to a much smaller part of their total agitation against the Hitler movement than Judeophobia played in the totality of Nazi propaganda.

Although SPD explanations of the origins of Nazi anti-Semitism implied that it was either unnecessary or impractical to treat Judeophobia per se as a problem of the first rank, they did not prevent the Socialists from displaying substantial awareness of the increased threat posed by Hitlerite agitation against

Matthias and Rudolf Morsey (eds.), *Das Ende der Parteien* (Duesseldorf, 1960), 133; Serge Chakotin, *The Rape of the Masses: The Psychology of Totalitarian Political Propaganda* (London, 1940), 190–231.

[26] Anna Siemsen, "Dass jeder tuechtige Mann aus Tahiti stammt," 44.
[27] NSDAP Hauptarchiv, fol. 800.

the Jews after 1929. Socialist concern was reflected in the sharp rise in the number of articles about anti-Semitism or Jewish matters published in *Vorwaerts* and *Der Abend* between 1929 and 1933. There were 511, or an average of 1 such item for every 5 issues, double the average for the years before 1929.[28] Comparable figures may be cited for three important provincial SPD newspapers—the *Fraenkische Tagespost*, the *Hamburger Echo*, and the *Leipziger Volkszeitung*—that were scrutinized for the years 1930–33. The *Freie Volkswacht* of Freilassing, a Socialist newspaper aimed at the rural and small-town population of Upper Bavaria, was examined for the full period of its short life (1929–31) to determine whether or how the Party altered its handling of the Jewish question when addressing Germans in an area more likely than any other in Germany to have been influenced by Austrian-style "Alpine anti-Semitism." While this triweekly SPD organ made an average of somewhat fewer comments on Judeophobia within its smaller format than the above newspapers, it contained nothing that could be considered anti-Jewish. Both *Die Gesellschaft* and the *Sozialistische Monatshefte* paid more attention to Judeophobia than ever before, the former printing 18 and the latter 28 articles on some aspect of the subject from 1929 to 1933. Socialist agitation against anti-Semitism was also well represented in lesser Party journals and in the small mountain of anti-Nazi pamphlets distributed by the SPD during those years.

It is difficult to generalize about whether Jewish or non-Jewish Social Democrats were responsible for most SPD denunciations of anti-Semitism. The ethnic backgrounds of many Socialist writers cannot now be verified, while comment in the Party press was largely anonymous. Nonetheless, it would appear from available data that a disproportionate percentage of such Party spokesmen were of Jewish background. Of those

---

[28] See Chap. 2, page 36. Dates are for the years 1929–33 inclusive. *Der Abend* was the evening edition of *Vorwaerts* during this period.

Socialists who openly opposed anti-Semitism after 1929, the ethnic backgrounds of eighteen have been verified. Of these, six had Jewish backgrounds. Although Jewish Socialists contributed a disproportionate share of SPD condemnations of anti-Semitism, they by no means monopolized the subject. Among prominent Socialist critics of Judeophobia were the non-Jews Carlo Mierendorff, Wilhelm Hoegner, Carl Severing, and Hermann Wendel. They were joined by Otto Friedlaender, Ernst Heilmann, Hermann Heller, and Erich Kuttner, Socialists with Jewish backgrounds.

Keeping most of their agitation against anti-Semitism on a rational plane, German Socialists repeatedly submitted factual material to counter Nazi contentions about Jews during the years 1929–33. Above all they felt it their duty to challenge National Socialist claims of Jewish racial inferiority, confronting these "deranged ideas . . . with knowledge and truth." [29] In their opinion, only with reliable information could Germans fully recognize "how unbelievably narrow and superficial the racial theories" of the Nazis were and therefore turn against "the deprecation of other races and peoples, which deepens into the most imbecilic racial hatred." [30] As they had done before, the Socialists maintained that science knew next to nothing about the influence of race on individuals. They concluded from what little was known that environment rather than race was of decisive importance and that differences between individuals were of greater significance than those between races.[31] Applying their analysis specifically to the

29 *Der Abend*, January 27, 1931.
30 *Fraenkische Tagespost*, January 25, 1932.
31 Paul Thorwirth, review of Friedrich Hertz, *Hans Guenther als Rasseforscher*, in *Sozialistische Monatshefte*, XXXVIII (1932), 84–85; Hugo Iltis, "Rassenforschung und Rassenfrage," *Sozialistische Bildung* (January, February, 1929), 12–21, 45–52; Ernst Boese, "Rassenproblem und Marxismus," *Sozialistische Bildung* (March, 1931), 65–70; H. Roe, "Rasse und Front," *Fraenkische Tagespost*, March 5, 1932, p. 5; Robert Schirokauer, "Vernunft oder Blut und Rasse?" *Das freie Wort*, III (June 28, 1931), 9–13; Albert Spitzer, "Volk und Rasse," *Schulfront*, II (March, 1930), 41–43.

Jews, German Social Democrats recognized history alone as the determinant of group characteristics. Hugo Iltis commented: "The character of the Jews has little to do with race but much to do with the centuries-long milieu of the ghetto and of oppression; Herr Guenther's forefathers, who shut up the Jews in ghettos to free themselves from competition, bear more of the guilt for such Jewish characteristics as commercialism, slyness, etc., than 'Jewish blood.'" Carl Tries also traced Jewish interest in trade and profits to past oppression. "If distasteful phenomena with respect to money stand out among the Jews, no one is less justified to be scandalized over them than those who caused them through their impudent barbarousness and brutality." [32]

The Socialists also continued to attack Nazi dogmas about a clearly identifiable Aryan race that was superior to all others. They repeatedly insisted that through the centuries Germany had been an "enormous hybridization laboratory" in which the races had become completely intermingled.[33] In 1932 Dr. J. Weinberg defended himself against an anti-Semitic insult by noting that since the time of the Crusades alone he and his contemporaries had had more than a million ancestors each, and these in times of mass migrations and indiscriminate intermarriage. "Racial purity is only a means to political agitation, and it is good for our intellectually less well endowed contemporaries only in so far as it shows a reaction to greatly intensified demands for recognition. The conceit of having descended from a nobler race substitutes for bank accounts and limousines, sweetens a lack of success in the struggle for existence, and provides an apparently moral pretext for immoral envy." [34]

[32] Iltis, "Rassenwissenschaft und Rassenschwindel," *Jungsozialistische Blaetter*, X (1931), 37; Tries, "Was wissen wir von den Rassen und der Juden?" *Das freie Wort*, IV (October 9, 1932), 18.
[33] Ernst Muehlbach, "Rasse und Volk," *Hamburger Echo*, October 22, 1931, p. 6.
[34] *Der Abend*, October 7, 1932.

The SPD press also publicized and underlined speeches by experts who discredited speculation about "pure" races; just days after Hitler became chancellor, *Der Abend* made deprecatory reference to Nazi racism in reviewing a lecture by Professor Eugen Fischer, director of Berlin's Institute of Anthropology, in which the history of man was portrayed as one of constant interracial crossbreeding. Indeed, the Socialists, following von Luschan, contended that interracial breeding was a source of strength to a nation. As Carl Tries put it in 1932: "The refreshment of blood through extensive interbreeding is an inescapable condition for blossoming and improvement." [35]

SPD writers also deprecated the Nazi notion that physical characteristics were reliable guides to a person's race and quality. In 1931 Hugo Iltis made a mockery of the Nazi fetish for long skulls by citing evidence that they were as common among primitive tribes of Africans, Australians, and Eskimos as among Germans.[36] Late the following year, in a special lecture delivered at Berlin's Free Socialist University, Halle professor Friedrich Hertz indignantly singled out two of the greatest Germans, Goethe and Beethoven, as examples of men whose physical characteristics corresponded most closely to the "inferior, eastern" racial type of National Socialist fantasies.[37] An anonymous Nuremberg Socialist was quoted in the *Fraenkische Tagespost* when he told of meeting a visiting Nazi who regaled him with boasts of his prowess as a race expert; to prove it the Hitlerite confidently picked out of a nearby group a "typical Jew," who was in fact a locally well-known Nazi agitator. A 1930 *Leipziger Volkszeitung* cartoon, entitled "The New

---

[35] *Ibid.*, February 3, 1933 (see also *Fraenkische Tagespost*, January 25, 1932); Tries, "Was wissen wir," 18. See also Ernst B. Weithass, "Schach dem Rassenwahn!" *Das freie Wort*, III (September 17, 1931), 13–16; Muehlbach, "Rasse und Volk," 6.
[36] Iltis, "Der Schaedelindex in Wissenschaft und Politik," *Die Gesellschaft*, VII (1931), 549–62.
[37] *Vorwaerts*, December 11, 1932; see also *ibid.*, July 14, 1931.

"Face and head, bad race, cross-breed. Low, retreating fore-head, ugly nose, broad cheek-bones, small eyes, dark hair; facial expression not that of a man in full command of himself, but of one fanatically excited." [47] In April, 1932, the *Fraenkische Tagespost* published Gruber's appraisal next to a list of recent Nazi outrages against Jews and scoffed, "Veil your mongrel head, Adolphus!" The *Hamburger Echo* laughed heartily when Nazi press chief Ernst Hanfstaengel defended his Fuehrer against such attacks by explaining that, although the hair on Hitler's head was black, that in his armpits was blond.[48]

Another choice target was Josef Goebbels, who, according to Jewish SPD Reichstag member Julius Moses, looked "like all the tribes of Israel had united to leave behind an absolutely typical prototype." [49] Criticizing Nazi racism in 1931, Oskar Niwel observed that a "racial outrage" like the Berlin *Gauleiter* could take some comfort in the fact that none of Germany's great men looked very Nordic. O. Heymann urged Socialists to ask the Nazis if Goebbels did not "look like the chairman of a Zionist organization who just came from Palestine." [50] The *Leipziger Volkszeitung* caricatured Goebbels with clearly Jewish features and printed a joke about an old Jew who found a place of honor at a Hitler rally by claiming he was Goebbels' grandfather.[51] To make it clear that the SPD needled Goebbels only to point out the incongruity of his racism, *Vorwaerts* commented during the first presidential campaign in 1932: "Little Goebbels—can he help it that he is physically ill-favored and looks rather Jewish? He can not help it, and no one would re-

[47] Konrad Heiden, *Hitler: A Biography* (New York, 1936), 298.
[48] *Fraenkische Tagespost*, April 2, 1932. For evidence of similar citations, consult Kurt Koszyk, *Zwischen Kaiserreich und Diktatur: Die sozialdemo-kratische Presse von 1914 bis 1933* (Heidelberg, 1958), 206. *Hamburger Echo*, March 4, 1932.
[49] *Hamburger Echo*, May 22, 1930.
[50] *Der Abend*, February 11, 1931; O. Heymann, "Winke fuer Diskussionen mit Nazis," *Das freie Wort*, III (August 16, 1931), 27–28.
[51] *Leipziger Volkszeitung*, December 28, 1932; February 21, 1933.

proach him for it in the slightest . . . if he were not the very same little man who wants to play his part with the leading anti-Semites, the champions of the Nordic-Germanic master race, and the representatives of national valor." [52]

Nor did the SPD ignore lesser Nazis. In 1930 Adolf Schlucks remarked that of the 107 new Nazi Reichstag deputies "not half a dozen" looked at all like Aryans. Two years later *Vorwaerts* gleefully told of a Nazi leader in Eutin who was exposed by a member of the *Tannenbergbund* as the illegitimate child of a Polish Jewish woman.[53] The alleged acceptance of a Negro into an NSDAP local in Nuremberg was headlined by the *Fraenkische Tagespost*: "A Negro as Hitler Man—But German Jews are 'Racially Inferior.' " Socialists in Freilassing pointed out that a local Evangelical curate fond of preaching Nazi racism possessed all the stereotyped Jewish physical characteristics. [54]

Nazi claims that great figures in German history had been anti-Semitic were fair game for SPD agitation. The Socialists were particularly eager to establish that Nietzsche had never hated Jews. Nietzsche's teachings about superior individuals were never intended to carry racial significance, according to Johannes Albert.[55] Hermann Wendel, an unusually prolific Socialist journalist and a gentile, repeated the claim and substantiated it with a number of quotations from the philosopher's writings, including Nietzsche's comment that "to meet a Jew is a blessing, provided that one lives among Germans. Their

---

[52] *Vorwaerts*, February 24, 1932.

[53] Schlucks, *Kampf dem Hakenkreuz* (Berlin, 1930), 4; *Vorwaerts*, August 19 and 21, 1932; I. R., "Nazi-Kreisleiter — Judenstaemmling," *Das freie Wort*, IV (August 28, 1932), 30–31. For a similar case in Saxony, see *Leipziger Volkszeitung*, July 2, 1932; "Nazi Fuehrer und polnischer Jude," *Das freie Wort*, IV (July 17, 1932), 28–29.

[54] *Fraenkische Tagespost*, August 27, 1930; *Freie Volkswacht*, March 3, 1931.

[55] Albert, "Nietzsche und Hitler: Zur Ideologie des Nationalsozialismus," *Sozialistische Bildung* (1930), 353–61.

[the Jews'] shyness hinders them from following us into madness, as, for example, into nationalism. They are themselves an antidote to this last sickness of the European intellect." [56] Werner Hegemann pointed out that the Nazi idol Frederick the Great had never displayed prejudice against Jews as a group and had granted privileges and court influence to several individual Jews. [57]

German Socialists also continued to defend Jews against imputations that they had betrayed Germany in the First World War. *Vorwaerts* expressed outrage over criticism of Field Marshal August von Mackensen after he had cheered a statement praising the role of Jews in the front lines. Rallies sponsored by the *Reichsbund juedischer Frontsoldaten* again gave the Socialist press opportunities to recall Jewish sacrifices for the Fatherland. [58] When the *Stahlhelm* defended its leader, Theodor Duesterberg, against slurs about his Jewish background by noting that his grandfather, Abraham Selig, had fought bravely for Germany in 1813, *Der Abend* commented: "To be sure, even the *Stahlhelm*, which extols the Jewish wartime volunteer Abraham Selig, deprecates . . . the twelve thousand Jewish dead from the years 1914–1918 and behaves in exactly as anti-Semitic a fashion as the Nazis whenever it does not happen to be a question of the grandfather of the organization's president." [59]

SPD spokesmen found no justification for Nazi claims of Jewish responsibility for economic instability and depression. If permanent improvement were to be achieved, they said, capitalism would have to be eliminated, not the Jews. "Assume that a Nazi-caused blood-bath . . . tomorrow were to exterminate all the Jews. The morning after not one worker would earn a

[56] *Der Abend*, July 25, 1932.
[57] *Ibid.*, July 30, 1932.
[58] *Vorwaerts*, August 7, February 15, 1929; November 19, 1932.
[59] *Der Abend*, September 12, 1932. See also *Vorwaerts*, September 4, 1932; R. P., "Noch ein Charakter," *Das freie Wort*, IV (October 9, 1932), 25.

penny more, or have his work-week shortened by a minute, or have a pound more meat to eat. . . . *the extermination of the Jews would eliminate neither competition nor wage-slavery.* 'White Jews' would step into the places left by the unbaptized." [60] They added that Jews often suffered from heightened competition as much as non-Jews. "As many Jewish as Christian shops are put out of business by the department stores. . . . Our enemy . . . , therefore, is not the Jew but rather capitalism, which destroys independent existences and proletarianizes the masses." [61] The Nazis' dichotomy of Jewish "greed capital" and Aryan "creative capital" betrayed their "complete economic ignorance" to Adolf Schlucks, who explained that money in the hands of banks and other capital investments embraced nothing more than deposits of creative, working capital.[62] Indeed, the Socialists argued that the Nazis and their sympathizers consistently practiced the kinds of fiscal immorality that they attributed to the Jews. In 1929 a *voelkisch* banker, Willi Bruss, was tried for having swindled his twenty thousand customers of their investments; a cartoon in *Der Abend* showed him explaining to the court why he felt no scruples about stealing from his fellow racists: "Oh, please, in return I have saved them from the clutches of usurous Jewish capital." [63] A National Socialist's public plea for a sizeable loan because "the Jew" was about to foreclose and take everything stimulated Isaak Kofsch to exclaim: "What a robber! First he borrows money or goods from the Jews and then, to show his thanks, he makes mincemeat of 'the Jew' because the latter has claimed his equal

---

[60] *Die vom Hakenkreuz: Hitler und Konsorten* (Berlin, 1929), 7. Emphasis in the original. Wilhelm Hoegner included the same message in a speech in the Upper Bavarian town of Traunstein on January 15, 1931. *Freie Volkswacht*, January 20, 1931.

[61] *Die Nazi-Fibel*, 10; for similar comments, see *Der Drache Marxismus* (Bernburg, 1930), 12.

[62] Schlucks, *Kampf dem Hakenkreuz*, 5. See also *Fraenkische Tagespost*, May 19, 1931; *Vorwaerts*, August 10, 1932.

[63] *Der Abend*, February 25 and 26, 1929.

rights." [64] When twelve printers unsuccessfully sued the former publishers of a defunct Koblenz Nazi newspaper for back wages, *Der Abend* wanted "to see the . . . speculating Jewish businessman who could be a match in this matter for Germany's racially pure saviors from supposed Jewish corruption." Under the ironic headline "National Socialist Jews," the *Fraenkische Tagespost* told of a Nazi press campaign against Jewish grain dealers who made a profit of 200 percent in favor of a Nazi firm that made one of 300 percent. [65]

While German Social Democrats remained convinced that the Nazi leadership cynically used anti-Semitism in its plot to weaken the republic, after 1929 they showed greater understanding of the psychological factors that underlay the spread of Judeophobia. Socialist spokesmen not only renewed their traditional emphasis on bourgeois anxiety over the failures of capitalism, but they also acknowledged the influence of anti-modernism and collective inferiority complexes in stimulating militant racism. Awareness that such irrational opinions were difficult to combat did not prevent the Socialists from intensifying their attacks on the major pillars of Nazi racial ideology.

[64] *Leipziger Volkszeitung*, December 1, 1930.
[65] *Der Abend*, May 28, 1931; *Fraenkische Tagespost*, October 18, 1931. See also *Vorwaerts*, December 4, 1930; Friedrich Wendel, "Die verjudete NSDAP," *Der Abend*, February 18, 1931, p. 5.

Chapter VI

Protection of the Rights of Jews
1929-1933

The SPD remained determined to protect Jews from attacks on their persons, their property, and their civil rights during the declining years of the Weimar Republic. Most often this determination took the form of hostile reactions in Party pamphlets, speeches, and press reports to the various anti-Semitic outrages. Occasionally the Socialists roused themselves to direct action against anti-Jewish violence. Although these efforts never were organized into a campaign against Judeophobia, they affirmed continued Socialist solidarity with the persecuted Jewish minority.

The Socialists regarded the desecrations of Jewish cemeteries as the most cowardly of all Nazi tactics. Typical of their reactions was the *Hamburger Echo*'s denunciation of such a desecration as "infamy and limitless degeneracy of feeling that cannot be stigmatized sharply enough."[1] When Nazis left a Jewish cemetery near Trebnitz in ruins, a *Reichsbanner*-sponsored protest meeting angrily passed a resolution excoriating the Hitlerites for having "sullied Germany's name and reputation in the world."[2] *Vorwaerts* had found that gangs of Nazi teenagers were frequently responsible for such acts,

[1] *Hamburger Echo*, January 7, 1932. See also *Vorwaerts*, September 30, 1928; June 5, 1931.
[2] "Gegen die Trebnitzer Friedhofsschaendung," *CV Zeitung*, IX (1930), 615–16.

and in 1929 one of its cartoons showed bourgeois parents scolding their son for spending time with girl friends when there were so many "beautiful Jewish cemeteries to be desecrated evenings." A Nazi story that Jews had spoiled their own cemeteries to discredit anti-Semites was emphatically rejected by the SPD organ; in every case in which the perpetrators had been arrested, it noted, they had been Nazis, Vikings, or *Stahlhelmern*.[3] "Of such deeds only 'the noble powers of the National Socialist Germany of the future' are capable," sneered the *Hamburger Echo*.[4] After the desecration of a Jewish cemetery in Georgensgmuend early in 1930, the police reported that the local SPD and *Reichsbanner* leader Hans Pfisterer was on such good terms with the Jewish community that the Nazis blamed him for trying to garner sympathy for the Jews by having committed the crime himself. A local authority further reported that political tensions generated by the incident had polarized the town between the local Jews and Socialists on the one hand and the Nazis and their right-wing allies on the other.[5]

Physical attacks against Jews stimulated equally negative reactions in the SPD. An abortive bomb attempt on the life of an actively anti-Nazi Jewish attorney in Lueneburg, one Dr. Strauss, produced a front-page outcry in *Der Abend*, the SPD central organ. When a group of Berlin Nazis celebrated their September, 1930, election success by forcing a Jewish-looking man out of the bus in which they all were riding, *Vorwaerts* reminded its readers that it was "the concern of all reasonable, thinking people to join together to repulse such attacks on personal freedom." Later, when two Jews defended themselves against a Nazi attack and wounded their tormentors, the *Fraenkische Tagespost* happily doubted that the Hitlerites

[3] *Vorwaerts*, February 29, 1928; January 30, March 15, 1929.
[4] *Hamburger Echo*, November 8, 1932.
[5] Police report to Bezirksamt Schwabach, February 2, 1930, Acten des Bayerischen Staats- Ministeriums des Innern, fol. 73725, no. 2019ba4; Prueckner to Ministry of Interior, *ibid.*, no. 2019ba5.

would quickly return to talk of "Jewish cowardice." [6] *Reichs-banner* units joined in denouncing violence against Jews. The organization's Kaiserslautern chairman, Robert Ruthmann, in 1929 sent his men two letters appealing for greater loyalty in the face of increased Nazi disorders against Jews. One letter cited recent anti-Semitic outrages that demonstrated "how serious the situation already is for our Jewish fellow citizens and what would impend should the Hitlerites succeed in grasping power." [7] Also in 1929, *Reichsbanner* leader Otto Hoersing sounded the alarm over the upswing in anti-Jewish violence and promised that he and his comrades would combat it with all their strength. [8]

In 1932 Albert Suedekum complained to Hermann Puender, Undersecretary of State in the Reichschancellory, about the intensification of anti-Semitism in East Prussia. His Jewish friends, he said, could no longer use the railroads there without harassment, and Jewish businessmen in the region were "frequently victims of inhuman persecution." He asked Puender to urge Chancellor Bruening to hit hard at the Nazis and their tactics in East Prussia during the presidential campaign. [9] If Bruening ever got the message, there is no evidence that he acted on the old Socialist's advice.

Violent Nazi demonstrations against Jews were rare before Hitler came to power. The only two worth noting occurred in Berlin in 1930 and 1931. The Berlin police, then under Socialist direction, were caught unprepared by the first but took vigorous action against the second. The Nazis' first large-scale, anti-Jewish street riot took place in Berlin when a new session of

---

[6] *Der Abend*, August 1, 1929; *Vorwaerts*, September 16, 1930; O. L., "Von Juden und Juristen," *Fraenkische Tagespost*, March 31, 1932, p. 4.

[7] *Voelkischer Beobachter*, July 31, 1929.

[8] Otto Hoersing, "Zur Abwehr entschlossen," *Abwehr-Blaetter*, XXXIX (February, 1929), 27.

[9] Suedekum to Puender, March 24, 1932, Nachlass Albert Suedekum, fol. 160a, nos. 4–6.

the Reichstag opened on October 13, 1930. Intended as a show of strength, the riot was carried out according to plan by SA men who assaulted Jewish-looking passersby and smashed the windows of Jewish shops and department stores. Responded *Vorwaerts*: "In its present situation Germany cannot afford the extravagance of anti-Semitic street riots. It must awaken and defend itself if it does not want to be murdered by the swastika-pestilence." One of its cartoons showed apes in SA uniforms hurling rocks through the windows of Jewish shops; the Nazis, its caption observed, had shown what they meant by "liberating deeds." [10] The Berlin police, then under the direction of Carl Zoergiebel (SPD), proved themselves unequal to the task of re-establishing order quickly. Minister-President Otto Braun therefore replaced him with a more able Social Democrat, Albert Grzesinski, in November, 1931.[11]

Much larger riots were instigated and carried through along the same lines on the Jewish New Year, September 12, 1931, outside the synagogue then located on Fasanenstrasse near the Kurfuerstendamm. This time, however, a more vigilant police force made fifty arrests.[12] *Der Abend* told its readers that the incident had damaged all Germans, not just the Jews. "For anti-Semitism, as it is pursued in Germany, meets with sympathy nowhere in the civilized world; and when the report comes from Berlin that Jews who have emerged from prayer on one of their feast days have been beaten in the streets, then once again in the world outside the picture of old Tsarist Russia arises, with its Black Hundred and its infamous Jew-baiting and pogroms." [13] Chief of Police Grzesinski called upon all Berliners to cooperate with his overworked forces to assure that matters would not "degenerate further into ideological and

10 *Vorwaerts*, October 14 and 15, 1930.
11 Grzesinski, *Inside Germany*, trans. Alexander S. Lipchitz (New York, 1939), 130.
12 *Vorwaerts*, September 13, 1931.
13 *Der Abend*, September 15, 1931.

religious persecution." He then banned Goebbels' *Der Angriff* for one week for running an anti-Jewish cartoon at that tense moment.[14]

The trials of the SA men began only days after their arrest and were closely followed in the SPD press. Without exception the accused denied that the riot was planned and tried to make it appear a spontaneous demonstration against the oppressors of the people. *Der Abend* mocked their testimony: "I went for walk in Wannsee; suddenly on the Kurfuerstendamm a Jew stole my cudgel and began hitting himself and shouting, 'Perish Judah!' " A more bitter *Vorwaerts* commented: "The Nazis have lost every feeling of shame over cowardly and absurd excuses." [15] Although moderately stiff sentences were quickly handed down on the lesser Nazis, the trial of the Berlin SA chief, Count Wolf von Helldorf, who had planned and directed the disturbance, dragged on for months, much to Socialist dismay.[16] Helldorf and eleven of his henchmen were eventually acquitted, verdicts that a disgusted *Vorwaerts* blamed on the courts for having let the defendants become "complete masters of the situation." It ran a cartoon showing Helldorf directing his pogrom under the shadow of a blindfolded goddess of justice and shouting, "Don't be afraid of the female, comrades! Of course she has a sword—but she's blind!" [17]

Nazi claims that the NSDAP neither advocated nor practiced violence against Jews were scornfully refuted by Social Democrats. Revolted by Nazi protests of innocence in a rash of anti-Semitic violence in Leipzig late in 1930, the local SPD organ pictured the Hitlerites as "innocent lambs" in a particularly blatant case of assault on a Jewish pedestrian in Leipzig's central marketplace. "In the first place we weren't in the marketplace at all. In the second place we didn't see any Jews there.

[14] *Vorwaerts*, September 17 and 18, 1931.
[15] *Der Abend*, September 22, 1931; *Vorwaerts*, September 26, 1931.
[16] *Der Abend*, December 17, 1931; *Vorwaerts*, January 8 and 9, 1932.
[17] *Vorwaerts*, February 10 and 11, 1932.

In the third place the Jew hit first." [18] The *Fraenkische Tagespost* reprinted three of the Nazis' favorite anti-Jewish songs to prove that the Hitlerites lied in denying their "intellectual parentage of the latest wave of pogroms." [19] In 1932 the Hamburg Party paper attacked Goebbels for his "mad incitements to murder" in *Der Angriff*: "And if stirred-up individuals then commit murder, Herr Goebbels 'disapproves' of the methods but remains himself unmolested; for he is, to be sure, 'innocent' and may go on writing and talking of execution, murder, and of heads rolling." [20] In a case involving young Nazis guilty of crimes of violence against Jews, the Socialists reserved their greatest censure for "the inhuman agitation of the National Socialist press." [21]

On at least one occasion SPD members employed more nearly direct measures to minimize violence against Jews. Breslau Socialists, shortly after noisy Nazi demonstrations against local Jews in June, 1932,[22] reacted to a giant poster —"Get Ready for Palestine"—advertising a speech by Goebbels with a threat to "seize upon relentless self-defense in the face of this brutalization of the political struggle" if city authorities did nothing to "prevent the posting of that kind of trash in the future." [23] Artur Schweriner had summarized the SPD view perfectly in 1928 in a speech before *Reichsbanner* functionaries: "Altogether, a more detestable form of agitation than Jew-baiting is inconceivable; therefore there is no longer any real difference between this kind of political action and the employment of revolvers, cudgels, and prussic acid." [24]

---

18 *Leipziger Volkszeitung*, October 22, November 26, 1930. See also *Hamburger Echo*, July 3, 1931.
19 *Fraenkische Tagespost*, September 28, 1931.
20 *Hamburger Echo*, August 25, 1932.
21 *Vorwaerts*, June 29, 1932.
22 *Ibid.*, June 3, 1932.
23 *Der Abend*, June 21, 1932.
24 Schweriner, *Von Tillesen bis Schmelzer* (Berlin, 1928), 4. See also Paucker, *Der juedische Abwehrkampf*, 120–21, 160–61.

Schweriner was a Jewish SPD member who until 1929 had been a leading member of the CV. In that year he gave up his official position in the Jewish organization to become editor of the anti-Nazi bimonthly (later weekly) *Alarm*, although he continued to cooperate with the CV.

German Social Democrats also reacted negatively to insults or lies hurled at Jews by the Nazis. In June, 1928, Goebbels began a vicious campaign in *Der Angriff* against Berlin's Assistant Chief of Police, Bernhard Weiss, the most prominent official of Jewish background in the municipal government and a Socialist.[25] At first the slurs were limited to insulting caricatures and name-calling—"Isidore"—and although Weiss successfully brought charges of libel against Goebbels and his assistant, Dagobert Duerr,[26] the SPD virtually ignored the matter as a Party. But when in July, 1932, the Nazis changed their tactics and demanded the dismissal of Weiss for allegedly accepting bribes from a Jewish industrialist, one Krojanker, and for tolerating or encouraging illicit relations between his wife and Krojanker, the Socialists rushed to his aid. In a letter to Weiss published in *Der Abend*, Carl Severing took note of "the hateful, purely demagogic defamation" of the policeman's wife. "Do not let yourself be downcast. This vulgarity is nearing the stage at which it dies of itself." [27] In its Reichstag election campaign of July, 1932, the SPD appealed for women's votes by citing the case as an example of "the unspeakable vileness of the National Socialist mob." [28]

Jews who were not specifically identified with the SPD were similarly defended. A Hamburg physician who was tried by his local professional organization for having heaped anti-Semitic abuse upon specific Jewish doctors in conversations with his patients was censured but acquitted of the charge of professional misconduct. The *Hamburger Echo* took strong

[25] Helmut Heiber, *Joseph Goebbels* (Berlin, 1962), 74–77.
[26] *Vorwaerts*, August 30, 1929.
[27] *Der Abend*, July 13, 1932.
[28] *Vorwaerts*, July 17, 1932.

exception to the decision, noting that the doctors hearing the case had encouraged a repetition of such practices by failing to root out "disgusting National Socialist and anti-Semitic agitation." [29] Jews as a group were also defended. *Vorwaerts* dismissed Hitler's charge that bolshevism was a Jewish plot by contending that "virtually no more Jews" were to be found among Bolshevik leaders and that only a "minute percentage" of the Jews accepted bolshevism. When unidentified anti-Semites distributed pamphlets signed by the fictitious *Juedische Glaubensgemeinschaft* (Jewish Religious Community) urging Jews to support the KPD, the Socialist organ exposed it as a ruse to confirm right-wing fables about Jewish inclinations toward bolshevism. It also protested the presence of a display of pictures insulting to Jews in the Nazi booth at Berlin's 1932 radio exhibition.[30]

Nor did the Socialists shrink from shielding Jewish capitalists from abuse. Hans Hackmack rejected as "an attrocious distortion of the facts" a Nazi claim that the collapse of the Continent's largest textile concern, the Nordwolle, was due to the maneuverings of Jewish banker Jakob Goldschmidt. On the contrary, he said, the three non-Jewish brothers, Carl, Heinz, and Friedel Lahusan, the Nordwolle's owners, had borrowed millions from Goldschmidt's Darmstadt and National Bank after having falsified their financial records; when they went broke, they dragged the bank down with them, making "Jewish finance capital" *their* victim. In 1932 the *Muenchener Post* complained bitterly that local Nazis were being allowed to give away large bills of paper currency from the inflationary period overprinted with a swastika and a comment about the "Jewish bank" that had appropriated the real money.[31]

Yet another aspect of the SPD's efforts against anti-Semitism

[29] *Hamburger Echo*, October 27, 1931.
[30] *Vorwaerts*, February 27, 1930; August 23 and 26, 1932.
[31] Hans Hackmack, "Lahusan und die verstummten Nazi," *Das freie Wort*, III (August 2, 1931), 7–11; *Muenchener Post*, November 19 and 20, 1932, in NSDAP Hauptarchiv, fol. 1559, no. 83.

during the period 1929–33 was its defense of Jewish religious and civil rights. Efforts by National Socialists in Northeim to prohibit as "inhumane" the slaughter of animals according to Hebrew ritual were opposed by the local SPD newspaper, and the Socialist in charge of Northeim's slaughterhouse brought suit against the Nazi organ in which the original charge had appeared.[32] Social Democrats in the Reichstag successfully opposed a Nazi proposal that fortunes made by a few *Ostjuden* since coming to Germany should be expropriated.[33] Socialists on the Leipzig city council crushed a Hitlerite plan to establish a new committee to screen applicants for permanent residency and keep out "racially undesirable" foreigners. The SPD spokesman against the proposal, one Frau Hammermeister, precipitated a small riot—including shouts of "Prostitute!"—when she poured contempt on Nazi racism and recalled Gruber's uncomplimentary judgment on Hitler's racial features.[34]

SPD spokesmen repeatedly complained that German courts violated Jewish civil rights and tolerated their violation by others. In 1930 Erich Kuttner complained in the general committee of the Prussian parliament about the large number of anti-Semitic judges in East Prussia, Silesia, and Pomerania. He illustrated his point with the story of a judge in Tilsit who—after acquitting a landowner of the charge of insulting, caning, and turning his dogs on a Jewish peddler—had used the opportunity to comment on the "coarse morals" of Jews.[35] The freeing of Nazis who had sung a song with the refrain, "When the Jews bleed, Germany will again be free!" was reported by a disgusted *Vorwaerts* under the headline: "The Swastika goes

[32] William Sheridan Allen, *The Nazi Seizure of Power: The Experience of a Single German Town, 1930–1935* (Chicago, 1965), 51–52.
[33] *Verhandlungen des Reichstags*, 44th Sess., 1929, CDXXIV, 1146; *ibid.*, 54th Sess., CDXLVI, 2085; *Vorwaerts*, February 6, 1931.
[34] *Leipziger Volkszeitung*, January 29, 1931.
[35] *Preussischer Landtag*, 127th Sess., 1930, III, 17–19; *Leipziger Volkszeitung*, March 5, 1930.

Unpunished—Even if it wants to see Jewish Blood." [36] The *Leipziger Volkszeitung* castigated a local court for letting so much time pass before trying Nazis who had beaten a Jewish shopkeeper that an effective case could no longer be made against them. The SPD organ in Nuremberg in March, 1932, protested the acquittal of a Nazi charged with having blackmailed an Austrian Jew. Noting that a blackmail letter signed by the defendant had been produced, the *Fraenkische Tagespost* sarcastically commented that the letter "was perhaps just a gentle request for a contribution to the race breeding fund or else an honorable attempt to . . . save two hundred shillings from the greedy hands of the Jews by placing it into the creative fists of the Hitler crowd." [37]

Social Democrats attributed the persistence of anti-Semitism in the courts to the presence of Nazis and Nazi sympathizers in the German judiciary. *Vorwaerts* in 1930 angrily fastened the label "party judge" on a jurist for acquitting a Nazi who had called Albert Grzesinski a "Jewish bastard." [38] Its cartoonist portrayed a panel of three judges wearing swastikas on their lapels, smiling benignly, and saying that "expressions of this kind correspond thoroughly with the convictions of the tribunal." [39] A defense attorney in another trial irrelevantly suggested that the discoverer of a medical treatment, for the use of which his client was on trial, might have been Jewish. The *Fraenkische Tagespost* found it a transparent diversionary

[36] *Vorwaerts*, February 23, 1929. See also *ibid.*, November 18, 1930; August 20, 1931; May 7, 1932; *Hamburger Echo*, August 10, 1930.

[37] *Leipziger Volkszeitung*, February 23, 1931; *Fraenkische Tagespost*, March 13, 1932; *Der Abend*, March 31, 1932. See also *Fraenkische Tagespost*, June 16, 1932.

[38] *Vorwaerts*, August 31, 1930. Grzesinski was an illegitimate child whose father may indeed have been Jewish. He himself has vigorously denied any Jewish ancestry, insisting he could trace back his " 'pure Nordic-Aryan' blood for almost two centuries," without explaining how. Grzesinski, *Inside Germany*, 18. But, as *Vorwaerts* commented, "What difference does it make, after all?" *Vorwaerts*, May 14, 1931.

[39] *Vorwaerts*, May 17, 1931.

measure that had a good chance of success because so many German judges were prejudiced.[40]

The Socialists repeatedly demanded the removal of anti-Semitic judges. When an East Prussian jurist addressed a defendant as "the Jew XYZ" and spoke of Jews as "foreign elements," the *Leipziger Volkszeitung* in January, 1930, demanded that the Ministry of Justice "see to it that this anti-Semitic sparrow flies out of the courts of law as soon as possible." [41] The same demand was raised after a well-known Nazi pastor was acquitted of insulting the republic with the cry "Jewish Republic"; in the opinion of the judges, Jews did indeed run the German government.[42] But realizing that nothing could be done to eliminate anti-Semitic judges without disrupting the whole legal system, the Socialists frustratedly reacted to yet another such prejudiced decision with the question: "What measures are to be taken against an 'irremovable' judge who . . . through such decisions openly offends against the national constitution and against accepted ideas of justice?" [43]

Almost as annoying to Socialists was the frequency with which Nazis succeeded in having Jewish judges removed from cases involving National Socialist misdeeds. *Der Abend* itself complained in 1930 that Jewish judges were too lenient with Nazi defendants and implored that the Hitlerites be judged only by non-Jews. The latter, *Der Abend* reasoned, could impose punishment without conflict of conscience or charges of racial prejudice.[44] But if that plea was meant to be taken seriously, it was never repeated. On the contrary, a few weeks later Hamburg Socialists decried the "unheard-of-scandal" when a Nazi defendant successfully demanded the removal of a Jewish judge

[40] *Fraenkische Tagespost*, November 8, 1931.
[41] *Leipziger Volkszeitung*, January 4, 1930. For a similar case involving a judge in Breslau, see *Der Abend*, January 9, 1929.
[42] *Der Abend*, April 21, 1931.
[43] *Vorwaerts*, December 27, 1931.
[44] *Der Abend*, June 21, 1930.

from the tribunal.[45] *Der Abend* scornfully suggested that Professor Guenther be brought in to make head measurements and pass on the race of all German judges, and *Vorwaerts* ran a cartoon showing a haughty Nazi giving blood tests to a panel of judges.[46] Socialists applauded subsequent rulings by the Prussian Ministry of Justice that Jewish judges and jurymen might be removed only when there was objective and specific evidence of prejudice against a particular defendant. When a Nazi on trial in Chemnitz managed to eliminate a Jewish juror, the Socialists repeated that such practices brought Germany ever nearer the National Socialist ideal of party justice.[47]

A favorite Socialist method of heaping shame on anti-Semitism was to quote from harshly worded judicial decisions against Judeophobes. When a prominent Nuremberg Nazi received a jail sentence for insulting members of the Leutershausen Jewish community, the *Fraenkische Tagespost* expressed pleasure that the bluntly phrased judgment censured the Nazi for "disseminating poison." The Nuremberg Party organ similarly endorsed a decision against the Nazi sponsors of a boycott against Jewish shops in Coburg, finding the stiff fine appropriate because of *"the obstinacy with which the accused pursue their speculation in base racial instincts for the furtherance of their political or commercial aims."* [48] When an SA reign of terror against the Jewish owner of a Berlin cafe was ended by a judicial decision, *Vorwaerts* applauded the judge's comment that the Nazi actions constituted "a disgrace against civilization of the first rank." [49]

The SPD also criticized civil servants who ignored or opposed Jewish rights. In 1929 *Vorwaerts* told of a Berlin Jewish

---

[45] *Hamburger Echo*, August 5, 1930.

[46] *Der Abend*, August 6, 1930; *Vorwaerts*, August 7, 1930.

[47] *Vorwaerts*, October 14, 1930; *Sozialdemokratische Partei-Korrespondenz* (February, 1932), 112.

[48] *Fraenkische Tagespost*, May 23, 1930; January 11, 1932.

[49] *Vorwaerts*, October 18, 1932.

doctor who had complained to a suburban municipal official about an excessive fine for a minor infraction of the traffic code; it protested the "anti-Semitic loutishness" of the official, who had replied that Jews might like to haggle but would not be allowed to do so over traffic fines. The *Fraenkische Tages-post* condemned a self-confessed Nazi on the administrative staff of the University of Cologne who had discouraged a Jew from studying law; Jews, the Nazi had promised, would have no future in that discipline. The Nuremberg Party organ commented that it was "decidedly an error" that such people were not ejected from high positions. The Socialists also condemned the penetration of anti-Semites into Germany's state-run radio network under the reactionary government of Franz von Papen (1932). *Der Abend* complained that a poem about persecuted Jews was altered to omit all mention of Jews when read over the air.[50] *Vorwaerts* reacted angrily when a Nazi editor from Munich, one Koehn, was allowed to deliver a radio talk filled with anti-Jewish vulgarities.[51] The Socialists held National Radio Commissioner Erich Scholz responsible for these developments. "As long as this complete cipher, this insignificant, reactionary political bureaucrat remains as director of the radio, catastrophes and disgraces of this kind will be foregone conclusions."[52]

Especially sensitive to anti-Semitism among the police, the Socialists found it "a peculiar view of the duties of the security police" when Nazis in Altenburg were allowed to escape after attacking Jews.[53] They also criticized the police in Bach for permitting a Nazi to hound and attack Jews while quickly arresting two workers who had given "the Nazi lout a sound,

[50] *Ibid.*, August 23, 1929; *Fraenkische Tagespost*, April 27, 1930; *Der Abend* October 18, 1932.

[51] *Vorwaerts*, October 23, 1932.

[52] "Der Vater des Koehn-Skandals," *Das freie Wort*, IV (October 30, 1932), 31–32.

[53] *Der Abend*, December 3, 1929.

well-deserved thrashing" for his anti-Semitic excesses. Socialists in Dinkelsbuehl bitterly complained that the police did nothing about the anti-Semitic demonstrations staged by Nazis before the homes of local Jews. *Der Abend* criticized Berlin police who, it said, had watched impassively while Nazis attacked Jewish students in January, 1933.[54] In an effort to bring police in the Prussian Province of Hanover to act against Judeophobes, Socialist *Oberpraesident* Gustav Noske on December 16, 1931, sent an order directing provincial administrators to have the police devote "particular attention" to preventing anti-Semitic outrages. If they occurred anyway, he concluded, the police were to "act forcefully and energetically to determine the identity of the culprits." [55]

The Socialists applauded and encouraged civil servants who respected Jewish civil rights. In 1930 Ernst Hamburger commended Albert Grzesinski for having helped German Jews to realize equal rights during his term as Prussian Minister of the Interior.[56] The Socialist majority in the assembly of Charlottenburg in Berlin put through a resolution barring anyone from public office in that borough who would not acknowledge equal rights for all citizens. In 1930 they successfully defended the policy against concerted Nazi attacks.[57]

The rights of Jews in public service also found supporters among SPD spokesmen. Nazi demands for the ouster of the Jewish chief doctor from the municipal hospital in Fuerth were successfully opposed by Socialist members of the city council, whose spokesman cited the doctor's long service to the community. The *Fraenkische Tagespost* agreed that the doctor

[54] *Fraenkische Tagespost*, January 21, July 15, 1932; *Der Abend*, January 17, 1933.
[55] Quoted in Herbert Michaelis, Ernst Schraepler, and Guenter Scheel (eds.), *Ursachen und Folgen: Vom deutschen Zusammenbruch 1918 und 1945 bis zur staatlichen Neuordnung Deutschlands in der Gegenwart* (Berlin, [1959–]), VII, 218.
[56] Hamburger, "Grzesinskis Leistung," *Die Gesellschaft*, VII (1930), 297.
[57] *Vorwaerts*, October 10, 1930.

enjoyed "the greatest confidence of the general population. It must be considered malicious to attempt to shake this confidence with racist nonsense." [58] In 1931 Carl Severing sprang to the defense of a certain Frau Rosenheim, an employee of the Naturalization Office in Berlin, whom Nazi Wilhelm Kube had accused of retarding the naturalization of Sudeten and Austrian Germans while expediting that of the *Ostjuden*. Not only was the allegation untrue, said Severing, but the woman was only a minor official who had no influence over policy.[59] Later the dismissal of one Dr. Kuerschner, a Hungarian-born Jew, from his post as director of the German radio's topical program section because of his foreign origin was denounced in *Der Abend* as a "public avowal of anti-Semitic racial theory" and a "flagrant contradiction" of the Weimar Constitution.[60]

Social Democrats were alert to evidence of anti-Semitism in the schools and universities and staunchly defended the equal educational rights of Jews. The Socialists understood that most German students stemmed from the middle class, and they believed them subject to the general bourgeois propensity for Judeophobia. Hedwig Steinkopf sadly acknowledged that nothing much had changed with university students since an 1897 Socialist indictment of their political aims: "To insult Jews, to elevate Teutonism, to revel in chauvinism, and to shout 'Hurrah!' at every patriotic show." [61] The establishment in 1930 of the anti-Semitic *Buendische Reichschaft* (National Federation), a central organization of various youth and student groups, gave the *Sozialistische Monatshefte* occasion to condemn the groups' equation of Western values and culture

---

[58] *Fraenkische Tagespost*, October 24 and 25, 1930.

[59] "Severing antwortet Kube," *CV Zeitung*, X (1931), 49.

[60] *Der Abend*, September 14, 1932.

[61] Heinrich Jakubowicz, "Die politische Entwicklung der deutschen Studentenschaft," *Sozialistische Bildung* (December, 1929), 356; Hedwig Steinkopf, "Student," *Sozialistische Monatshefte*, XXXVII (1931), 1047.

on the one hand and Jews and moral inferiority on the other.[62] In 1927 Germany's most important student organization, the *Deutsche Studentenschaft* (German Students' Association), had been denied official recognition and financial support by Prussia's SPD-led coalition government because it would not renounce the Aryan clause for membership in its Austrian counterpart, with which it had recently merged. A subsequent effort to pursuade the Socialists to relent was unsuccessful. When in 1931 the organization urged its local chapters to work for the limitation of Jewish enrollment in the schools, *Vorwaerts* fumed that it had deteriorated into a Nazi agitation society.[63]

The Socialist central organ deplored a resolution passed by the student government of Oldenburg's Engineering Academy which stated that limits should be placed on the number of Jewish students admitted there, and the newspaper condemned the arbitrary exclusion of Jewish students from debate on the question.[64] Socialists in the Saxon parliament led the majority of that body in quashing a Nazi proposal to limit the number of Jewish students in the University of Leipzig and other institutes and academies in that state.[65] Speaking before the Bavarian parliament, where he was a leading figure in the SPD delegation, Wilhelm Hoegner blasted the student government at the Friedrich Alexander University in Erlangen for having adopted bylaws that virtually excluded Jewish students from membership.[66] A decision by Leipzig students to exclude Jews

[62] "Voelkisches Programm," *Sozialistische Monatshefte*, XXXVI (1930), 1151–53.
[63] George L. Mosse, *The Crisis of German Ideology*, 270; *Der Abend*, April 22, 1930; *Vorwaerts*, February 15, 1931. See also Martin Boettcher, "Unsere Studenten," *Der Abend*, October 9, 1930, p. 5.
[64] *Der Abend*, December 30, 1930.
[65] *Leipziger Volkszeitung*, January 29, 1930.
[66] *Verhandlungen des Bayerischen Landtags*, 85th Sess., 1930, IV, 308–309. Hoegner, a non-Jew, was also a Socialist Reichstag Deputy.

from the university's social council was labelled "Nazi idiocy" by the local SPD organ, which begged for a return to sanity. About that same time *Vorwaerts* damned a similar move by Rostock University students.[67]

German Socialists also attacked students who were responsible for violence against their Jewish colearners. The University of Berlin's anti-Semitic "National Socialist rabble" was a constant source of irritation to the SPD central organ.[68] Early in 1932 Nazi students physically attacked a group of badly outnumbered Jewish students along with their Republican colleagues who had tried to defend them, precipitating the closing of the university.[69] Similar behavior, accompanied by demands for the expulsion of Jewish students, stimulated the Socialists to urge the Prussian government to "move against this dark, medieval terrorism with the most energetic measures."[70] In January, 1933, *Der Abend* endorsed the university rector's announced intention to expel the leaders of anti-Jewish brawls. Aware that racist students did not confine their violence to Jewish students, the SPD's Cologne newspaper, *Rheinische Zeitung*, in a special edition before the July, 1932, Reichstag election, imagined one group of students greeting another with "What's up? Shall we study today or take on the Jews?"[71]

Nor did the Socialists neglect the rights of Jewish teachers and other teachers who opposed anti-Semitism. Otto Friedlaender found a Nazi charge that German education was being "Judaized" a "grotesque comedy for all who know how difficult it is for a young university lecturer of Jewish extraction to get onto a faculty."[72] Hamburg Socialists answered a Nazi conten-

---

[67] *Leipziger Volkszeitung*, December 9, 1932; *Vorwaerts*, December 11, 1932.
[68] *Der Abend*, June 30, 1932.
[69] *Ibid.*, January 23, 1932; see also *Vorwaerts*, January 23, 1932.
[70] *Vorwaerts*, July 1, 1932.
[71] *Der Abend*, January 31, 1933; *Rheinische Zeitung*, July, 1932.
[72] *Vorwaerts*, February 8, 1931. Friedlaender, who was of Jewish background, was a Socialist journalist, secretary of the Socialist Student International, and chairman of the League of Socialist Students.

tion that the local adult education school had too many Jewish
teachers by citing the scientific contributions of Einstein and
Paul Ehrlich, resolving that the school had *"no reason simply
to exclude Jewish professors when they mean something to the
intellectual world."* [73] When anti-Jewish students attacked Kiel
Professor of Theology Otto Baumgarten as a "philo-Semite,"
the *Verein zur Abwehr des Antisemitismus* lauded the local
SPD organ for treating the scandal objectively and prominently
while non-Socialist newspapers in the area ignored it or gave it
only passing notice.[74] *Der Abend* commented dourly on the
resignation of the Jewish director of the Wismar Engineering
Academy, made under pressure from Nazi students and approved by local politicians who feared violence and economic
pressure: "If the Wismar example finds imitators, in the future
the most dull and barbarous element of the students will determine who may and who may not teach in German colleges and
universities." [75]

The most prominent case of discrimination against a Jewish
teacher occurred when young Ernst Cohn was called to the
chair of civil law at Breslau University in the last months of
the Weimar Republic.[76] From the moment he began teaching,
the new professor could not make himself heard because of the
din raised by Nazi students in the lecture hall, and his lectures
were immediately suspended. *Vorwaerts* applauded when the
rector of the university bravely declined to remove Cohn, re-
scheduled his lectures, and closed the school when the Nazis
repeated their performance. "All who are in earnest about freedom of the mind must offer energetic resistance," the news-

[73] *Hamburger Echo*, June 14, 1932. Emphasis in the original.
[74] Martin Hobohm, "Der Kieler Bach-Baumgarten-Skandal," *Abwehr-Blaetter*, CL (November/December, 1930), 141–42.
[75] *Der Abend*, November 7, 1931; *Fraenkische Tagespost*, November 15, 1931.
[76] Karl Steinhoff, "Rechtswissenschaft," *Sozialistische Monatshefte*, XXXVIII (1932), 1057–58.

paper stated, holding that Cohn's removal "would be a most severe blow against academic freedom" and one that "freedom-loving circles of the German people will not accept calmly." [77] Cohn was dismissed after admitting that he had advocated giving Leon Trotsky asylum in Germany, implying that an "intellectual" such as the Russian Communist was always worthy of protection. The Socialists, while annoyed over Cohn's indiscretion, were certain that he would not have gotten into trouble if he had not been Jewish and expressed disgust that the university had violated the principle of academic freedom. Restored to his chair after a swift investigation by Prussian officials, Cohn made an abject apology for his statement about Trotsky; Vorwaerts was unhappy that he had renounced his right and duty to speak out on controversial matters but was even more furious that pressure to do so had been put on the young professor by the academic senate. When Nazi students renewed their demonstrations against Cohn, the newspaper returned to its denunciations of the perpetrators. [78]

Equally anathema to the SPD were anti-Semitic teachers. Wilhelm Tiegins disparagingly remembered from his own university career a professor whose favoritism for "Aryan" students was matched by his insulting intolerance for Jewish learners. [79] An anonymous Socialist reproved a Nazi secondary-school teacher who had sneered to a new group of pupils, "There are Jews in the class!" [80] A racist professor at the University of Leipzig was portrayed by the Leipziger Volkszeitung as a coward for refusing to debate with "Jews and Marxists" and as an incompetent psychology instructor because he would not deal with the ideas of Freud, Katz, and Stern. [81]

[77] Vorwaerts, November 11, 12, and 18, 1932.

[78] Der Abend, December 24, 1932; January 24, 1933; Vorwaerts, January 5 and 15, 1933.

[79] Tiegins, "Die Faschisierung der deutschen Hochschulen," Sozialistische Bildung (February, 1931), 40–41.

[80] "Verhetzung der Schuljugend durch nationalsozialistische Lehrer," Sozialdemokratische Partei-Korrespondenz (June/July, 1932), 365.

[81] Leipziger Volkszeitung, December 10, 1932.

German Socialists kept an especially watchful eye on National Socialist Wilhelm Frick in the sixteen months he held the joint appointment as Thuringia's Minister of the Interior and Minister of Public Instruction, from December, 1929, to April, 1931. Frick's appointment in 1930 of racial "scientist" Hans F. K. Guenther to a chair at the University of Jena, against the will of the faculty, aroused Socialist ire.[82] A cartoon in *Der Abend* showed two Nazi students conversing: "An outrage! They let Haeckel teach here that we are descended from monkeys. But now, when Guenther has proved that we are the best of the exalted Nordic race, the faculty won't have him!" [83] *Vorwaerts* adjudged Guenther's inaugural lecture as one filled with primitive racism "clothed in scientific form," and it lamented that the Thuringian university was being turned into a Nazi propaganda agency.[84] When it became known that only a handful of students had registered for the racist's lectures, Herbert Kuehnert recalled that Frick had justified the appointment on the basis of student interest in the racial question.[85] A *Vorwaerts* cartoon showed Guenther lecturing to an almost empty hall: "My theory of why the genuine blue-skulled, blond-eyed, long haired Nordic super-race died out frequently finds confirmation in the present day." In May, 1931, the Thuringian parliament adopted an SPD-sponsored resolution condemning Guenther's appointment as serving "no real scholarly need" and as extravagant in view of the university's strained financial condition.[86] According to the Nazis, an unsuccessful attempt on Guenther's life at about the same time was the work of a Jew or someone incited by "Jewish instigators." In reality it was the work of a mentally disturbed lad who

---

[82] August Siemsen, "Die Kultur- und Schulpolitik des Nationalsozialismus," *Jungsozialistische Blaetter*, X (1931), 5.

[83] *Der Abend*, June 3, 1930.

[84] *Vorwaerts*, November 16, 1930.

[85] Kuehnert, "Thueringen," *Sozialistische Monatshefte*, XXXVII (1931), 796–97.

[86] *Vorwaerts*, January 23, May 30, 1931.

had become infected with the "Nazi spirit," according to the SPD's central organ, which went out of its way to show that the would-be assassin was neither a Jew nor a "red." [87]

Frick's executive order establishing five prayers with anti-Semitic overtones for use in schools throughout the province received instant Socialist condemnation.[88] The SPD deputies in the Thuringian parliament demanded that the provincial government annul Frick's order and, with some exaggeration, lashed out at the prayers as "partisan, political hate-prayers" that propagated "the vilest anti-Jewish agitation" and therefore violated the national constitution.[89] SPD Reichstag Deputy August Froelich of Weimar told his fellow parliamentarians that the prayers constituted pure and simple slander "against the Jews and against the Social Democrats." [90]

Meanwhile the Socialist press unstintingly took Frick to task. The *Fraenkische Tagespost* expressed impatience when Reich Minister of the Interior Josef Wirth, replying to an appeal from Thuringian Jews, instructed them to send him particulars of all actions that infringed upon their rights; it sarcastically inquired if Wirth had heard about Frick's hate-prayers. One Socialist cartoon showed Frick composing his prayers as the devil whispered in his ear, "More hatred!" Another pictured Frick as "the second Luther," flinging an inkwell in terror at a Jewish devil that had interrupted his prayer-writing.[91] *Der wahre Jacob*, the SPD's humor magazine, offered a "Thuringian School Prayer" of its own:

[87] *Voelkischer Beobachter*, May 12, 1931; *Der Abend*, May 13, 1931; *Vorwaerts*, May 13 and 14, August 28, 1931.

[88] For the full text of all five prayers, see "Fricks amtliche Juden- und Marxistenhetze durch Schulgebete," *Sozialdemokratische Partei-Korrespondenz* (June, 1930), 376–78.

[89] *Vorwaerts*, May 8, 1930. See also *ibid.*, May 21 and 23, 1930; *Der Abend*, May 8, 1930.

[90] *Verhandlungen des Reichstags*, 177th Sess., 1930, CDXXVIII, 5516.

[91] *Fraenkische Tagespost*, June 14, 1930; *Der Abend*, May 16, 1930; *Vorwaerts*, May 27, 1930; see also *Vorwaerts*, June 6, 1930.

Our Father, who art in Valhalla,
if you place value on having your name hallowed,
then first destroy all foreign races that you
          created in a moment of weakness.
The Third Reich come,
Frick's will be done,
on the whole earth as it is in Weimar.
Give us this day our assembly-riot,
and forgive us our debts as we forgive your
          Son for having been born in Bethlehem.
Lead us not into inspection,
but deliver us from the Republic;
for ours is the power and the big mouth and
          the tiny brain,
now and forever.

Amen.[92]

Socialists rejoiced when the Supreme Court in Leipzig in July, 1930, found the three most intemperate prayers unconstitutional for implying that Jews were traitors and deceivers of the people.[93]

German Socialists responded to anti-Semitic incidents with unambiguous condemnation in the last years of the Weimar Republic. The bulk of this agitation was verbal, but Socialists also made use of police powers that were at their command to combat anti-Jewish violence. Anxiety about Judeophobia's contributions to the spread of anti-Socialist and antirepublican sentiments was uppermost in Socialist minds. Party denunciations of anti-Jewish outrages, however, almost invariably stressed the desirability of maintaining equal rights for Jews and made no reference to larger political considerations.

[92] "Thueringer Schulgebet," *Der wahre Jacob*, LI (August 30, 1930), 7.
[93] *Fraenkische Tagespost*, July 12, 1930. For the text of the decision see Kuehnert, "Thueringen," *Sozialistische Monatshefte*, XXXVI (1930), 801.

Chapter VII

Socialist Agitation against Anti-Semitism 1929-1933

In defending Jews from the attacks of their detractors, German Socialists acted in response to specific charges or incidents that potentially or actually abrogated the equality of rights guaranteed to all citizens in the Weimar Constitution. They also showed themselves eager to take the offensive against anti-Semitism by attacking it without waiting for such catalysts. The primary target was, naturally enough, the NSDAP, whose Judeophobia they attacked most often with a mixture of contempt, disgust, and moral indignation. Nevertheless, no political party that encouraged Jew-baiting or that harbored anti-Semites was excluded from Socialist condemnation.

German Socialists joined in formal, direct appeals to the German people to shun anti-Semitism. A May, 1930, declaration signed by Erhard Auer and thirty-two other prominent Bavarians asked Germans to eschew Judeophobia as "unworthy of a civilized people of the rank of the Germans" for religious, patriotic, and humanitarian reasons.[1] At that time, too, another Bavarian Social Democrat, Wilhelm Hoegner, was among those who issued public statements against anti-Semitism. He noted that the Jewish people long had been "prominently represented" in an "invisible community of noble spirits whose deeds are for the common good of humanity. . . . Anti-Semitism,

[1] "Mahnwort," *Abwehr-Blaetter*, CL (May, 1930), 1.

which on principle denies to the entire Jewish people all decent, human characteristics and attributes to it everything evil, is therefore deplorable madness. It leads to crimes against humane ideals whenever, as today in Germany, it is pursued as a political trade." [2] Shortly before the Reichstag elections of September, 1930, Artur Crispien and Carl Severing joined twenty-four prominent non-Jewish, non-Socialist moderates in signing a plea "To the German People" sponsored by the League for Human Rights. It branded anti-Semitism "a cultural disgrace of the first order," asserted that attempts to hold the Jews responsible for the depression "must be utterly rejected by every decent human being," and urged "the entire German nation to turn away from uncivilized anti-Semitic agitation." [3]

On the fortieth anniversary of the *Verein zur Abwehr des Antisemitismus* in 1931, the prominent Germans who sent messages of greeting included Social Democratic leaders Paul Loebe, Hermann Mueller, Philipp Scheidemann, and Wilhelm Sollmann. Loebe extolled the opponents of Judeophobia as "the noblest and finest minds in the German nation" but lamented that "a considerable element of confused people" remained unmoved by their efforts. Mueller urged the *Verein* not to lose heart over the proliferation of Nazi anti-Semitism, which he promised would disappear when the economic despair that gave it impetus died away. "History teaches that those who purvey reactionary ideas . . . cannot in the long run arrest the progress of mankind." Scheidemann depicted the struggle against Nazi Judeophobia as a continuation of the SPD's traditional opposition to racism, in which he considered himself a pioneer: "It must be hammered into the heads of the deluded masses that every anti-Semitism, regardless of the name or form it takes, is detestable and unworthy of a civilized nation.

---

2 "Bayerische Stimmen gegen den Judenhass," *ibid.*, 2. At that time Hoegner was a Reichstag deputy.
3 "Aufruf," *ibid.*, CL (October, 1930), 125.

Anti-Semitism is not only the 'Socialism of the fool,' . . . it is also not only a brake to all cultural progress, it is an outrage and a disgrace." Sollmann agreed that to fight against anti-Semitism was "not only a political duty but also a human and moral duty." [4]

These general appeals were supplemented by reminders to German Christians that anti-Semitism was incompatible with the moral and doctrinal tenets of their faith. In 1930 the *Leipziger Volkszeitung* rained contempt on Nazis who wanted to "reform heaven" by eliminating the "Jewish-tainted" Old Testament.[5] A 1932 *voelkisch* proposal that August Winnig fashion a synthesis of Christianity and anti-Semitic National Socialism was reported in *Vorwaerts* under the headline "Christianity as Words Alone." Shortly after some of the participants in a symposium of Evangelical theologians at the University of Goettingen expressed enthusiasm for National Socialism, an astounded and angry *Vorwaerts* reasoned that nazism was, in the last analysis, an anti-Christian movement that replaced Christ with Wotan and Christian love with anti-Jewish dogmas "conceived of entirely in the sense of a crudely mechanistic science." Emil Fuchs agreed: "What is Christianity if one no longer recognizes the essence of humanity in foreigners, in Jews, in the feeble, and in other groups of our own people who have been cast into misery by the mighty ones?" In yet another article addressed to Christians, *Vorwaerts* recalled that, while Nazi racism negated the ideal of brotherly love, the apostle Paul had admonished Christians that there were neither Jews nor Greeks, servants nor free men, but brothers alone.[6]

Johannes Albert applauded the 1931 New Year's message of

---

[4] *Abwehr-Blaetter*, CLI (March, 1931), 37–48.
[5] *Leipziger Volkszeitung*, August 13, 1930.
[6] *Vorwaerts*, March 24, May 13 and 15, December 27, 1932. Fuchs, a non-Jew, was a Socialist Protestant theologian.

Cardinal Bertram, chairman of the Bishops' Conference in Fulda, which underscored the incompatibility of Nazi anti-Semitism with Roman Catholicism.[7] Theodor Siegfried welcomed a similar declaration by the General Curate of the Catholic Bishopric of Mainz, who had given his statement substance by excluding members of the NSDAP from the sacraments.[8] However, at least one Leipzig Socialist, one Bergholz, dissented from the majority opinion, holding confessional schools responsible for the acceptance of anti-Semitism: "In its propaganda German Fascism makes use of anti-Semitism, that utterly crack-brained movement that holds men responsible for their ancestry. Psychologically this anti-Semitism is possible only through our 'Christian' religious education, which sets growing young people against the Jews." [9]

Each year the Socialists saved some of their sharpest barbs for the Christmas season. Answering an attack by the press service of the Evangelical Church on Jewish shops that displayed Christmas trees on the Christian holiday, *Der Abend* wondered how it could have been made in the name of the Prince of Peace and Love at a time when the church remained silent about the sale of such symbols of murder as toy pistols and rockets as gifts for children.[10] In 1930 an SPD cartoon pictured "A New Christmas Manger Scene for the German People" into which a Nazi intruded to shout "Out with the Jews!" [11] When a judge in Osnabrueck freed the Nazi sponsors of a Christmas boycott against Jewish stores because he found it reasonable to deprive Jews of profits from a Christian holiday, *Der Abend* felt that true Christians must have found the judgment "downright em-

[7] Albert, "Politischer Katholizismus und Nationalsozialismus," *Sozialistische Bildung* (January, 1931), 7–8.

[8] Siegfried, "Religionswissenschaft," *Sozialistische Monatshefte*, XXXVII (1931), 183.

[9] *Leipziger Volkszeitung*, October 29, 1930.

[10] *Der Abend*, December 23, 1929. See also *Vorwaerts*, December 25, 1929.

[11] *Der wahre Jacob*, LI (December 20, 1930), 16.

barrassing," asking: "What do you suppose Jesus himself would have said about that?" [12]

Yet another way that German Socialists condemned anti-Semitism in the present was to point out its pernicious effects of the past. In 1929 *Vorwaerts* retold a story, *Eine Stunde ein Jude* ("A Jew for an Hour") by the nineteenth-century realist Berthold Auerbach, about the poet Peter Hebel, who was mistaken for a Jew while visiting a strange town and was subjected to such dreadful abuse that he became a friend of the Jews out of compassion for their fate. The Socialist organ, pleading for empathy that would wipe away racial hatred, agreed that all who could experience how it felt to be persecuted as were the Jews would be quick to put away their prejudices.[13] The Dreyfus Affair was not forgotten, and Jean Jaurès, the French Socialist who had led his comrades in cooperating with bourgeois Dreyfusards to combat the unjust conviction of the Jewish captain, was represented as a hero.[14] Hermann Wendel identified the nineteenth-century Socialist Eugen Duehring as one of the men who had laid the foundations for nazism by propagandizing for a combination of authoritarian socialism and anti-Semitism.[15] On the fiftieth anniversary of the death of Richard Wagner, another Socialist drew attention to the composer's anti-Semitic attack on his patrons and promoters, Meyerbeer and Heine, in his "shabby pamphlet" *Das Judentum in der Musik (Jewry in Music)*.[16]

That anti-Semitism was basically a medieval phenomenon, completely incongruous in a scientific world, was another theme of SPD agitation against Judeophobia. In 1929 *Vor-*

---

[12] *Der Abend*, April 25, 1929.

[13] *Vorwaerts*, February 28, 1929.

[14] Max Hochdorf, "Die Affaere Dreyfus," *ibid.*, January 4, 1930, p. 5; *ibid.*, February 6, 1930; Felix Stotzinger, review of Bruno Weil, *Der Prozess des Hauptmann Dreyfus*, in *ibid.*, August 9, 1930, p. 5.

[15] *Vorwaerts*, January 12, 1933.

[16] H. H., "Der Richard-Wagner Kultus," *Sozialistische Bildung* (February, 1933), 31.

waerts marked the three-hundredth anniversary of the discovery of the compound microscope by recalling that the Jews were frequently persecuted as poisoners of water supplies before the device was used to prove otherwise. It reproduced a 1493 document signed by Frederick the Strong, Margrave of Meissen, which attributed the cause of a plague to the Jews and commanded that they be burned en masse. The *Fraenkische Tagespost* ran a long, illustrated article about the history of the Jews of Nuremberg, which it pictured as one of intermittent persecution, especially in the fifteenth century and before.[17] Max Bernhardi told the story of the Court Jew for Joachim II, Elector of Brandenburg. Lippold, the Jew, was broken on the wheel after being unjustly accused of poisoning the Elector.[18] Announced Nazi proposals for a compulsory two-year "work service" for all young Germans except Jews, who were to pay a special tax instead, seemed appropriately medieval to *Vorwaerts*, which recalled the special Jew-tax that had been collected in feudal Germany.[19] When the Socialists commemorated the tenth anniversary of the assassination of Walther Rathenau, they pointed out that Nazi-style Judeophobia had inspired the murderers: "A medieval belief in superstition, transplanted into the political struggles of the twentieth century, was the only motivating force for the murderer—the fairy tale of the 'Elders of Zion,' who brought about the World War, caused Germany's downfall, and founded Bolshevism for the purpose of destroying the Germanic race." [20]

Social Democrats often treated anti-Semites with contempt and loathing. Typical was Helmuth von Gerlach's comment on the eightieth birthday of Eduard Bernstein in 1930 when he praised "the Marxist Jew Bernstein" as "one of the most Ger-

---

[17] *Vorwaerts*, February 24, 1929; *Fraenkische Tagespost*, September 17, 1930.
[18] *Vorwaerts*, December 21, 1930. For a similar story, see A. K., "Nur ein Jude," *Leipziger Volkszeitung*, February 10, 1930, p. 5.
[19] *Vorwaerts*, July 1, 1932; see also *Der Abend*, October 27, 1930.
[20] *Vorwaerts*, June 24, 1932.

man of all Germans" and deplored "the damage done to Germany's reputation by the backward anti-Semitic movement." [21] When a tribe of American Indians made Albert Einstein an "honorary chief," a Socialist cartoon contrasted this action with a mob of Nazis shouting "Jew-pig!" at the scientist.[22] A nauseated *Fraenkische Tagespost* told of a man in Altenfeld who besmirched the memory of Walter Rathenau by speaking of him as "this man with the synagogue nose and the flat feet." A Nazi charge that Jews entered into "unnatural" sexual relationships prompted an anonymous Socialist to inquire if the Nazi leader Ernst Roehm (known to be a homosexual) were Jewish.[23] Another unnamed Social Democrat accused the *voelkisch* Queen Louise League of distributing common pornography under the guise of exposing the heinousness of Jewish race-mixing.[24]

Socialists showed their contempt for anti-Semitism by hurling insults at it. A Nazi story of Jewish ritual-murder they dismissed as a "horror fairy tale." The *Hamburger Echo* scorned as cowards members of the *Stahlhelm* who would not confess to having destroyed a fashion exhibition created by a Jewish designer, which was staged on the Baltic island of Fehmarn.[25] Nazi economist Gottfried Feder's discovery that Jewish symbols had been planted on German coins and coats of arms was sarcastically discarded as "profound swastika-wisdom . . . ; so

---

[21] *Fraenkische Tagespost*, January 8, 1930. Gerlach, a pacifist and a non-Jew, stood close to the SPD but was not a Party member.

[22] *Der wahre Jacob*, LII (April 25, 1931), 5; see also *Der Abend*, July 23, 1930; *Hamburger Echo*, October 28, 1930.

[23] *Fraenkische Tagespost*, September 14, 1931; "Ist Roehm Jude?" *Das freie Wort*, IV (October 23, 1932), 28. See also Robert Schirokauer, "Die Frau Hitler," *Das freie Wort*, IV (November 6, 1932), 4–9; A. Rier, "Hitlerianische Sitten," *Leipziger Volkszeitung*, March 8, 1932, p. 9.

[24] H. F., "Treudeutsche Sittenhueter," *Sozialistische Bildung* (February, 1930), 64.

[25] *Muenchener Post*, July 29, 1929, NSDAP Hauptarchiv, fol. 1559, no. 7; *Hamburger Echo*, March 5, 1930.

much twaddle at once—that is more than the police allow!" [26]
In 1932, on the centennial of Goethe's death, Carl Severing
wrote in the *Wiener Freie Presse*: "The wild songs of hate, . . .
which are prompted by the barbarism of racial and national
incitement, show us to our dismay the great disparity that lies
between the humanitarian ideals of Goethe and reality." [27]
Later *Vorwaerts* deplored an upsurge of nazism's "filthy anti-
Semitism" in Oldenburg.[28]

A prime recipient of Socialist indignation was the wildest of
the Nazi anti-Semites Julius Streicher, the editor of Nuremberg's semipornographic racist newspaper *Der Stuermer*. Its
1929 stories of the ritual-murder of a gentile child in Manau bei
Hofheim were given the lie by the Socialist newspaper in
Wuerzburg, which printed the official medical report showing
the child was the victim of a sexual pervert and concluded: "It
is a sad mark of political bankruptcy and moral degeneracy
when a deeply depressing, abominable crime is used to specu-
late on mankind's lowest instincts." [29] The *Fraenkische Tagespost* rejoiced over a two-month jail sentence given Streicher for
the untrue allegations, expressed pleasure that for once the
racist had not gotten away with "heaving every bit of rubbish
at humanity," and reprinted the full text of the decision with
the hope that it would open the eyes of the citizenry to the real
nature of *Der Stuermer*.[30]

When the death by accident or suicide of the seriously ill
Paul Levi was mocked in the racist organ as having occurred
because he "could no longer stand the smell of his own race,"
Otto Landsberg denounced Streicher's "bestial brutality" be-

---

[26] *Vorwaerts*, November 30, 1930.
[27] *Wiener Freie Presse*, March 17, 1932, Nachlass Severing, fol. A–16.
[28] *Vorwaerts*, May 29, 1932.
[29] *Fraenkische Volksfreund* (Wuerzburg), April 18, 1929, Acten des Bayerischen Staats- Ministeriums des Innern, fol. 73725, no. 2019ba9. See also
Muenchener Post, September 6, 1929.
[30] *Fraenkische Tagespost*, November 5, 1929, NSDAP Hauptarchiv, fol. 499.

fore the Reichstag, lamenting that the dead Levi could not make Streicher pay for it in court.[31] Streicher's behavior in court during his 1930 trial for having portrayed Jewish men as seducers of gentile women was reported by the *Fraenkische Tagespost* as ranging from cowardly—successfully pinning the blame on his assistant editor—to belligerent—threatening the public prosecutor with physical harm.[32] The Socialist organ delightedly reported a Jewish professor's success in suing Streicher's paper for having accused him of sabotaging his school's subscription to the *Voelkischer Beobachter* and dealing unfairly with Nazi students.[33] Later the Socialist paper contemptuously told of Streicher's about-face when he learned that the "Jewish doctor" who had treated a non-Jewish patient "like an animal" and let her die was in fact a Christian physician with a Jewish-sounding name while the dead patient was a Jew.[34] A disgusted *Der Abend* noted that an able Jewish soccer coach had resigned as the result of a campaign against him in *Der Stuermer*. The SPD organ found it ironic that he should have found it more comfortable to return to his native Hungary under the anti-Jewish Horthy-Goemboes dictatorship than remain in Germany.[35]

While heaping contempt on anti-Semitism's immorality, German Socialists gladly ridiculed its more absurd aspects. Nazi racism made the most vulnerable target. Letting a racist speak for himself, *Vorwaerts* laughingly reprinted his newspaper advertisement for a wife of "Aryan-Germanic race, blond hair, long skull, conceived and born of parents firmly dedicated to a vegetarian life, nursed on her mother's breast." A cartoon

[31] *Der Abend*, February 10, 1930; *Verhandlungen des Reichstags*, 141st Sess., 1930, CDXXVII, 4449–50.

[32] *Fraenkische Tagespost*, May 24, 1930. See also *ibid.*, May 19, 1931; "Licht gegen Finsternis," *Schulfront*, II (1930), 119.

[33] *Fraenkische Tagespost*, November 22, 1930. For a similar case see *ibid.*, January 14 and October 16, 1931.

[34] *Ibid.*, February 25, 1931; see also *ibid.*, October 16, 1931.

[35] *Der Abend*, August 11, 1932.

in *Der wahre Jacob* showed a "racial scientist" pointing to the tip of South America and assuring Hitler that the Patagonians of the region had never known a Jew. A delighted *Hamburger Echo* told of a local worker's reply to a Nazi's anti-Semitic comment on a streetcar: "Rubbish! You Nazi upstart! What do you know? You're just running off at the mouth, and what's more, you're a Jew, too!" When he reminded the Nazi that the story of Noah and the flood proved Hitler, Goebbels. Ludendorff, and everyone else had descended from the same Jewish family, everyone within hearing distance exploded in approving laughter that set the luckless Nazi to flight. Hitler's Aryan swastika was identified as an "Indian homosexual sign" in a *Reichsbanner* publication.[36] Theodore Kunze so enjoyed the "sport" of baiting the Nazis over their racism that he urged other Socialists to join the fun, advising them to remind the Nazis of a contention that Aryans had inspired the building of the Great Wall of China.[37]

Socialist scoffing greeted the announcement in January, 1932, that a special "race council" would pass on the racial purity of any woman who intended to marry an SS man. The *Fraenkische Tagespost* gleefully printed the nine racial laws governing SS marriages, and later it ran a cartoon showing a plump Brunhilde having her skull measured and her blood tested by a team of lecherous racial scientists under an enlarged picture of the "bacillus judaensis." [38] A delighted *Muenchener Post* told of Hitler making the mistake of including anti-Semitic comments in a letter to a prominent Jewish Italian Fascist, who replied that he would not take offense because he knew the Aryan and Semitic races were descended from the same mon-

[36] *Vorwaerts*, June 13, 1929; *Der wahre Jacob*, LI (January 18, 1930), 4; *Hamburger Echo*, November 22, 1930; *Das Reichsbanner*, April 9, 1932 (cited in Rohe, *Das Reichsbanner Schwarz Rot Gold*, 407).

[37] Kunze, "Rassenwahn," *Das freie Wort*, III (August 2, 1931), 19–20.

[38] *Vorwaerts*, January 9, 1932; *Fraenkische Tagespost*, January 17, March 11, 1932.

keys.[39] The publication of an anonymous book, *Semi-Imperator Wilhelm II*, that purported to show the "Jewish ancestry" of the Hohenzollerns prompted *Der Abend* to gloat over DNVP discomfort over the revelation and to wonder if Prince August Wilhelm would be expelled from the Nazi Party as a Jew.[40] Alice Ekert-Rolholz satirized a performance of Lessing's *Nathan the Wise* in the Third Reich of the future in which the Jew Nathan was played by an unsuspecting Communist, who was subjected to an orgy of hatred by the audience before being murdered by the other actors, all "true to the highest axiom of the new national repertory: *Pogrom instead of Program!*"[41]

Drolly maintaining that the Nazis owed unacknowledged debts to the Jews, *Der Abend* traced their salute of the outstretched right arm to the Jewish greeting "shalom," accompanied by a similar gesture, which was first borrowed by the Romans, imitated by Mussolini, and finally copied by Hitler. *Vorwaerts* found that a Frankfurt am Main *Stahlhelm* local owed a more tangible debt to a synagogue in which these superpatriots took refuge from a rampaging band of Communists just as the feast of the tabernacle was about to be celebrated. A cartoon pictured the anti-Semites cowering behind a rabbi, who welcomed them benevolently: "I am truly pleased, little children, that you have come to visit me."[42] Peter Igel told the story in rhyme:

> They came from much flag-waving,
> they shouted 'loud, Hurray!

[39] *Muenchener Post*, January 25, 1932, NSDAP Hauptarchiv, fol. 1559, no. 69.

[40] *Der Abend*, November 12, 1929. See also Michel Brand, "Aus Naphtalis Stamm," *ibid.*, October 31, 1928, p. 5; *Leipziger Volkszeitung*, February 29, 1932.

[41] *Der Abend*, July 30, 1932. Emphasis in the original. For similar cases, see *ibid.*, October 31, 1928; August 25, 1932; "Rassen Praxis," *Der wahre Jacob*, LI (December 6, 1930), 3; "Wie ist das mit den Juden?" *Das freie Wort*, V (1933), 221.

[42] *Der Abend*, September 18, 1930; *Vorwaerts*, October 8, 1930.

They answered Germany's craving,
they drove the Jews away.
But then *they* needed saving
in a synagogue that day.[43]

Friedrich Wendel sardonically suggested that the Hitlerites should thank the Jews—or rather the Nazi stereotype of the Jews—for providing them with an exact prototype for their own behavior, including avarice, ethnocentrism, putschism, demagogy, and criminality.[44]

An abortive bomb attempt on Paul Josef Goebbels' life in 1931, which Goebbels attributed to his Jewish enemies, presented *Vorwaerts* with an opportunity to ridicule the little man for garnering sympathy with the public by sending himself a bomb in the names of "Rosa Rosenbaum" and "Sacha Nathan." *Der wahre Jacob* offered its readers a "Little Nazi Dictionary" with these definitions:

Race, Nordic: An object of inspiration for people of the
          Southern type.
National Socialism: Capitalism without any Jews.
Jew: A person who has wrongly attained the kind of sol-
          vency after which you strive in vain.[45]

Stories that Hitler's stepsister was employed as a cook in a Jewish student cafeteria stimulated Socialist visions of an unemployed Adolf reduced to assisting her as a "ritual-soup cook";[46] should that happen, laughed the *Hamburger Echo*, the Fuehrer could always endorse Theodor Franke's book *Erdkunde*, which portrayed the ancient Jews as Aryans and hailed

[43] *Fraenkische Tagespost*, October 12, 1930.
[44] Wendel, "Die verjudete NSDAP," 5. See also *Freie Volkswacht*, January 17, 1931.
[45] *Vorwaerts*, March 17 and 19, May 6, 1931; *Der wahre Jacob*, LII (May 9, 1931), 3.
[46] *Fraenkische Tagespost*, October 4, 1931.

Saul as a "Germanic-Gothic prince" and David as a blond-haired, blue-eyed hero.[47] Suggesting that *voelkisch* nonsense proceeded from stupidity, an amused *Der Abend* told of a certain Albert Bruehahn who swindled anti-Semites of enormous sums by promising to perfect a death ray with which they could kill all the Jews in Berlin in three minutes simply by assembling them at Tempelhof Airdrome.[48] When a practical joker persuaded *Der Angriff* to print an excerpt from *All Quiet on the Western Front* with a new title and fictitious author, an anonymous Socialist derisively noted that it was clear the Nazis had not read a line of the book they defamed so often. "Just how much 'the Jew' is guilty for that certainly escapes our knowledge." [49]

The Socialists also took their sense of humor with them into the Reichstag. When in 1929 the Nazi Count Ernst zu Reventlow demanded the public labeling of every Jewish civil servant, they interrupted his short speech eleven times with laughter and shouted witticisms; when he read a list of such Jews, they gleefully added him to the list with the cry, "The Jew Reventlow!" SPD Deputy Carl Litke of Berlin added a bit of life to an otherwise dull speech by Berlin Nazi Franz Stoehr by shouting: "Do tell us about racial degeneration!" When Stoehr rose to the bait, the Socialists roared back with jeers and catcalls.[50] Replying to an anti-Semitic tirade by Gregor Strasser, Socialist Wilhelm Hoegner twitted him for "a lack of consideration" for "former princely masters" who had become Nazis and were able to pay their party dues only because their ancestors had

[47] *Hamburger Echo*, October 25, 1931.

[48] *Der Abend*, July 3, 1929.

[49] A. S., "Die boshaften Juden and die armen Nazis," *Sozialistische Bildung* (May, 1931), 159–60. For a similar case, see *Der Abend*, April 23, 1931.

[50] *Verhandlungen des Reichstags*, 96th Sess., 1929, CDXXV, 2979; 143rd Sess., 1930, CDXXVII, 4504. See also *ibid.*, 178th Sess., 1930, CDXXVIII, 5600–601. Litke was non-Jewish. This was also a favorite sport of the Socialists in the Bavarian Parliament. See, for example, *Verhandlungen des Bayerischen Landtags*, 18th Sess., 1929, I, 491; 46th Sess., 1929, II, 307.

borrowed money from the ancestors of German Jews in order to save their mortgaged castles, lands, and crowns.[51]

While recognizing ridicule as an effective weapon against irrational anti-Semitism, the Social Democrats were more often in dead earnest over it. In Leipzig they went so far as to recommend boycotts as a direct means of combating Judeophobia. In 1932 the *Leipziger Volkszeitung* told of the reading matter one could find in the waiting room of a local dentist: "The reader is astounded. He believes he has sought out, in the interest of his health, an intelligent man and finds—shameless absurdities of National Socialist anti-Semitism." It gave the dentist's name and address and urged its readers to keep them in mind should they need dental care. Later the Leipzig paper proposed a boycott of a local cafe that catered to a right-wing crowd, members of which had attacked and seriously wounded a Jewish customer whom they could not force to pay their bill. On the other side of the coin, when Leipzig's Hitler Youth distributed a list of Jewish shops with a call to boycott, the SPD organ reprinted the list and intimated that patronage of the shops would help frustrate the Nazis' "unclean fusion of politics and business." [52]

By reproving Judeophobia in other lands, the Socialists indirectly attacked the same phenomenon in Germany. Their frequent attention to anti-Jewish incidents in Poland, Lithuania, and Rumania attempted to connect them with the undeniably backward status of these countries and to play on widespread German contempt for the Slavs.[53] After a near pogrom in the Polish city of Lemberg, *Der Abend* contemptuously dubbed it a "Hitler Paradise." A cartoon accompanied the newspaper's report that Prince Starhemberg, leader and prin-

---

[51] *Verhandlungen des Reichstags*, 6th Sess., 1930, CDXLIV, 135.

[52] *Leipziger Volkszeitung*, October 13, 1932; December 7, 1932; September 9, 1932.

[53] See especially *Vorwaerts*, June 13, 1929; July 22, 1930; November 15, 1931; May 25, 1932; *Der Abend*, June 25, 1929.

cipal financier of Austria's Fascist and anti-Semitic *Heimwehr*, had filed for receivership. The old aristocrat worried, "Child, child, what are we to do if Kohn does not extend our credit?" His son answered: "Hmm, very simple! A small putsch accompanied by a pogrom, just as our ancestors did when they found themselves too deep in the red to Jews." [54]

Although the Nazis were the most frequent targets of SPD agitation against anti-Semitism, others, including the Communists, were not neglected. In 1929 *Vorwaerts* called attention to clearly anti-Jewish remarks made in a letter from Josef Eisenberger, a member of the pro-Moscow faction of the KPD, to Rosa Aschenbrenner, a former leader of that party's right wing. [55] A year later the KPD revived its policy of National Bolshevism and again included anti-Semitism among its appeals to nationalistic radicals. [56] That May, *Vorwaerts* indignantly reported that Communist delegates on Berlin's City Council had joined Nazis in shouting "Out with the Jews!" to prevent members of the moderate parties from being heard. [57] When a few months later *Die rote Fahne* printed a snide denunciation of "Jewish stock-market jobbers," the Socialist central organ accused it of competing with Hitler in anti-Jewish fervor, recalling Ruth Fischer's 1923 outburst against Jewish capitalists. [58] The Communists and Socialists also fought over the status of the Jews in Russia, the former sketching an idyllic view of happy Jewish workers and peasants freed from persecution, [59] the latter repeatedly contending that the lot of Russian Jews remained at least as bad as it had been under the Tsars and suggesting that communism in general failed to guarantee Jews equal rights. [60]

[54] *Der Abend*, November 29, 1932; *Vorwaerts*, March 31, 1932.

[55] *Vorwaerts*, August 24, 1929.

[56] Klemperer, *Germany's New Conservatism*, 146–50.

[57] *Vorwaerts*, May 16, 1930.

[58] *Die rote Fahne*, August 27, 1930; *Der Abend*, August 28, 1930.

[59] See, for example, *Die rote Fahne*, March 5, 1929.

[60] *Vorwaerts*, January 3, August 26, 1928; March 29, 1929; April 3, 1930;

Among non-Nazi anti-Semites on the political right, the DNVP, which had taken the brunt of Socialist criticism before 1929, later earned little attention in that context. Typical was *Der Abend*'s reaction when a DNVP member was unjustly assailed as a Jew; the Socialist organ saw it as poetic justice because the man had helped to spread anti-Semitism and therefore shared in "the guilt for such moral degeneration." [61] The DDP's sharp turn to the right in 1930, when it combined with Artur Mahraun's anti-Jewish *Jungdeutscher Orden* to form the State Party, marked its absorption of "demagogic anti-Semitism" for the Socialists. They remarked that only masochistic Jews could remain true to a party that had come to regard them as second-class citizens.[62] According to the *Leipziger Volkszeitung*, Georg Bernhard, editor of the *Vossische Zeitung*, was excluded from the State Party's list of candidates for the 1930 Reichstag election because he was "a Jew, . . . a real democrat, and . . . a decisive opponent of every National Socialist policy and all National Socialist obscurantism." [63] Two years later at least one Socialist reacted sensitively to a certain Father Muckermann's charges that Jews threatened to break down Germany's spiritual, moral, and physical existence, asking if it was the cleric's purpose "to build a 'spiritual' foundation for an eventual coalition between the Center Party and National Socialism." [64]

Socialist electioneering against anti-Semitism was directed only at the far-right parties. By 1930 the SPD had come to realize that the NSDAP alone threatened to conquer the republic with propaganda that included anti-Jewish appeals. In

---

Otto Maenchen-Helfen, review of Otto Heller, *Der Untergang des Judentums*, in *Die Gesellschaft*, IX (1932), 461–62; Friedrich Weigelt, review of Otto Heller, *Der Untergang des Judentums*, in *Sozialistische Monatshefte*, XXXVIII (1932), 1041.
[61] *Der Abend*, February 26, 1930.
[62] *Vorwaerts*, August 6, 1930.
[63] *Leipziger Volkszeitung*, August 18, 1930.
[64] H. F., "Ein Vorkaempfer der Nazis im Zentrum," *Sozialistische Bildung* (July, 1932), 159.

the Reichstag elections of that year the readers of the *Fraen-kische Tagespost* were reminded that the Nazis loved to "incite the most wretched and contemptible race-hatred." Leipzig Socialists fought part of a local election campaign by pointing out the inanity of dividing capitalists into ethical Aryans and unethical Jews, reminding readers that the Nazi racial ideals of blond hair and blue eyes were not uncommon among Jews and Slavs, and exploiting a Nazi's affair with a Jewess. In a local election campaign in Hamburg, the *Hamburger Echo* drew unfavorable attention to a case in Schleswig-Holstein; there the Nazis had attempted to derail a trial in which several of their number were defendants by intimating that the prosecuting attorneys were Jews.[65]

In both presidential elections in 1932, the SPD supported the reelection of Hindenburg to prevent the victory from falling to Hitler. Or, as Carl Severing put it: "We will vote for Hindenburg because we want to strike at the barbarism of racial hatred and the system of lies and slander." [66] The *Fraenkische Tagespost* exposed Nuremberg's bourgeois *Fraenkische Kurier* as the printer of pro-Hitler, anti-Semitic campaign leaflets. Reproducing some of the attacks made on Jews, it blasted the *Kurier* for placing itself at the disposal of the party of "pimps, murderers, sex-offenders, and desecraters of Jewish graves" and urged Jewish citizens to disassociate themselves from the publication and its causes.[67] The Socialist paper also warned that the Nazis' "bestial theory of racial breeding" could lead to mass infanticide of racial undesirables if Hitler were given his way.[68] When the Nazis in Bavaria distributed a pamphlet that designated the KPD and its candidate Ernst Thaelmann as agents of the Jews, the SPD local in the Munich suburb of Groebenzell

[65] *Fraenkische Tagespost*, September 10, 1930; *Leipziger Volkszeitung*, June 5, 7, and 14, 1930; *Hamburger Echo*, October 11, 1930.
[66] Severing, *Mein Lebensweg* (Cologne, 1950), II, 327.
[67] *Fraenkische Tagespost*, March 10, 1932.
[68] *Ibid.*, April 8, 1932.

denounced it in a leaflet of its own as an affront "of the shabbiest sort." Reprinting and correcting parts of the Hitlerite attack, it did its best to demonstrate that only "political stupidity and historical ignorance" could have found a significant connection between Communists and Jews.[69] During the campaigns for elections to the provincial parliaments in April, 1932, the Social Democrats again attempted to debunk Nazi claims about Germany's "Jewish government" with facts and figures about the small numbers of Jews among provincial governors, district magistrates, high-ranking civil-servants, and educators.[70] Socialist propaganda in the November, 1932, Reichstag election carried an appeal to women voters by Henni Lehmann: "Mary was a Jewish mother. Must her motherly sorrow . . . be made to appear inferior according to the National Socialist racial standpoint?" [71]

Not content with responding to anti-Jewish incidents, German Socialists agitated against anti-Semitism without waiting for Judeophobes to act. They used a wide variety of techniques —ranging from ridicule to contempt—against the NSDAP and other parties that employed Jew-baiting. Such propaganda left the unmistakable impression that decent Germans must regard anti-Semitism as barbaric, inhuman, and unpatriotic.

[69] NSDAP Hauptarchiv, fol. 798.
[70] *Fraenkische Tagespost*, April 19, 1932; *Hamburger Echo*, April 20, 1932.
[71] NSDAP Hauptarchiv, fol. 799, no. 4.

Chapter VIII

The SPD and the Jews
1929-1933

German Socialists regarded the Jews with no less cordiality after 1929 than before, but they were considerably less overt about it. Fearing the consequences for both groups if Nazi propaganda about Socialist-Jewish collusion were made to seem plausible, the Social Democrats frequently avoided open associations with non-Marxist Jews. They doubted that such neglect would harm the Jewish cause, for most of them remained certain that they themselves as Socialists were the real targets of anti-Semitic agitation. While underestimating the long-term dangers to Jews from Nazi Judeophobia, Socialists kept their ranks relatively free from anti-Jewish prejudice throughout the years of Hitler's rise to power.

German Social Democrats often expressed positive opinions of Jews as a nonpolitical entity and of Jewish Socialists. When a Nazi *Sturmfuehrer* was injured during an anti-Semitic brawl and given emergency treatment at a Jewish hospital, Socialist Hellmuth Falkenfeld doubted that the racist had reasoned away his hatred. Nevertheless, Falkenfeld sardonically thought that the Nazi might well have concluded that his was a hopeless cause "because this infamous people always understands how to win the confidence of its host and because this race has the unprecedented shrewdness always to wash wounds—even those

184

of its enemies, rather than inflict them." [1] Other Socialists esteemed what they called "the independent religious value of Judaism and . . . its creative meaning for modern intellectual life." [2] In 1933 Socialist theologian Paul Tillich maintained that the Hebrew religion had provided Christianity with an account of the Creation that was both general and symbolic; by eliminating polytheism and animism it had rendered Christianity, rightly understood, "the inevitable and eternal enemy of political romanticism," while anti-Semitism, which he deplored, was "essentially established with the latter." Giving practical expression to Socialist respect for Judaism, *Der Abend* in 1929 voiced displeasure that the trial of a man accused of burglarizing the home of a rabbi was held on a Saturday, when the cleric could not attend.[3]

The Socialist press encouraged amicable relations with the Jewish community by announcing dozens of meetings of Jewish organizations and reporting developments among the Jews. Sports, veterans, and charitable group meetings were most numerous among the former. For example, when Hamburg Jews established their own sports association because other such groups excluded them, the local SPD organ published invitations for new members and informed its readers about the growth of the organization. Also typical was the Hamburg paper's comment that the unity against anti-Semitism expressed at a joint meeting of Jewish and non-Jewish war veterans proved "that at this time, when crude racial hatred and a stifling Nazi spirit seem to be trump, intellectual arguments are still possible." [4] Naturally, the SPD press gave special attention to

[1] *Hamburger Echo*, September 14, 1930.

[2] Herbert Kuehnert, review of Richard Coudenhove-Kalergi, *Held oder Heiliger*, in *Sozialistische Monatshefte*, XXXVI (1930), 72.

[3] Tillich, *Die sozialistische Entscheidung* (Rev. ed.; Offenbach, 1948), 30–31. (This book was originally published in 1933, but it was confiscated after only a few copies had been sold.) *Der Abend*, March 5, 1929.

[4] *Hamburger Echo*, November 11, 1931; October 21, 1932; September 30, 1932; July 13, 1932.

activities of the Poale Zion Party, a small group of Jewish Zionist Socialists.[5] But the press devoted even more attention to a wide variety of subjects from non-Socialist Jewish sources: a display of plans for a new synagogue, the death of a local rabbi, a performance of Jewish folk songs, a Jewish cabaret, activities at Jewish secondary schools, a new Jewish polyclinic for the poor of all religions, and readings of Jewish poetry.[6]

Ostjuden in Germany continued to receive sympathetic treatment at Socialist hands. As the Nazis railed at the newcomers for their strange customs and for aggravating the unemployment problem, SPD spokesmen retold the story of Jewish deportation and suffering during and after the war.[7] In 1930 Rudolf Breitscheid told a meeting of the *Hilfsverein der deutschen Juden* that the detractors of *Ostjuden* had forgotten "under what unspeakable misery, under what endless torment, under what hardship, under what persecution, under what injustice these Eastern European Jews have had to live for generations . . . and in part are forced to live even today." [8] An insulting portrayal of *Ostjuden* in one of Frank Allen's highly popular detective novels drew fire from Paul Mochmann in 1931.[9] The value of Yiddish, the High German dialect used by most of the newcomers, and the desirability of preserving its literature and

[5] See, for example, *Vorwaerts*, November 30, 1930; *Leipziger Volkszeitung*, January 18, 1932.

[6] See, for example, *Hamburger Echo*, January 28, July 10, 1930; January 21, 1932; *Vorwaerts*, December 3, 1929; *Der Abend*, November 12, 1929; *Leipziger Volkszeitung*, May 19, 1930; *Fraenkische Tagespost*, March 23, 1931; March 8, 1932.

[7] Georg Engelbert Graf, review of Ilya Ehrenburg, *Das bewegte Leben des Lasik Roitschwantz*, in *Jungsozialistische Blaetter*, VIII (1929), 160; Willibald Kater, "August 1914! Juden fluechten!" *Leipziger Volkszeitung*, August 1, 1931, p. 18; Erich Kunter, "Pogrom," *Vorwaerts*, October 22, 1931, p. 10.

[8] *Kundgebung fuer das Werk des Hilfsvereins der deutschen Juden* (Berlin, 1930), 6. See also Nathan Gurdus, "Judenstaedtchen Z.," *Vorwaerts*, July 15, 1930, p. 9.

[9] *Der Abend*, August 12, 1931.

promoting its theater were advanced by Socialist publications.[10] Socialists lavished approval on the work of the *Hilfsverein der deutschen Juden*, especially insofar as it aided Jewish refugees to cope with a multitude of problems during their stay in Germany. Rudolf Breitscheid named its work "the noblest form of humanitarianism" because it helped create "the prerequisites that are necessary so that in the future these *Ostjuden* can be regarded as valuable individuals even by those who neither think nor reflect." [11]

Many Social Democrats continued to regard Zionism as the best solution to the problems of *Ostjuden* in and outside of Germany. Leading Socialists who stood closest to Zionism were Fritz Naphtali, Oscar Cohn, and Eduard Bernstein, the last of whom was joined by Rudolf Breitscheid and Paul Loebe on the Socialist Committee for Working Class Palestine, which was founded by the Second International at its Brussels Congress in 1929.[12] Bernstein argued that Zionism presented the only practical means of guaranteeing the "inalienable human rights" of Eastern European Jews and maintained that Arab resistance to Jewish settlement in Palestine was the work of a minority of religious fanatics who could be pacified before long. There was "no better book for an appreciation of the Jewish situation," wrote Franz Hering of a pro-Zionist volume that contrasted the indigence and misery of Jews in Eastern Europe with the success and optimism of those who were building a new home in Palestine.[13] Approving interest in the development of a strong

10 *Leipziger Volkszeitung*, January 6, 1930; *Vorwaerts*, November 11, 1930; February 11, 1931.

11 *Vorwaerts*, March 9, 1928; April 20, 1930; *Der Abend*, December 9, 1930; *Kundgebung fuer das Werk*, 7.

12 Franz Hering, review of Albert Londres, *Jude wohin?* in *Sozialistische Monatshefte*, XXXVIII (1932), 463; Naphtali, "Das arbeitende Palaestina," *Sozialistische Monatshefte*, XXXV (1929), 115–19; *Vorwaerts*, May 9, 1929; Silberner, *Sozialisten zur Judenfrage*, 284–85.

13 *Vorwaerts*, December 8, 1929; Hering, review of *Jude wohin?* 463.

socialist movement in the new Jewish homeland was general through much of the SPD press.[14]

Other Socialists were less optimistic about Zionism's chances for success. Aging theoretician Karl Kautsky was still its most outspoken Socialist detractor. Correctly gauging the nationalistic reaction of the Arabs to an influx of Jews—a factor that pro-Zionist Jews grossly underestimated—he reasoned that the settlers could remain only with the protection of British bayonets and would be slaughtered when Arab nationalism prevailed.[15] *Vorwaerts* cautiously agreed that substantial Jewish immigration to Palestine would spell disaster but expressed the hope that Jews then in the Holy Land would stop treating Arabs as "inferiors" and establish the groundwork for peaceful cooperation with them.[16]

While debating about how best to solve the problems of the *Ostjuden*, German Socialists consistently showed respect for their own Jewish leaders. A particularly beloved Social Democrat was Eduard Bernstein. When he died in 1932, he was eulogized by Wilhelm Sollmann in a tribute that was reprinted in much of the SPD press: "By race Bernstein was a Jew. He was probably not a synagogue-goer. But this much I know—I have met few men who acted as much like a Christian as he." [17] A lesser, unnamed Jewish leader was treated as a hero for returning to a Nazi meeting from which he had been excluded pre-

[14] See especially Rudolf de Haas, "Das moderne Palaestina," *Der Abend*, April 13, 1929, p. 5; M. Y. Ben-Gavriel, "Bilder aus Palaestina," *ibid.*, March 23, 1931, p. 5; *Hamburger Echo*, October 5 and November 13, 1930; V. K., "Die Arbeiterbewegung in Palaestina," *Gewerkschafts-Zeitung*, XXXVIII (1928), 380–81; Julius Kaliski, "Die Zukunft der juedischen Palaestinaarbeit," *Sozialistische Monatshefte*, XXXVI (1930), 990–95; Theodor Kappstein, "Rund um den Zionismus: Eindruecke auf einer Palaestinafahrt," *Sozialistische Monatshefte*, XXXVII (1931), 759–69.

[15] *Vorwaerts*, October 4 and 6, December 15, 1929. See also, for example, Julius Kaliski, "Palaestina und der Sozialismus," *Sozialistische Monatshefte*, XXXV (1929), 783–90; Markus Joffe, "Juden und Araber," *Sozialistische Monatshefte*, XXXVII (1931), 577.

[16] *Vorwaerts*, August 18, 1928; August 28, 1929; April 13, 1930.

[17] Nachlass Sollmann, fol. 11, no. 5.

viously, answering the main speaker with a half-hour rebuttal, and finally inducing most of the audience to forsake the hall with him.[18] Not a single Jewish Socialist to whom the present writer has spoken or written knows of or experienced any form of discrimination against Jews in the Party during the period 1929–33. Even in the last dark days of the republic, when some Socialists attempted to compromise with the Nazis in hopes of avoiding legal suppression, Jews were not asked to move into the background, although the possibility of their doing so for tactical reasons was discussed. Before the tense national and provincial elections of March 5, 1933, when most of the SPD press had been banned, Wilhelm Keil and his colleagues in Stuttgart discussed barring a Jewish comrade, Berthold Heymann, from running for reelection to the Wuerttemberg parliament. They wanted to do so to minimize the effectiveness of anti-Semitic propaganda against the Party, but in the end they decided against it. In Keil's opinion those who voted to exclude Heymann were old Party opponents with personal or ideological grudges. Keil has also told of a Party comrade, identified only as a Stuttgart attorney, who wrote him at that time that Jews should be encouraged to disassociate themselves from the Party for the duration of the emergency, while adding: "It obviously will not do for our Party to slip into the anti-Semitic channel." [19] The candidacy of Ernst Hamburger, SPD deputy in the Prussian Parliament from the highly anti-Jewish province of Silesia, was renewed by the provincial Party organization in March, 1933, without a dissenting vote. In February and March of that year, officials of the Silesian Party locals asked Hamburger to address meetings throughout the province, although the Nazis prohibited him from speaking more than twice.[20]

18 *Der Abend*, September 10, 1930.
19 Keil, *Erlebnisse eines Sozialdemokraten* (Stuttgart, 1947), II, 497, 613. Keil, a non-Jew, was a leading figure in the Wuerttemberg SPD.
20 Hamburger, personal letters, February 8, May 18, 1967.

Although maintaining openly cordial relations with non-political and pro-Socialist Jews throughout the last years of the Weimar Republic, German Social Democrats tended to shrink from public association with Jewish self-defense organizations and with Jewish voters, especially after 1930. These were tactical retreats, made to avoid giving apparent substance to the Nazi story that Socialists were "Jewish shock troops." The SPD worked more closely with the Jewish *Centralverein* after 1929 than it had earlier, but did so in greatest secrecy. The CV, recognizing the SPD as one of its firmest bulwarks against the rising tide of nazism, contributed "considerable amounts" to the Party.[21] Exact information is extremely hard to come by, but a few examples have been verified. In 1928 or 1929, the CV in Saxony financed the printing of SPD election posters.[22] Two CV publications, *Anti-Anti*, which refuted anti-Jewish propaganda, and *Anti-Nazi: Redner- und Presse-Material ueber die NSDAP* (*Anti-Nazi: Speaker and Press Material Concerning the NSDAP*), were made available free of charge to the Party, the trade unions, and the *Reichsbanner*.[23] Such material was regularly reprinted in Socialist publications, especially the *Sozialdemokratische Parteikorrespondenz*. The *Buero Wilhelmstrasse*, which was the CV's propaganda agency, actively supported Serge Chakotin's attempts to employ highly emotional propaganda methods in the SPD's 1932 election campaigns, supplying the Party with pamphlets and brochures.[24] One of the most valuable members of the "Abegg Committee," a brain trust of republican politicians who advised the CV on how best to deal with the Nazi threat, was Helmuth Klotz. His experience in the Nazi Party before becoming a Socialist

[21] Rudolf Callmann, personal letter, February 14, 1967.
[22] Alfred Hirschberg, personal letter, March 16, 1967.
[23] Hans Reichmann, "Der drohende Sturm," in Tramer, *In zwei Welten*, 566–68.
[24] Paucker, "Der juedische Abwehrkampf," 431, 470–71; Chakotin, *The Rape of the Masses*, 192–233.

in 1924 was put to use in the fight against Judeophobia.[25] In the summer of 1930 the CV secretly supported a series of anti-Nazi rallies at which Carlo Mierendorff was the featured speaker.[26] This cooperation between the SPD and the CV extended to local organizations, where individuals who were members of both bodies acted as intermediaries. In Bocholt, for example, Jeanette Wolff held membership in the directing committees of both the Party and the *Verein* and regularly provided the former with information from the latter about the status of the Jews.[27] The CV and the *Reichsbanner* also cooperated closely. On at least one occasion, in Kaiserslautern, the Jewish organization financed new uniforms for the *Reichsbanner*.[28] CV leader Alfred Hirschberg was the author of two anonymous anti-Nazi pamphlets published under the signature of the *Reichsbanner*, with introductions by Otto Hoersing.[29]

While the CV and SPD cooperated closely behind the scenes, they displayed only moderate friendship in public. Occasionally Social Democrats praised or defended the Jewish organization. On the tenth anniversary of the *CV Zeitung* in 1932, Carl Severing's cordial greeting, which urged the CV not to lose courage in the face of the Nazi challenge, was given a place of honor in the publication.[30] The *Leipziger Volkszeitung* warmly recommended a 1932 collection of *Anti-Anti* issues as the best source of information about the Jewish question.[31] The *Hamburger Echo* revealed as fraudulent a leaflet ostensibly signed by the CV urging support for the DNVP in the No-

[25] Reichmann, "Der drohende Sturm," 570–71.

[26] Eugen Jacobi to Berthold Sender, June 30, 1930, reproduced in Paucker, *Der juedische Abwehrkampf*, 174.

[27] Interview with Jeanette Wolff, March 12, 1967.

[28] Paucker, *Der juedische Abwehrkampf*, 452.

[29] Hirschberg, personal letter, March 16, 1967. For a more detailed description of CV–SPD cooperation against anti-Semitism, consult Paucker, *Der juedische Abwehrkampf*, 87–90, 94–99.

[30] "Glueckwuensche zu unserem Jubilaeum," *CV Zeitung*, XI (1932), 235.

[31] *Leipziger Volkszeitung*, August 2, 1932.

vember, 1932, Reichstag election. On the day before the Hamburg organ was suppressed, it debunked a Nazi claim that a raid on the CV's Berlin headquarters had uncovered evidence of Communist financial support for the organization, noting that the CV was nonpartisan but predominantly bourgeois and therefore more likely to accept aid from the political right than from the KPD.[32] The SPD press also continued to report the contents of speeches against Judeophobia delivered at CV meetings. In 1931 *Vorwaerts* summarized a talk about anti-Jewish racial ideology given by Dr. Bruno Weil before the Berlin CV. It also welcomed the CV's 1931 "Day of Culture" and endorsed speeches for the occasion that extolled Jewish contributions to German civilization and called for the preservation of these contributions.[33] But it is significant that Social Democrats expressed open approval of the CV much less frequently after 1929 than they had before; although the SPD central organ called attention to sixteen meetings of the Jewish organization from 1919 to 1928, it did so for only four from 1929 to 1933. As noted above, the primary consideration of the Socialists was to avoid confirming Nazi claims that Jews controlled the Party.[34]

But it is also true that the depression had stimulated a certain amount of resentment in Socialist ranks against the bourgeois CV. This resentment was strong enough to influence even some younger Jews in the SPD. In 1931 CV member Heinz Cohn felt obliged publicly to urge his fellow Jewish Social Democrats to forget about the CV's bourgeois complexion and work with it as another means of combating nazism.[35] One important source of Socialist annoyance with the CV may have been the

[32] *Hamburger Echo*, November 2, 1932; March 2, 1933.

[33] *Vorwaerts*, November 22, 1931; December 5, 1931. See also *Der Abend*, December 14, 1928.

[34] Interview with Dr. Eva Reichmann, September 14, 1966; interview with Dr. Ernst Fraenkel, February 2, 1967.

[35] Hirschfeld interview; Heinz Cohn, "Kann ein Sozialdemokrat CV.er sein," *CV Zeitung*, X (May 29, 1931).

Jewish organization's reluctance to supply the *Reichsbanner* with more than money and propaganda material. For example, in 1930 the Wuerzburg CV local decided to set up its own self-defense organization, rejecting the plea of *Reichsbanner* member Josef Adler that the Jews join his organization for the protection of *all* prorepublican groups. Only Leo Friedmann expressed this resentment openly. He criticized the *Central-verein* for taking a high moral stand against anti-Semitism and the irrational arguments on which its stand rested, yet failing to take positive action against the social conditions that gave rise to such sentiments.[36] It is clear that some Social Democrats had returned to the demands of their pre–World War I comrades that Jews become Socialists and fight for general, not just Jewish, emancipation.

The *Verein zur Abwehr des Antisemitismus*, another organization whose membership was primarily Jewish, rated Socialist notice only once during the period under review. When the group held its annual meeting in Munich in 1930, Socialist Paul Thorwirth approvingly quoted from its concluding resolution: "Anti-Semitism represents an offence to the ethical concepts of Christianity, of justice, and of truth, and it is a menace to public order at home and to Germany's reputation abroad."[37] However, two important non-Jewish Social Democrats, Albert Suedekum and Gerhard Seger, were members of the *Verein*'s national executive board in the late Weimar Republic, and Seger, who was a Socialist editor and Reichstag deputy, has indicated that "many" lesser Social Democrats belonged to the organization.[38]

[36] Wuerzburg police report to the Bavarian Ministry of the Interior, Acten des Bayerischen Staats- Ministeriums des Innern, fol. 73725, no. 2019ba11; Friedmann, "Politische Bewegungen im Judentum der Gegenwart," *Jung-sozialistische Blaetter*, X (1931), 49–50.

[37] Thorwirth, "Anthropogeographie," *Sozialistische Monatshefte*, XXXVI (1930), 927.

[38] *Abwehr Blaetter*, XXXVIII (October, 1928), 140; Seger, personal letter, June 29, 1966.

A decline in Socialist appeals for Jewish support and votes reflected another aspect of SPD reluctance to appear a "Party of the Jews." This decline, however, became noticeable only after 1930; before that the SPD had actively solicited Jewish help. Appeals to Jewish voters were particularly numerous during the campaign for the 1930 Reichstag election. Franz Kuenstler, chairman of the Berlin SPD organization, assured the readers of the *CV Zeitung*: "Social Democracy judges a man according to his conduct and his behavior towards his fellow men, not according to race or religion." [39] The same message was brought to a meeting of Jewish veterans by Erich Kuttner.[40] In a flyer addressed to their fellow Jewish voters, twenty-five Berlin Jews, some of whom were Socialists or fellow travelers, reviewed the history of the Party's militant opposition to anti-Semitism, presented the SPD as the strongest bulwark against a Nazi takeover, and concluded: "The SPD has never hesitated to present Jewish candidates for the Reichstag and the provincial parliaments; it has never yielded to opportunistic fears or even to anti-Semitic tendencies. Even today Jews in Berlin are present on the SPD's list of candidates, foremost among them Hugo Heimann." [41] The *Leipziger Volkszeitung* printed a declaration implying that Jews who planned to vote for any party but the Socialist would be committing symbolic suicide.[42]

After 1930, however, only the *Hamburger Echo* continued to publicize Party appeals for Jewish support. In 1931 it reprinted Edith Hammerknack's assurances to a women's auxiliary of the Hamburg CV that "the Jew as a member of a particular race and cultural community will find no political party in Germany that provides such immunity from opportunism

[39] Kuenstler, "Die Sozialdemokratie kaempft gegen Hitler," *CV Zeitung*, IX (1930), 483. Kuenstler was not Jewish.
[40] *Der Abend*, September 4, 1930.
[41] ADGB Akten, fol. NB–104, no. 88.
[42] *Leipziger Volkszeitung*, September 11, 1930.

on the subject of equal rights for Jewish citizens as the Social Democratic Party of Germany." Soon thereafter it published Otto Ruschke's vigorous attack on Nazi anti-Semitism, made before the regular CV organization, which ended with the promise that Jews would "always find Social Democracy at their side in their defensive struggle against the National Socialists." Just before the Reichstag elections held in November, 1932, the Hamburg organ published a declaration entitled "The Jews and November Six" which stated the SPD's determination "that no one may be denied his political and social rights because of his descent or his religious convictions. The Social Democratic Party is the party of all the oppressed, regardless of the race or religion to which they belong." [43]

SPD support for legislation strongly opposed by Bavarian Jews may also have been influenced by the Socialists' nervousness over being labeled *Judenknechte*. In January, 1931, the Socialist deputies in the Bavarian parliament voted with the majority of that body to require slaughterhouses in Bavaria to stun all animals prior to bloodletting, which made it impossible for orthodox Jews to practice ritual-slaughter methods. The Bavarian People's Party, the Bavarian branch of the Center Party, opposed the bill as an infringement on the religious rights of Hebrews, but Socialist spokesman Wilhelm Hoegner insisted that humanitarian considerations should be kept uppermost and suggested that modern methods—presumably electrification —could make ritual-slaughter compatible with the proposed law.[44] Hoegner has admitted that he and his colleagues were by no means of one mind on this issue; the Munich SPD organ printed protests by local Jewish groups and an article by Jewish Social Democrat Philipp Loewenfeld that condemned the

[43] *Hamburger Echo*, September 8, 1931; April 15, November 2 and 3, 1932; March 7 and 27, 1931.
[44] *Muenchener Post*, January 23, 1930; *Verhandlungen des Bayerischen Landtags*, 51st Sess., 1929, II, 484–86; *Verhandlungen des Bayerischen Landtags*, 57th Sess., 1930, III, 106–20.

Party's stand as ill-considered and likely to be mistaken as anti-Semitic.[45] The parliamentary delegation maintained discipline, however, and only one Socialist deputy, Rosa Aschenbrenner, failed to vote with the Nazis and Communists in favor of the bill, which became law on October 1, 1930.[46] The vote was 70 to 34, which made the 28 SPD votes decisive.

Socialist reluctance to be associated too closely with the Jews was intensified by two "scandals," similar to the Barmat case, that were fully exploited by the Nazi press throughout the declining years of the republic. In 1926 the SPD had borrowed 800,000 marks from Jakob Goldschmidt's Darmstadt and National Bank to buy a substantial piece of property in Berlin. A year later the Nazis had charged that the money was a gift from the Jewish banker to *Vorwaerts*—evidence, they said, of Socialist complicity in an international Jewish conspiracy. After the Nazis intensified their propaganda about the 800,000 marks and the Communists picked up the story for their own purposes, SPD spokesmen publicized the facts about the loan.[47] On no less than seven occasions in the next four years the Party brought charges against Nazi publications for repeating the untrue story of a gift from Goldschmidt.[48] Socialist uneasiness over the accusations was illustrated at the SPD's 1929

---

[45] Interview with Hoegner, June 19, 1969; *Muenchener Post*, January 21, 1930. Loewenfeld, "Zum Gesetz ueber die Betaeubung der Schlachttiere," *Muenchener Post*, January 28, 1930. As Loewenfeld pointed out, Socialists in other parts of Germany were opposed to laws restricting the slaughter of animals according to Hebrew ritual. And he was right about the Socialist position being misunderstood. In 1931 Social Democrat Edith Hammerknack was asked to account for the Bavarian SPD's vote while addressing a Jewish group in Hamburg. *Hamburger Echo*, March 7, 1931.

[46] Aschenbrenner, an ex-Communist noted for her contentiousness, abstained on the ballot, earning for herself the *Muenchener Post*'s rebuke and apparent excommunication from the SPD. *Muenchener Post*, January 30, 1930.

[47] *Voelkischer Beobachter*, May 10, 1927; *Die rote Fahne*, October 11, 1928; *Vorwaerts*, October 12, 1928; "Jakob Goldschmidts 800,000 Mark," *Sozial-demokratische Partei-Korrespondenz: Ergaenzungsband, 1923-1928*, 461-64.

[48] See, for example, *Vorwaerts*, October 26, 1930; July 24, 1931; *Der Abend*, May 18, 1932.

Party Congress in Magdeburg. Here Konrad Ludwig was forced to interrupt his financial report and explain the Gold-schmidt case in response to the shouted demand from the floor of an unidentified delegate.[49]

Still more damaging to the Socialists was the 1929 revelation of corruption in Berlin's SPD–DDP coalition city administration involving the Jewish brothers Max, Leo, and Willi Sklarek, two of whom were SPD members. The Sklareks were clothing dealers who had obtained huge loans from the municipal bank and a monopoly in supplying clothes to city institutions in return for certain favors to city officials. These shady dealings, which might have gone undetected in good times, were uncovered when the depression made it impossible for the brothers to repay their loans. The disclosure was a signal for the Nazis to unleash another storm of anti-Semitic abuse against the Socialists, who defended themselves by pointing out that no Socialist official had been directly implicated in the scandal and promising to expel any convicted of complicity in the matter.[50] SPD spokesmen also tried to turn the tables on the political right by alleging that the Sklareks had cultivated excellent contacts in the DNVP and had contributed to its campaign funds.[51] A further allegation was made that the brothers had even paid the vacation expenses of a Nationalist Reichstag deputy.[52] When two of the Sklareks were convicted and given four-year sentences, *Vorwaerts* washed its hands of the brothers, concluding that they were worthless opportunists whose former relations with the SPD were "regrettable." But the So-cialist central organ went out of its way to denounce the exploi-

[49] *Protokoll: Sozialdemokratischer Parteitag, Magdeburg 1929* (Berlin, 1929), 44–45.
[50] Walter Pahl, "Die oekonomischen und politisch-moralischen Lehren der Sklarekaffaere," *Sozialistische Monatshefte*, XXXV (1929), 907–14; Landauer, *European Socialism*, II, 1365–66; *Der Abend*, September 27 and 28, 1929.
[51] *Vorwaerts*, November 6 and 7, 1929; *Der Abend*, November 16, 1929.
[52] Erich Flatau, *Zum "Sklarek Skandal"* (Berlin, 1929), 11–15; *Vorwaerts*, October 11, 1929; February 6, 1930.

tation of the scandal by Judeophobes, noting that the sins of the Jewish Sklareks were as nothing compared with the crimes of "good Christian, Evangelical, even nationalistic celebrities," for which it cited the Raiffeisen scandal as proof.[53]

In view of Nazi exploitation of the Goldschmidt and Sklarek cases, it is surprising that German Socialists made almost no tactical retreats from the war against anti-Semitism. CV leader Alfred Hirschberg recalls "one or two" cases of lower echelon, local SPD bosses having toned down their attacks on anti-Semitism in order to minimize the effectiveness of right-wing denunciations of the Party. Unfortunately he no longer recalls any details aside from having taken up the matter with high Party leaders, who proved cooperative.[54] In the summer of 1930 SPD officials on the Berlin city government, bowing to the anti-Jewish demands of their DVP colleagues, dropped Bern Meyer as their candidate for the directorship of the municipal bank. Instead they endorsed a non-Jew. Although the Socialists blamed the People's Party for the move, at least one Jewish publication, the *Juedische Rundschau*, held the SPD responsible for having acquiesced to the DVP's anti-Semitic demand.[55] These are the only instances of SPD compromise on the subject of anti-Semitism that have come to light.

While their occasional tactical retreats from contacts with Jews did not prevent most German Socialists from opposing anti-Semitism, a great many of them underestimated the long-term Nazi threat to the Jews. One measure of this underestimation was the minor place given to arguments against anti-

[53] *Vorwaerts*, June 29 and 30, 1932. In 1927 it was revealed that the Raiffeisen Bank, an organization of rural and conservative cooperatives, had a deficit that would cost various Prussian and national institutions losses of around 40,000,000 marks. This scandal was decidedly one of the political right and was the result of bad faith or gross negligence on the part of the bank's officers, but little public outcry accompanied its revelation. Landauer, *European Socialism*, II, 1365, 1714–15.

[54] Hirschberg, personal letter, March 16, 1967.

[55] *Leipziger Volkszeitung*, June 14, 1930; Knuetter, "Die Linksparteien," 339.

Semitism in official SPD booklets that suggested the best ways for Party spokesmen to attack nazism. Of nine such booklets, only three touched on the problem of Judeophobia, and all of these emphasized Nazi opportunism on the subject.[56] Before the September, 1930, Reichstag election, it was common for Socialists to depreciate the chances of a Nazi takeover, while both before and after the election a great many SPD spokesmen expressed doubt that the Nazis would carry out their anti-Semitic program if given the chance. During the former period it was common for Social Democrats to think of the NSDAP as a reincarnation of the old political anti-Semitism of the 1890's, with no greater chances for success. As Albert Grzesinski told a *Reichsbanner* rally in 1929, the Nazis constituted "nothing more than a quite ordinary anti-Semitic boom party [*Konjunkturpartei*]." [57]

CV leader Hans Reichmann held a news conference in the summer of 1928 in which he pointed out the dangers presented by the spread of nazism, but Otto Landsberg later assured him that he had seen such movements come and go and that no one had anything to fear from the latest wave of animosity toward Jews. "It would be wrong to take these people seriously in politics," Landsberg concluded.[58] In 1930 Otto Buchwitz told SPD leaders that the Party should take more energetic measures against the Nazis, to which Landberg commented: "My dear Buchwitz, I have already survived three anti-Semitic waves, and I will also endure the fourth." Carl Severing quickly added his agreement.[59] The Reichstag election that September quashed

56 *Materialsammlung gegen die Nationalsozialisten: Fuer Redner und Funktionaere* (Goerlitz, 1930), 24–26; *Kampf dem Hakenkreutz: Rededisposition ueber die faschistische Gefahr* (Berlin, [1930]), 15; *Referentenmaterial zur hessischen Landtagswahl am 19. Juni 1932* (n.p., n.d.), 18. See below, pages 201–205.

57 Interview with Walter G. Oschilewski, February 2, 1967; *Muenchener Post*, December 28 and 29, 1929, NSDAP Hauptarchiv, fol. 1906.

58 Reichmann, "Der drohende Sturm," 562–63.

59 Buchwitz, *Fuenfzig Jahre Funktionaer*, 119–20.

their optimism as the Nazis won 107 seats and in less than two years went on to replace the SPD as Germany's largest party.

A more important determinant of Socialist underestimation of Nazi Judeophobia was the impression that the Hitlerites had no intention of following through on their threats against the Jews. Wilhelm Hoegner, for example, admits that he doubted the Nazis sincerely hated Jews and assumed that the Hitlerites merely used this old method of political agitation to terrorize the bourgeoisie.[60] As it had before 1929, this impression went hand-in-hand with the SPD's "plot theory" of anti-Semitism; if the Nazis railed at the Jews only to win votes and political power, they might never carry out their anti-Semitic program once they were in control. A number of German Socialists expressed the opinion that Nazi anti-Semitism was a fraud. In 1930 Erich Kuttner indicated that he thought only a few racist leaders really believed what they said about the Jews. Of the majority he wrote: "They are crude placeseekers who laugh themselves to death inside over the whole hocus-pocus; they are hard-boiled, indifferent demagogues whose tirades are nothing other than carefully weighed means of keeping their following obedient and intellectually dependent." [61] A certain Dr. Sussheim wrote of the Nazis' anti-Semitism: "Their endlessly repeated assertion that the Jews are guilty of all distress is a senseless phrase designed solely for purposes of agitation; for them agitation is an end in itself, not a means to a programatical end." [62] Hermann Heller maintained that Nazi racism was designed to hurt Socialists, not Jews: "The political and social significance of ... *voelkisch* racial ideas rest by no means in anti-Semitism, as is asserted in mass agitation, but rather in anti-Socialism, that is, in the doctrine of the racial superiority of the

---

[60] Fraenkel interview; Hoegner interview.
[61] Kuttner, *Pathologie des Rassenantisemitismus*, 30.
[62] Sussheim, "Die nationalsozialistische Seuche," 25.

ruling classes." [63] In Wilhelm Sollmann's estimation, the Nazis wanted power and used anti-Semitism to that end alone. According to the *Freie Volkswacht* an unidentified Nazi leader admitted as much in a letter to a Weimar factory manager by excusing National Socialist attacks on capitalism and Jews as slogans to seduce the workers.[64] Fritz Baer, a Socialist student at the University of Berlin, testified that among Nazi students the question of anti-Semitism "stays in the background and hardly ever becomes a major point of attack." Wilhelm Tiegins said of Nazi students: "They talk about the Jews, but they mean the Socialist movement. . . . They talk about the Jews, but they strike at the Social Democrats." Hans Vogel said much the same thing about the Nazis in general: "It is incorrect to regard National Socialism as a movement solely or even primarily against the Jews. It turns itself against Marxism with much greater severity than against the Jews. National Socialism says 'Jew' and by it means 'Marxism'; it says 'Jewry' and by it really means the concept of the class struggle." [65]

The Social Democrats found confirmation of this impression in dozens of examples of Nazi opportunism on the Jewish question. They identified pecuniary, political, and personal motives for this opportunism. As a 1930 SPD pamphlet put it: "Certainly the National Socialists agitate against the Jews in word and in print; but if they think they can get any kind of material advantage from the Jews, then something else can be expected from them." [66] The Socialists believed that Nazis encouraged

[63] Heller, "Nationaler Sozialismus," *Neue Blaetter fuer den Sozialismus*, II (1931), 156.

[64] Sollmann, "Der politische Antisemitismus," 270–71; *Freie Volkswacht*, June 24, 1930.

[65] Baer, "Sind die Nazis wirklich Sozialisten?" *Das freie Wort*, IV (May 29, 1932), 17; Tiegins, "Die Faschisierung der deutschen Hochschulen," 40–41; Vogel, *Faschismus–Nationalsozialismus* (Berlin, 1930), 15. Vogel, a non-Jew, was a member of the SPD's central committee from 1927 to 1933. In 1931 he was elected Party chairman.

[66] *Materialsammlung gegen die Nationalsozialisten*, 24.

contributions from Jews. In a 1930 Party pamphlet they sought to prove that Hitler's Judeophobia was a sham by contending that he accepted a thousand marks per month from a Hamburg Jew, one Frau Neffman; at the same time he maintained a plush apartment in Munich with a six-thousand-mark gift from a Jewish director of the firm Held and Franke, a certain Riess. *Der Abend* pointed out that Hitlerites in Breslau actually sent letters to Jews appealing for money. Later the SPD central organ interpreted a decline in Nazi newspaper attacks on Jewish artists as a play for advertisements from Jewish film studios, a policy *Der Abend* called "cultural fascism." [67] Nazi newspapers gladly accepted Jewish advertisers and used the threat of boycott to encourage reluctant Jewish merchants to take out ads, said the *Leipziger Volkszeitung*. In 1932 the *Muenchener Post* commented on the case of a Jew who was subjected to Nazi harassment until she purchased protection from the Hitlerites for three thousand marks: "Jews who can pay up will have nothing to fear in the Third Reich: they'll be grabbed by the purse, not by the gullet." [68]

National Socialist business dealings with Jews strengthened the SPD view that Nazis were more interested in money than in anti-Semitism. The Socialist press frequently drew attention to Nazi purchases of uniforms, weapons, insignia, and even busts of Hitler from Jewish firms.[69] In 1930 a Party pamphlet reported that a Nazi town councilor in Stralsund had offered to act as an agent for a Jewish bank in order to secure foreign credit for the city government.[70] In 1932 a Socialist in the

[67] *Die Nazi-Fibel*, 9; *Der Abend*, September 17, October 6, 1932. See also *Vorwaerts*, July 25, 1930; *Hamburger Echo*, July 27, 1932; *Leipziger Volkszeitung*, May 12, 1930.

[68] *Leipziger Volkszeitung*, June 11, December 8, 1930; March 16, September 9, 1932 (see also *Freie Volkswacht*, December 17, 1929); *Muenchener Post*, February 16, 1932, NSDAP Hauptarchiv, fol. 1559, no. 73.

[69] *Leipziger Volkszeitung*, July 7, 1931; July 18, 1932; *Fraenkische Tagespost*, March 21, July 29, 1932; *Der Abend*, August 19, November 4, 1932.

[70] *Materialsammlung gegen die Nationalsozialisten*, 24.

Franconian town of Roth observed of an outspokenly anti-Jewish local Nazi leader: "He appears to have nothing against letting his wife bring home wine and groceries that she has purchased from a Jew, as was often the case during the past year." [71] Nazi intimacy with "cooperative" Jewish businessmen led the *Fraenkische Tagespost* to deny Hitler's 1930 claim that his movement was "anti-Semitic to the last consequence" by pointing out that in Plauen the Nazis had become "an armored shield for Jewish capitalists." When Hamburg Nazis appeared to have rented a building from a Jew, the local SPD paper remarked: "Their Judeophobia ceases the moment they can make a favorable business deal." [72]

Desire for political advantage was another source of Nazi opportunism on the Jewish question, according to Socialist observers. During the period of close NSDAP–DNVP cooperation in 1929 and 1930, the Social Democrats pointed out that Nationalist leader Alfred Hugenberg's close business dealings with Jews did not seem to bother the Nazis. A cartoon in *Der wahre Jacob* showed Hitler sitting on Hugenberg's lap before a rug on which a swastika was woven within a Star of David; to Hugenberg's inquiry if Hitler were annoyed about those Jewish business contacts, the Fuehrer cooed: "With the prospects you have opened to me, not in the least." [73] When the Hugenberg press eulogized a Berlin Jewish banker, Arthur Salomonsohn, on the occasion of his death in 1930, *Der Abend* knew Hitler would not object: "Hitler plus Salomonsohn—two stitches are better than one. Out with the Jews! In with the Jews! Down with Jewish finance capital! Heil Hitler! Three cheers for Salomonsohn!" [74] Similarly, when in October, 1930,

[71] *Fraenkische Tagespost*, February 22, 1932; see also *Vorwaerts*, February 6, 1929; *Hamburger Echo*, January 10, 1932.
[72] *Fraenkische Tagespost*, August 19, 1930; *Hamburger Echo*, January 5, 1933.
[73] *Der Abend*, January 20, 1930; *Der wahre Jacob*, L (September 28, 1929), 1.
[74] *Der Abend*, June 16, 1930.

the Nazi deputies supported the candidacy of DVP member Dr. Ernst Scholz for the presidency of the Reichstag even though his wife was Jewish, the Socialists contrasted it with a recent Nazi proposal for a law to punish anyone who "polluted" German blood with Jewish. Helmut Klotz told the story and put quotation marks around his sarcastic description of Hitler as an "anti-Semite." [75] Also in 1930 Socialists reported that Hitler had renounced anti-Semitism in an interview with an American reporter; an anonymous Social Democrat concluded that Hitler had wanted to "secure a favorable impression among the rich Jews of America." [76] The *Leipziger Volkszeitung* agreed, noting that the Nazis changed their attitude toward Jews as often and as quickly as they might change their shirts. A leaflet distributed at a 1931 SPD rally in Munich pointed out that Hitler had recently addressed Hamburg's "National Club" even though its president was a Jew. Later the *Muenchener Post* revealed that Hitler had greeted the Jewish wife of a visiting Italian trade envoy with a bouquet of red roses.[77] When Hitler made Franz von Papen his vice-chancellor in 1933, the *Leipziger Volkszeitung* prominently drew attention to earlier Nazi attacks on von Papen for having set a "Jewish trap" for Hitler by trying to bring him into von Papen's "Jew-ridden" government.[78]

German Socialists also observed that the Nazis let a variety of personal considerations get in the way of their anti-Semitism. Paul Loebe noted that Hermann Goering retained amicable private relations with prominent Jews while publicly delivering

---

[75] *Kampf dem Hakenkreuz*, 15; Klotz, *Hitlers Sozialismus* (Berlin, 1931), 8.
[76] *Materialsammlung gegen die Nationalsozialisten*, 26.
[77] *Leipziger Volkszeitung*, July 19, 1930, NSDAP Hauptarchiv, fol. 1894; *Muenchener Post*, January 9 and 10, 1932, NSDAP Hauptarchiv, fol. 1559, no. 63. See also *Freie Volkswacht*, October 23 and 25, 1930.
[78] *Leipziger Volkszeitung*, February 4, 1933. The story also appeared in the *Bayerisches Wochenblatt*, February 25, 1933, NSDAP Hauptarchiv, fol. 798.

the fiercest anti-Jewish speeches. *Vorwaerts* called attention to Goering's patronage of Berlin's Wertheim Department Store, which frequently had been the target of anti-Semitic Nazi propaganda. In 1930 the Socialist organ took satisfaction in Nazi discomfort over the discovery that English Fascist Viscount Harold S. H. Rothermere had been denounced as a Jewish plutocrat by Alfred Rosenberg ten years earlier. It also pointed out that a local Nazi leader in Gleiwitz was the only non-Jew arrested when police raided a club where illegal gambling was going on.[79] *Der Abend* trumpeted that Vienna *Gauleiter* Alfred Frauenfeld had a Jewish physician and had chosen a Jewish hospital when he needed an operation. The *Muenchener Post* thought it significant that a Munich Nazi had gone to a Jewish medical specialist on the advice of his non-Jewish general practitioner. A Nuremberg Nazi's anti-Semitic speech during the campaign for the first 1932 Reichstag election did not deceive the local SPD press, which noted that both the partners in the Nazi's law firm were Jews.[80]

Although most Socialist commentators expressed doubts that the Nazis seriously planned to carry out their anti-Semitic program, a minority of SPD spokesmen took the opposite view. An anonymous Socialist, observing ambiguity in the Nazi attitude toward Jews, concluded that the Nazi's anti-Semitic riots of October, 1930, plainly demonstrated that they meant to persecute.[81] Writing in 1949, Otto Braun claimed that the anti-Jewish disorders of 1930 and 1931 convinced him that the Nazis intended to back up their anti-Semitic slogans with deeds. In 1930 the *Fraenkische Tagespost* predicted that the expulsion

[79] Loebe, *Der Weg war lang*, 140; *Vorwaerts*, March 1, 1932; October 4 and 23, 1930. See also *Freie Volkswacht*, September 30, 1930.

[80] *Der Abend*, December 13, 1932; *Muenchener Post*, December 10 and 11, 1932, NSDAP Hauptarchiv, fol. 1559, no. 84; *Fraenkische Tagespost*, April 22, 1932.

[81] "Zwei Nazifuehrer — zwei Judenrezepte," *Sozialdemokratische Partei-Korrespondenz* (November, 1930), 713.

of Jews would be made a prime task of any future Hitler dictatorship.[82] Wilhelm Hoegner, drawing on Hitler's draft constitution of November 9, 1923, for evidence, decided that the Jews could expect to have their property expropriated by the bosses of a Third Reich.[83]

None of the Social Democrats who assumed that nazism was fully in earnest about anti-Semitism sensed that it would one day resort to extermination as a "final solution" to the Jewish question. In fact, so far as the author has been able to determine, the Nazis did not explicitly propose the extermination of Jews at any time before 1933. Such a threat seems to have been made for the first time by Hitler in a speech made in January, 1939, when he promised the "annihilation of the Jewish race in Europe" should "international-finance Jewry inside and outside of Europe . . . succeed once more in plunging nations into another world war." [84] The most nearly complete Socialist prediction about Nazi intentions was provided by the *Hamburger Echo*, which claimed to have acquired the text of a top secret Nazi document containing Hitler's plans for the Jews. These it summarized as follows: Jews were to be excluded from the civil service, the press, the legal profession, all German schools and universities, and stripped of their citizenship; all who had come to Germany after August, 1914, were to be expelled regardless of whether they had been naturalized or not; ritual-slaughter methods were to be denied them, as was recourse to law courts; they would not be permitted to marry non-Jews or be witnesses in trials; Jewish doctors would not be allowed to treat gentile patients; state subsidies to and official recognition of the Jewish community would be withdrawn, and a special law code and special taxes would take their place; the state

[82] Otto Braun, *Von Weimar zu Hitler*, 180; *Fraenkische Tagespost*, August 13, 1930.
[83] *Der Abend*, December 8, 1931.
[84] Raul Hilberg, *The Destruction of the European Jews* (Chicago, 1961), 257.

would place important Jewish-owned concerns under strict supervision as a prelude to eventual expropriation; a "final solution" would impress Jews for forced labor to cultivate marginal land in the East.[85] However, these infrequent contentions that the Nazis meant business about anti-Semitism were neither characteristic of the Socialist point of view nor as significant as SPD assertions of Nazi insincerity on the Jewish question.

Although inclined to underestimate the potential of Nazi Judeophobia, German Socialism remained generally free from intrusions of direct anti-Semitism in the years 1929–33. Only two Social Democrats are reported to have used anti-Jewish phrases in that period. One, surprisingly, was Erhard Auer, the same Bavarian SPD leader whose earlier opposition to anti-Semitism had been unambiguous and outspoken. Imprisoned by the Nazis in May, 1933, he shared the same prison cell for a time with Bavarian monarchist Erwein von Aretin, with whom he established good personal relations despite their conflicting political views. According to Aretin, Auer complained that the Nazis had destroyed some of his very important files, which among other things contained the document by which King Ludwig III, after the revolution, had released Bavarian officials from their oath of allegiance (Auer had been the first postrevolutionary Minister of the Interior). He then continued, according to Aretin's account of 1955: "You can believe me, the king's signature was much too valuable for me to hand it over to the Berlin Jew Eisner [the Prime Minister]. He got only a copy!" [86] Carl Landauer has attributed this comment, if really made, to Auer's utter despair over his imprisonment and to his personal antipathy for the radical USPD intellectual Kurt Eisner.[87]

[85] *Hamburger Echo*, December 7, 1931.
[86] Aretin, *Krone und Ketten: Erinnerungen eines bayerischen Edelmannes* (Munich, 1955), 216.
[87] Landauer, personal letter, May 24, 1966.

In a case rather similar to that of Richard Fischer, discussed in Chapter I, Wilhelm Sollmann is also reported to have used mildly anti-Jewish phraseology in his dealings with radical journalists in meetings of administrators of the Social Democratic press. Ernst Hamburger, however, reports that Sollmann does not seem to have said or done anything further which was unfavorable to Jews and that he enjoyed the esteem of most SPD members, both Jews and non-Jews alike.[88] Certainly Sollmann's opposition to anti-Semitism during the Weimar years was fully as incontestable as Auer's.[89]

Some Social Democrats have expressed the opinion that part of the Socialist proletariat regarded Jewish intellectuals in the SPD leadership as "too intelligent" and as obstacles to the advancement of "real workers," but no evidence has been found of any case in which such feelings led to open discrimination against Socialist or non-Socialist Jews.[90] Nevertheless, left-wing Socialists were particularly sensitive to such prejudices against leftist SPD Jewish intellectuals. When Wilhelm Sollmann urged the delegates to the 1929 Party Congress to end entirely their propaganda against religion, he summarized the wide range of religions and philosophies represented in the Party: "We have atheists, monists, positivists, philosophical idealists, philosophical materialists, neo-Kantians, Evangelicals, Catholics, sectarians, yes, we even have Jews in the Party." Cheers

[88] Hamburger, *Juden im oeffentlichen Leben*, 150; Hamburger, personal letter, July 9, 1969.

[89] See above, pages 33, 106, 126, 167, 168. It is also true, however, that after 1936 Sollmann was suspected of holding anti-Semitic convictions by some of his fellow SPD exiles in the United States, including Paul Hertz. These suspicions were serious enough to inspire a lengthy but inconclusive Party investigation and the refusal of some left-wing groups to sponsor Sollmann as a public speaker. Nachlass Paul Hertz, fols. 25–C and 29–A. For a brief and rather eulogistic sketch of Sollmann's career, see Felix E. Hirsch, "William Sollmann, Wanderer Between Two Worlds," *South Atlantic Quarterly*, LII (1953), 202–27.

[90] Wolff and Oschilewsky interviews; Hedwig Wachenheim, personal letter, February 9, 1967.

and laughter met his last remark, but Frau A. Torhorst did not think it funny. She arose and professed to be shocked that "the Party Congress of the Social Democratic Party, which is based on Marx and Lassalle and other distinguished Jewish leaders, [had witnessed] applause induced by a remark that came close to sounding a faintly anti-Semitic note." The congress erupted with shouts of "Unbelievable!" and "Unheard of!" Chairman Otto Wels reprimanded Torhorst; such a comment, he remarked, was quite uncalled for.[91]

Socialist indulgence in indirect anti-Semitism, on the other hand, intensified somewhat during the last years of the republic. As it had earlier, it took the form of a few intemperate attacks on Jewish capitalists, but the attacks bore a faint resemblance to the Nazi agitation against the Jews. Writers in the *Leipziger Volkszeitung* gave the word "worker" too narrow a definition as they proved that Jews were "workers" by pointing to the East European Jewish proletariat and the working-class *Ostjuden* in Germany. That Germany's bourgeois Jews were not really productive workers was implied by the definition, thus feeding the myth that those outside the proletariat were parasites.[92] In 1930 Adolf Schlucks, misreading Marx, identified a peculiarly capitalistic spirit among Jews when he suggested that Nazi Judeophobia proceeded from self-hatred: "One remembers the words of Karl Marx, that those Christians who have been Judaized by capitalism can first take exception to the Jews when they have previously dejudaized themselves and freed themselves from capitalism." [93] *Der wahre Jacob* caricatured a greedy, malevolent Jewish pawnbroker as an incidental figure in an otherwise harmless sequence of cartoons. Over the caption "That's life during Fasching," it showed a man picking up

[91] *Protokoll . . . Magdeburg 1929*, 75–77, 88.
[92] E. G., "Im Warschauer Judenviertel," *Leipziger Volkszeitung*, August 8, 1931, p. 8; Fritz Heller, "Juden ohne Geld vom Mittelalter zum Klassenkampf," *ibid.*, August 14, 1931, p. 13.
[93] Schlucks, *Kampf dem Hakenkreuz*, 4.

a rich man's suicide gun, pawning it, and using the proceeds to enjoy the carnival.[94]

Although occasional Socialist representations of Jews as grasping capitalists resembled Nazi anti-Semitic propaganda, they were motivated by factors quite foreign to any the Hitlerites would have accepted. The Nazis criticized Jewish capitalists as the source of all abuses of the capitalist system. Socialists, while vehemently rejecting the Nazi point of view, reproved some Jewish capitalists for aiding or ignoring the Hitlerites and others for opposing Nazi anti-Semitism without helping to ameliorate the social conditions that made nazism possible. SPD spokesmen believed that capital "often of notably Semitic origins" helped to finance the NSDAP.[95] The *Muenchener Post* complained that one Misrachi, whom it identified as a wealthy Jewish cigarette manufacturer, had given sizable gifts to the Nazi Party, while an anonymous Social Democrat identified Jewish banking houses as sources of loans to the National Socialists.[96] The *Leipziger Volkszeitung* reported in 1930 that Jewish banker Jakob Goldschmidt had met with Hitler and received an "entirely excellent impression" of his personality and aims. Later it observed that some Jewish capitalists seemed to be preparing places for themselves in the Third Reich, noting that Jewish members of Duesseldorf's Industry Club had received Hitler cordially when he spoke to club members early in 1932.[97]

Dr. Julius Moses found much to criticize in the attitudes of certain Jews toward a Reichstag investigation he headed into the deaths of fifty-five babies in Luebeck. Moses and the major-

[94] *Der wahre Jacob*, L (February 2, 1929), 13.

[95] Georg Engelbert Graf, *Die faschistische Gefahr* (Leipzig, n.d.), 23. The impression was not without foundation. See Grzesinski, *Inside Germany*, 196; Edgar Ansel Mowrer, *Germany Puts the Clock Back* (New York, 1933), 116–17, 127.

[96] *Muenchener Post*, January 11, 1933, NSDAP Hauptarchiv, fol. 1559, no. 88; see also, "Selbstherrschung der Nationalsozialisten," *Das freie Wort*, V (January 15, 1933), 90–91.

[97] *Leipziger Volkszeitung*, September 10, 1931; May 20, June 2, 1932.

ity of his committee had fixed the blame on a local doctor who
had approved the use of a controversial medication that caused
the disaster. But the Nazis tried to exploit the case politically by
assigning guilt to higher government officials, calling the findings of Moses' committee a "Jewish sham," and sponsoring a
committee of their own as a front organization to promote
these ideas. When Moses appeared at the Nazi committee's press
conference to demand the withdrawal of the anti-Semitic attack, two Jewish members of the group defended the Nazi
position. A disgusted Dr. Moses excoriated the Jewish turncoats
in the *CV Zeitung*, expressing amazement that the men could
not comprehend the implications for all Jews in the anti-Semitic
attack they defended.[98] Berlin's Assistant Chief of Police Bernhard Weiss bristled when an unidentified Berlin Jewish newspaper editor privately criticized him for directing police measures against unruly Nazis in the Reichstag at a time in 1932
when Chief of Police Grzesinski was out of town. The editor
had argued that for a Jew to lead the police against the Hitlerites
merely added fuel to Nazi propaganda, and he had urged Weiss
never to do so again. Weiss wrote that such a step would negate
a decade of Jewish emancipation and render out-of-bounds all
administrative positions in which a Jew might run afoul of the
Nazis. He reminded his critic that Article 23 of the National
Socialist program, which demanded that only "racial comrades"
edit German-language publications, rendered the editor as vulnerable to Nazi anti-Semitism as anyone. Accusing the man of
"political obsequiousness, or better put, an utter lack of political dignity" and of having lost "every feeling of self-assurance,"
he begged Jews to unify themselves against every concession to
Nazi demands. It is significant that the Socialists reserved both
of these complaints about bourgeois Jews for Jewish publica-

[98] *Der Abend*, May 17, June 5, July 11, 1930; Moses, "Selbst das Luebecker
Kindersterben wird parteipolitische ausgeschlachtet," *CV Zeitung*, IX (1930),
382.

tions; *Der Abend* reported the incident involving Dr. Moses without revealing that the men who defended the anti-Semitic attack were Jewish, while the SPD press ignored Weiss's complaint altogether.[99]

Other Socialists criticized Jews for being hypersensitive to anti-Semitism but insensitive to the social and economic problems that sparked the Nazi upsurge.[100] In 1930 Hermann Mueller replied to the complaint of an unidentified Jew about his use of the term "Jewish school" in referring to Nazi hecklers in the Reichstag. He explained that at the time he made that remark the Nazis were making so much noise he decided to silence them with an ironic inquiry if they had been raised in a "Jewish school," which in Mueller's South German homeland referred to any loud talk similar to the repetition of prayers in Jewish classrooms and synagogues. Protesting his friendship for the Jews, Mueller reproved their tendency to be oversensitive to anti-Semitism—a sensitivity he felt to be "grist in the mills of the National Socialists and anti-Semites." [101] Socialists found a still more pernicious consequence of Jewish hypersensitivity to Judeophobia in the far-right League of German Nationalist Jews, whose "exaggerated anxiety over anti-Semitism" in their opinion produced "precisely the same methods" as the Nazis.

What was missing, in the opinion of some Socialists, was Jewish concern over the economic causes of the proliferation of nazism and anti-Semitism. At a 1932 meeting of Jewish Socialists in Hamburg, a Professor Berendsohn criticized bourgeois Jews for living in a vacuum and for failing to realize that human rights were not special rights for Jews alone. A speaker at a similar meeting in Leipzig flayed the "capitalistic Liberals" who

[99] Bernhard Weiss, "Mehr Selbstbewusstsein," *CV Zeitung*, XI (1932), 233–34; *Der Abend*, July 12, 1930.

[100] Paucker, "Der juedische Abwehrkampf," 451–52; *Verhandlungen des Reichstags*, 4th Sess., 1930, CDXLIV, 48.

[101] Mueller to [?], November 3, 1930, in Nachlass Hermann Mueller, fol. 7; *Der Abend*, March 10, 1931.

led the local Jewish community for spending their time debating whether or not to use an organ in worship services or to appropriate money for new synagogues when many members of the community were destitute.[102] This Socialist irritation over Jewish social unconsciousness was also apparent in the larger political sphere. During the campaign for the 1928 Reichstag election, Fritz Heller had attacked the "old headmasters and Jewish clothiers" who remained true to the DDP's magic eighteenth-century phrases about the rights of man even though "under the rule of capitalism hundreds of thousands of workers" wanted for bread, and Berlin's bourgeois Jews raised "a storm against granting equal rights to their co-religionists who immigrated [*sic*] from what was once German Posen—from which they themselves came thirty years earlier." [103]

Later, when one of the directors of Berlin's Jewish community, Georg Kareski, ran for a Reichstag seat on the Center Party list (the bourgeois parties had already faded badly), an anonymous Socialist commented: "The homeless Jewish bourgeoisie has in great part sought shelter with the Center Party—Christ and the first Pope were Jews, so why not? Wretched individuals who do violence to their ideas and purposes out of anxiety over 'Socialist expropriation.' What Hitler is to the Christians, the Center Party is to the Jews." [104] In 1928 Albert Salomon had made the point more directly: "In the present world situation the Jews of this generation can give only one political decision, that for the proletariat." [105] The fact that very many German Jews disagreed, and failed to change their minds even during the post-1929 period of economic and political crisis,

[102] *Hamburger Echo*, April 15, 1932; *Leipziger Volkszeitung*, April 10, 1931.
[103] Fritz Heller, "Die Wahlverwandten," *Jungsozialistische Blaetter*, VII (1928), 146.
[104] "Deutsche Juden, waehlt Zentrum!" *Schulfront*, II (1930), 135. See also *Der Abend*, September 1, 1930; *Leipziger Volkszeitung*, September 13, 1930.
[105] Salomon, review of Rudolf Kaulla, *Der Liberalismus und die deutsche Juden. Das Judentum als konservatives Element*, in *Die Gesellschaft*, V (1928), 471.

rankled the Socialists but never induced them to abandon their opposition to anti-Semitism.

At no time in the declining years of the Weimar Republic did the SPD as a party slacken its opposition to Judeophobia or resort to anti-Jewish phrases. Fear of seeming to confirm Nazi propaganda about Jewish control over the Party made Socialists reluctant to associate openly with Jewish organizations or to appeal openly for Jewish votes, but it never induced them to shrink from close secret cooperation with Jews in the fight against anti-Semitism. The marginal infiltration of anti-Jewish opinions among individual Social Democrats remained almost unmeasurable. On the other hand, the persistence in belief among Socialists of the "plot theory" of anti-Semitism and evidence of Nazi opportunism on the Jewish question produced Socialist doubts that the Nazis were ideologically committed to Judeophobia or seriously intended to carry out any substantial part of their anti-Semitic program. Moreover, indirect anti-Semitic attacks on bourgeois Jews increased with the Nazi challenge, partially because Socialists persisted in believing Jews had a special obligation to work for general emancipation with or through the SPD. But these attacks were of much less importance than was Socialist opposition to anti-Semitism during the Nazi rise to power.

Chapter IX

Truth and Error of a Moderate Party

SPD attitudes toward the Jews and anti-Semitism in the Weimar Republic must be seen as a reflection of the total character of the Party. The events of 1918–19 facilitated the triumph of revisionism in the SPD. The giving of power and responsibility to Socialists made them more willing than ever before to work for social and political democracy through existing channels. They also changed the SPD from the chief party of opposition in Germany to the principal defender of the democratic Weimar Republic against its opponents on both the right and the left.

German Socialist attitudes toward anti-Semitism from 1919 to 1933 tended to reflect the SPD's moderate stance. Orthodox Marxism's pre-1914 apathetic view of Judeophobia, which assigned the task of Jewish emancipation to the coming socialist revolution, virtually disappeared from Party thinking. Instead, Socialist spokesmen insisted upon equal treatment for Jews within the framework of the existing state. They countered racist contentions about Jews with carefully reasoned arguments showing the fallacies of anti-Semitism. At the same time they exposed anti-Jewish ideology and actions to slashing ridicule. The Socialists poured disgust on *voelkisch* bullies who attacked Jews physically, and they inveighed against anti-Semitic incidents in the army, the courts, and the government service. They extended special sympathy and hospitality to the homeless, friendless *Ostjuden* who were stranded in Germany after World War I. Nor did Social Democrats always wait for specific attacks on Jews in order to criticize anti-Semitism; they regularly exposed the activities of *voelkisch* groups and parties in a most unfavorable light, and they pointedly injected attacks upon these groups into local and national election campaigns. Although these SPD measures against Judeophobia were most numerous in the periods of greatest danger to the Jews—in the years 1919–20, 1922–24, and 1929–33—they were common throughout the life of the Weimar Republic.

Socialists rarely took direct action against anti-Semites. Not only were there few cases of outright violence against Jews, but Social Democrats regarded these few instances as matters for the police to handle. Caught off guard by the anti-Jewish riots of October, 1930, Berlin's Socialist-led police department quickly placed itself on the alert and took vigorous action against similar riots staged by the Nazis in September of the following year.

Jewish Socialist intellectuals, who occupied leading positions in the SPD in numbers disproportionate to the number of Jews in Germany, were especially active in the fight against anti-Semitism. While at most 1.5 percent of the German population was Jewish, roughly 10 percent of the Party leadership had Jewish backgrounds. Most Socialist Jews considered themselves "emancipated" from the Jewish community, but that did not prevent them from condemning anti-Semitism in disproportionately greater numbers than their non-Jewish comrades. Around one-third of the Socialist attacks on Jew-baiting came from Party members who were Jews. Although few individual German Socialists consistently singled out Judeophobia for special emphasis, among the more outspoken opponents of anti-Semitism were such Socialists of Jewish backgrounds as Otto

Friedlaender, Ernst Hamburger, Hermann Heller, Erich Kuttner, and Ernst Heilmann. Others were their non-Jewish comrades Artur Crispien, Erhard Auer, Carlo Mierendorff, Carl Severing, Wilhelm Hoegner, and Wilhelm Sollmann.

Militant SPD opposition to anti-Semitism was most basically determined by Socialist egalitarian ideas. But an equally important determinant of socialism's attitude was its conviction that bigotry toward the Jews was an effective means by which the political right rallied the gullible against the republic and its supporters. Party spokesmen warned of unscrupulous demagogues who stirred up racial prejudices to make the Jews into scapegoats for problems that the old ruling classes had bequeathed to Germany. Anti-Semitism, the Socialists said, was a plot to trick even the workers into thinking that Jews had lost the war for Germany, fomented a Bolshevik revolution, and systematically undermined the economy. Although Party members showed remarkable understanding of the psychological pathologies that motivated rank-and-file anti-Semites, especially after 1929, few of them believed that the leaders of Judeophobia shared these maladies.

The tying of the vital interests of Socialists and republicans to the struggle against organized hatred of Jews gave rise to the "plot theory," which was instrumental in turning the SPD against racism and immunizing it against anti-Jewish encroachments. But it also weakened somewhat the Socialist front against Judeophobia, for Social Democrats who viewed anti-Semitism as a scheme to undo the republic and emasculate the Socialist Movement also tended to underestimate the sincerity—and thus the great danger—of the Nazi animus toward Jews. Most Social Democrats believed that right-wing leaders who played on bourgeois psychoses in Machiavellian style were too intelligent themselves to believe such racist nonsense. Only a minority thought it likely that Jews would be subject to severe persecution in the event of a Nazi take-over, and none sensed that the Nazis might eventually resort to genocide. The majority view was strengthened by evidence of National Socialist opportunism about Jews; it appeared to Socialist observers that the Hitlerites cynically set aside their racism whenever it seemed to their advantage. Social Democracy's militant opposition to anti-Semitism, therefore, was chiefly the product of concern for its immediate effects rather than for its long-term possibilities. This Socialist underestimation of Judeophobia had far-reaching implications. It restrained Socialists from developing their opposition to anti-Semitism into a major part of their organized campaign against nazism. Except for propaganda against Jew-baiting reprinted in the *Sozialdemokratische Partei-korrespondenz*, virtually no directives from Party leaders instructing functionaries how best to fight anti-Semitism have come to light. Denunciations of Judeophobia consistently played a minor role in SPD propaganda against the Nazis. Hence the politically strongest opponents of nazism and racism, leading spokesmen of the Social Democratic Party, failed adequately to alert fellow Germans that the persecution of Jews was an important Nazi goal. If Socialist doubts about Nazi ideological commitment to anti-Semitism strengthened feelings that the Nazis would become much more conservative and responsible once in power, it is possible that they made it easier for some Germans to support National Socialism. It is also true, of course, that this was not exclusively a Social Democratic failing, for very few people—inside Germany or out—took Nazi anti-Semitism very seriously until long after 1933.

While German Socialists underestimated the potential of Nazi anti-Semitism, few individual Social Democrats expressed anti-Jewish opinions during the Weimar period. The unhappy events of the period 1918–20 drove a number of nationalists and anti-Semites out of the SPD. This was the fate of August Winnig, Emil Kloth, Emil Unger, and other men such as they. Exactly how many of these men there were is not known, but their number was probably not large. Judeophobes who remained within the Party, of whom Eduard David may have been one, never publicly uttered anti-Jewish phrases, and the spokesmen and organs that formed and represented the Party's policies consistently opposed and discouraged anti-Semitism. Resentment in Socialist ranks against Jewish intellectuals and theoreticians, especially those in the SPD's left wing, persisted into the Weimar Republic, but the few known isolated examples of this prejudice suggest that it, too, was of slight importance. Socialist freedom from significant infiltrations of anti-Semitism reflects the success of Party agitation against racism.

It is difficult to estimate how rank-and-file Social Democrats and nonmembers who voted for the SPD viewed the Party's stand on anti-Semitism. What is certain is that no Party supporter could have mistaken the SPD's stand against Judeophobia and that it showed a remarkable relative ability to retain a loyal following in the face of the rise of nazism. In the Reichstag election of March 5, 1933, the Socialists won only 22 percent fewer votes than they had received in May, 1928. They remained Germany's largest party until July, 1932, and were second only to the Nazis until the Party was suppressed in June, 1933. Among the republican parties, only the confessionally based Center Party boasted a better record. In contrast, the Democratic Party lost 78 percent of its votes between 1928 and 1933, and the People's Party virtually ceased to exist after 1930. The more than seven million German voters who remained loyal to the SPD until the bitter end must have ignored, tolerated, or endorsed its opposition to anti-Semitism.

It is even more difficult to assess the SPD's overall impact on German attitudes toward anti-Semitism and the Jews. At the very least, one may suggest that the Socialists' underestimation of Nazi Judeophobia contributed to an assumption, widespread among Jews as well as non-Jews, that the deportation after 1939 of Jewish citizens to the east would lead to resettlement rather than to extermination. And, once the truth was made known, popular support for West Germany's substantial postwar reparations to Jewish victims of Nazi persecution was shaped and promoted by Social Democrats whose aversion for racism and friendship for the Jews had not changed since 1933 and who were not unsuccessful in renewing those sentiments among their countrymen. Indeed, the decrepitude of German anti-Semitism since 1945 owes much to SPD suasion.

The attitudes of the SPD toward Jews were, if anything, even more clear and consistent than was its position on anti-Semitism. Party leaders fostered good relations with the Jewish community by showing interest in its activities and applauding its efforts to combat Judeophobia. Behind-the-scenes cooperation with Jewish self-defense organizations was an important aspect of the Socialist struggle agains racism. The SPD's tendency toward public aloofness from nonmember Jews, especially after 1930, was dictated by fears that Germans would believe Nazi stories of Jewish domination of the Party. It is even possible that Party leaders feared that some rank-and-file Socialists would be lost to the NSDAP should the SPD show too much open friendship for non-Marxist Jews, although no one is known to have raised this point. However, such fears did not significantly diminish Socialist efforts to overcome anti-Semitism.

On the other hand, occasional vitriolic attacks on apathetic or anti-Socialist Jews during Hitler's rise to power continued to manifest German socialism's occasional susceptibility to indirect, anticapitalist Judeophobia. Jews who supported, financed, or apologized for right-wing or bourgeois parties came in for SPD censorship after 1929, when Social Democrats cast blame for the depression and the rise of nazism on the timid and ineffectual policies of the middle-class parties. In the opinion of German Socialists, Jews had a special obligation to renounce capitalism and support Social Democracy simply because the SPD, more than any other party, promised them full social emancipation and an end to anti-Semitism. In cursing those who did not support them, Socialists infrequently contributed to the stereotype of Jews as grasping capitalists who were more interested in profits than in justice. This was also a familiar part of the stronger and broader Nazi stereotype of the Jew. But those Germans who were influenced by SPD propaganda should not have regarded these Socialist attacks as anti-Semitic in any racial sense. Socialist spokesmen repeatedly attributed unsavory "Jewish characteristics" to the pernicious effects of past persecution, and they rejected all personifications of greedy capitalists in general as Jewish profit takers. These Socialist criticisms of Jewish capitalists are better viewed as being part of their general propaganda against capitalism than as being concessions to anti-Semitism. The Party's militant, unambiguous, and unwavering opposition to anti-Semites and their deeds in the Weimar era was far more important. When the SPD was outlawed in 1933 by the Nazi dictatorship, Germany's Jews lost their most important source of organized support in German society.

Bibliography

UNPUBLISHED PAPERS

Most unpublished manuscript collections proved to be of secondary value in this study. Most helpful, however, was the NSDAP Hauptarchiv, on file at the Bundesarchiv in Koblenz and at the Hauptstaatsarchiv in Munich and available on microfilm from the Hoover Institution. It contains a wealth of SPD and Nazi propaganda, press clippings from a variety of sources, and Munich police reports about SPD activities. Similar material is in the Acten des Bayerischen Staats- Ministeriums des Innern in the Bayerisches Hauptstaatsarchiv, Munich. Also useful were the Allgemeiner Deutscher Gewerkschaftsbund Akten in the August Bebel Archive, Kurt Schumacher House, West Berlin. These contain about 120 folders of union correspondence and publications. The Acta der Friedrich-Wilhelms-Universitaet zu Berlin, available at the renamed (Humboldt) university in East Berlin, hold a few thin folders with membership lists and correspondence of Socialist and Jewish student groups.

The Nachlaesse of several leaders of the Weimar SPD are in the International Institute of Social History in Amsterdam. The Bernstein collection of correspondence, manuscripts, and documents is primarily from the period before 1918, as is the extensive Nachlass Karl Kautsky. The Nachlass Paul Hertz contains material almost exclusively from the period of his post-1933 emigration. On the other hand, the papers of Otto Braun, Albert Grzesinski, and Wolfgang Heine pertain primarily to the Weimar period.

The Archive of the Central Committee of the Social Democratic Party of Germany in Bonn has two of the largest and most important collections, those of Carl Severing and Hermann Mueller.

Also there is the Nachlass Wilhelm Dittmann. The papers of Albert Suedekum, including his diary, are on file in the Bundesarchiv, Koblenz. The Nachlass Otto Landsberg, also in the Bundesarchiv, is limited to the years 1921–22. Rudolf Wissell's papers, which deal mostly with the period before 1924, are held by the (West) Berlin Historical Commission. The Nachlass Wilhelm Sollmann is in the Friends Historical Library of Swarthmore College, Swarthmore, Pennsylvania. Most of this collection concerns the period of his emigration, but a few folders pertain to the last years of the Weimar Republic.

PUBLISHED DOCUMENTS

Keil, Heinz, ed. *Dokumentation ueber die Verfolgung der juedischen Buerger von Ulm/Donau.* Ulm: Hergestellt im Auftrage der Stadt Ulm, 1961.

Michaelis, Herbert, Ernst Schraepler, and Guenter Scheel, eds. *Ursachen und Folgen: Vom deutschen Zusammenbruch 1918 und 1945 bis zur staatlichen Neuordnung Deutschlands in der Gegenwart.* 12 vols. Berlin: Dokumenten-Verlag Dr. Herbert Wendler and Co., [1959–].

Sitzungsberichte des preussischen Landtags. 1921, 1922, 1930.

Sozialdemokratische Partei Deutschlands. *Protokoll: Sozialdemokratischer Parteitag, Magdeburg 1929.* Berlin: J. H. W. Dietz Nachfolger, 1929.

————. *Protokoll: Sozialdemokratischer Parteitag, Leipzig 1931.* Berlin: J. H. W. Dietz Nachfolger, [1931].

Statistisches Jahrbuch fuer das deutsche Reich: 1928, 1929, 1930, 1931, 1932, 1933, 1934. Berlin: Verlag von Reimar Hobbing, 1929–35.

Treue, Wolfgang, ed. *Deutsche Parteiprogramme 1861–1956.* Goettingen: Musterschmidt Verlag, 1956.

Verhandlungen des Bayerischen Landtags: Stenographische Berichte. 1920–21, 1928–33.

Verhandlungen des Reichstags: Stenographische Berichte. 1928–33. Berlin: Druck und Verlag der Reichsdruckerei, 1928–33.

NEWSPAPERS AND PERIODICALS

Der Abend. January, 1928–February, 1933. Berlin. The evening editions of *Vorwaerts.*

Abwehr-Blaetter: Mitteilungen aus dem Verein zur Abwehr des Antisemitismus. Vols. XXXVI–XLI, 1926–31. Berlin.

Die Buecherwarte: Zeitschrift fuer sozialistische Buchkritik. 1929–33. Berlin. A minor publication of the *Reichsausschuss fuer sozialistische Bildungsarbeit* (National Committee for Socialist Education).

Central-Verein Zeitung: Blaetter fuer Deutschtum und Judentum. Vols. VII–XI, 1928–32. Berlin. The official CV weekly.

Fraenkische Tagespost. January, 1930–July, 1932. Nuremberg/ Fuerth.

Freie Volkswacht: Blatt fuer die schaffenden Staende des Inn-, Chiem- und Rupertigaues. Amtsblatt fuer die Gemeinde Freilassing. October, 1929–September, 1931.

Das freie Wort. 1929–33. Berlin. This "Social Democratic Discussion Forum" was edited by Ernst Heilmann, who was Jewish.

Die Gesellschaft. Vols. I–X, 1924–33. Berlin. Successor to *Die neue Zeit* as the official SPD theoretical monthly.

Gewerkschafts-Zeitung. Vols. XXXVIII–XLIII, 1928–33. Berlin. Official weekly of the ADGB.

Hamburger Echo. January, 1930–March, 1933.

Jungsozialistische Blaetter. Vols. VII, VIII, and X, 1928, 1929, 1931. Berlin. Official monthly of the "Young Socialists."

Der Klassenkampf. Vols. I–V, 1927–31. Berlin. Semi-monthly organ of the left-wing opposition in the SPD.

Leipziger Volkszeitung. January, 1930–March, 1933.

Neue Blaetter fuer den Sozialismus. Vols. I–IV, 1930–33. Potsdam. An official journal of young, right-wing Socialist intellectuals, edited by Eduard Heilmann, Paul Tillich, and Fritz Klatt.

Die neue Zeit. Vols. XXXVII–XLI, 1919–23. Stuttgart. The official SPD theoretical journal.

Schulfront: Organ der sozialistischen Hoeheren Schueler. Vols. I–II, 1929–30. Berlin.

Sozialistische Bildung, 1929–33. Berlin. Official monthly of the *Reichsausschuss fuer sozialistische Bildungsarbeit.*

Sozialistische Erziehung. 1929–32. Berlin. Monthly organ of Social Democratic elementary and secondary teachers.

Sozialistische Monatshefte. Vols. XXV–XXXIX, 1919–33. Berlin. Widely read unofficial journal of the SPD's right wing, edited by Jewish Social Democrat Joseph Bloch.

Sozialdemokratische Partei-Korrespondenz. 1923–33. Berlin. The official publication for SPD functionaries.

Vorwaerts. January, 1919–February, 1933.

Der wahre Jacob. Vols. L–LII, 1929–31. Berlin.

DIARIES, MEMOIRS, AND CORRESPONDENCE

Aretin, Erwein von. *Krone und Ketten: Erinnerungen eines bayerischen Edelmannes.* Munich: Sueddeutscher Verlag, 1955.

Bernstein, Eduard. *Entwicklungsgang eines Sozialisten.* Leipzig: Felix Meiner Verlag, 1930.

Boree, Karl Friedrich. *Semiten und Antisemiten.* Frankfurt on the Main: Europaeische Verlags-Anstalt, 1960.

Braun, Otto. *Von Weimar zu Hitler.* Hamburg: Hammonia Norddeutsche Verlagsanstalt, 1949.

Buchwitz, Otto. *Fuenfzig Jahre Funktionaer der deutschen Arbeiterbewegung.* Berlin: Dietz Verlag, 1949.

Gerlach, Hellmut von. *Von Rechts nach Links.* Zuerich: Europa-Verlag, 1937.

Grzesinski, Albert C. *Inside Germany.* Translated by Alexander Lipchitz. New York: E. P. Dutton and Co., 1939.

Heimann, Hugo. *Vom taetigen Leben.* Berlin: Arani Verlag, 1949.

Hirsch, Paul. *Der Weg der Sozialdemokratie zur Macht in Preussen.* Berlin: Otto Stollberg Verlag, 1929.

Hitler, Adolf. *Mein Kampf.* Translated by Ralph Manheim. Boston: Houghton Mifflin Co., 1943.

Hoegner, Wilhelm. *Der schwierige Aussenseiter: Erinnerungen eines Abgeordneten, Emigranten und Minister-praesidenten.* Munich: Isar Verlag, 1959.

Kaisen, Wilhelm. *Meine Arbeit, mein Leben.* Munich: Paul List Verlag, 1967.

Kampffmeyer, Paul, ed. *Friedrich Ebert: Schriften, Aufzeichnungen, Reden.* 2 vols. Dresden: Carl Reissner Verlag, 1926.

Keil, Wilhelm. *Erlebnisse eines Sozialdemokraten.* 2 vols. Stuttgart: Deutsche Verlags-Anstalt, 1947–48.

Kloth, Emil. *Einkehr: Betrachtungen eines sozialdemokratischen Gewerkschaftlers ueber die Politik der deutschen Sozialdemokratie.* Munich: Deutscher Volks-Verlag, 1920.

Leber, Julius. *Ein Mann geht seinen Weg: Schriften, Reden und Briefe von Julius Leber.* Berlin: Mosaik Verlag, 1952.

Loebe, Paul. *Der Weg war lang.* Berlin: Verlags G. M. B. H., 1954.

Loewenstein, Prince Hubertus zu. *Conquest of the Past: An Autobiography.* Boston: Houghton Mifflin Co., 1938.

Matthias, Erich, and Susanne Miller, eds. *Das Kriegstagesbuch des Reichstagsabgeordneten Eduard David 1914 bis 1918.* Duesseldorf: Droste Verlag, 1966.

Mayer, Gustav. *Erinnerungen.* Zuerich: Europa-Verlag, 1949.

Mueller-Franken, Hermann. *Die November Revolution: Erinnerungen.* Berlin: Verlag der Buecherkreis G. M. B. H., 1931.

Mueller, Richard. *Vom Kaiserreich zur Republik.* 2 vols. Vienna: Malik Verlag, 1925.

Niekisch, Ernst. *Gewagtes Leben: Begegnungen und Begebnisse.* Cologne and Berlin: Kiepenheuer und Witsch, 1958.

Noske, Gustav. *Erlebtes aus Aufstieg und Niedergang einer Demokratie.* Offenbach on the Main: Bollwerk Verlag, 1947.

Puender, Hermann. *Politik in der Reichskanzlei, Aufzeichnungen aus den Jahren 1929–1932.* Stuttgart: Deutsche Verlags-Anstalt, 1961.

Scheidemann, Philipp. *The Making of the New Germany.* 2 vols. Translated by J. E. Michell. New York: D. Appleton and Co., 1929.

Seger, Gerhart. *A Nation Terrorized.* Chicago: Reilly and Lee Co., 1935.

Sender, Toni. *The Autobiography of a German Rebel.* New York: Vanguard Press, 1939.

Severing, Carl. *Mein Lebensweg.* 2 vols. Cologne: Greven Verlag, 1950.

Stampfer, Friedrich. *Erfahrungen und Erkenntnisse: Aufzeichnungen aus meinem Leben.* Cologne: Verlag fuer Politik und Wirtschaft, 1957.

Unger-Winkelried, Emil. *Von Bebel zu Hitler: Vom Zukunftsstaat zum Dritten Reich. Aus dem Leben eines sozialdemokratischen Arbeiters.* Berlin: Verlag Deutsche Kultur, 1934.

Winnig, August. *Heimkehr.* Hamburg: Hanseatische Verlagsanstalt, 1935.

————. *Der weite Weg.* Hamburg: Hanseatische Verlagsanstalt, 1932.

Wolff, Theodor. *Through Two Decades.* Translated by E. W. Dickes. London: William Heinemann, 1936.

SPD PUBLICATIONS

Antisemitismus und Sozialdemokratie. N.p., [1920].

Auer, Erhard. *Sozialdemokratie und Antisemitismus: Rede des Abgeordneten E. Auer, ehemaliger Minister des Innern, am 15. Dezember 1920 im grossen Saale des Muenchener Kindl-Kellers.* Munich: G. Birk and Co., n.d.

Brammer, Karl. *Das Gesicht der Reaktion 1918–1919.* Berlin: Der Firn Verlag, 1919.

Breitscheid, Rudolf, and Hermann Mueller. *Gegen den Rechtskurs.* Berlin: Vorwaerts Buchdruckerei, 1925.

Der Drache Marxismus. Bernburg: Bernburger Buchdruckereigesellschaft, 1930.

Flatau, Erich. *Zum "Sklarek Skandal."* Berlin: Vorwaerts Buchdruckerei, 1929.

Graf, Georg Engelbert. *Die faschistische Gefahr.* Leipzig: SPD Gross Leipzig, n.d.

Die vom Hakenkreuz: Hitler und Konsorten. Berlin: Vorwaerts Buchdruckerei, 1929.

Handbuch fuer sozialdemokratische Waehler. Berlin: Buchhandlung Vorwaerts, 1924.

Heilmann, Ernst. *Die Sozialdemokratie in Preussen.* Berlin: Vorwaerts Buchdruckerei, 1928.

Hirsch, Paul. *Fuer Republik und Demokratie: Gegen Reaktion und Terror!* Berlin: Buchhandlung Vorwaerts, 1919.

[Hirschberg, Alfred.] *Das wahre Gesicht des Nationalsozialismus.* Magdeburg: W. Pfannkuch and Co., [1929].

Jahrbuch der deutschen Sozialdemokratie fuer das Jahr 1927; 1928; 1929; 1930; 1931. Berlin: Vorwaerts Buchdruckerei, 1928–32.

Kampf dem Hakenkreuz: Rededisposition ueber die faschistische Gefahr. Berlin: no publisher indicated, [1930].

Kampffmeyer, Paul. *Der Faschismus in Deutschland.* Berlin: J. H. W. Dietz, 1923.

_____. *Juedischer Marxismus.* Berlin: J. H. W. Dietz, 1923.

_____. *Der Nationalsozialismus und seine Goenner.* Berlin: J. H. W. Dietz, 1924.

_____. *Wer ist schuld an Not und Elend?* Berlin: Vorwaerts Buchdruckerei, 1922.

Kautsky, Karl. *Die materialistische Geschichtsauffassung.* 2 vols. 2nd ed. rev. Berlin: J. H. W. Dietz, 1929.

_____. *Rasse und Judentum.* 2nd ed. rev. Stuttgart: J. H. W. Dietz, 1921. (English translation: *Are the Jews a Race?* New York: International Publishers, 1926.)

Klotz, Helmut. *Hitlers Sozialismus.* Berlin: Trommler Verlag, 1931.

Kultur und Erziehung unter dem Hakenkreuz: Referenten Material. Berlin: Volksblatt-Druckerei, 1931.

Kuttner, Erich. *Pathologie des Rassenantisemitismus.* Berlin: Philo-Verlag, 1930.

_____, and Franz Kluhs. *Die politischen Parteien in Deutschland.* Berlin: Reichsausschuss fuer sozialistische Bildungsarbeit, [ca. 1924].

Materialsammlung gegen die Nationalsozialisten: Fuer Redner und Funktionaere. Goerlitz: Arbeiter-Druckerei, 1930.

Mierendorff, Carlo. *Arisches Kaisertum oder Judenrepublik?* Berlin: Vorwaerts Buchdruckerei, [ca. 1924].

Die Nazi-Fibel: Eine Handvoll Naziluegen und ihre Widerlegung. Darmstadt: Genossenschaftsdruckerei, [1930].

Pflueger, Paul. *Der Sozialismus der israelitischen Propheten*. Berlin: Buchhandlung Vorwaerts Paul Singer, [ca. 1920].

Referentenmaterial zur hessischen Landtagswahl am 19. Juni 1932. N.p., n.d.

Schlucks, Adolf. *Kampf dem Hakenkreuz*. Berlin: J. H. W. Dietz, 1930.

Sender, Toni. *Grosse Koalition?* Frankfurt on the Main: Union Druckerei und Verlagsanstalt, 1923.

SS Diktator. Halle on the Saale: Hallesche Druckerei-Gesellschaft, 1931.

Vogel, Hans. *Faschismus — Nationalsozialismus*. Berlin: Reichsausschuss fuer sozialistische Bildungsarbeit, 1930.

Was muss das schaffende Volk vom politischen, wirtschaftlichen, religioesen Juden- und Rassenhass des reaktionaeren Faschismus wissen? Fuer Redner und Funktionaere herausgegeben von der Sozialdemokratischen Partei Deutschlands, Ortsverein Hannover. Hanover: E. A. H. Meister and Co., [1924].

OTHER PRIMARY SOURCES

Bahr, Hermann, and others, eds. *Der Jud ist Schuld . . . ? Diskussionsbuch ueber die Judenfrage*. Basel: Zinnen Verlag, 1932.

Bernstein, Eduard. *Die Aufgaben der Juden im Weltkriege*. Berlin: Erich Reiss Verlag, 1917.

Blos, Wilhelm. *Von der Monarchie zum Volksstaat*. Stuttgart: Bergers Literarisches Buero und Verlagsanstalt, 1923.

Blueher, Hans. *Deutsches Reich, Judentum und Sozialismus: Eine Rede an die Freideutsche Jugend*. Prien: Anthropos Verlag, 1920.

Braun, Heinz. *Am Justizmord vorbei: Der Fall Koelling-Haas*. Magdeburg: W. Pfannkuch and Co., 1928.

Daedelow, Walter. *Michel wach auf!* Berlin: Otto Wilhelm Wolff, [1931].

Ebert, Paul. *Der internationale Karl Marx*. Hamburg: Deutschvoelkische Verlagsanstalt, 1920.

Fendrich, Anton. *Der Judenhass und der Sozialismus*. Freiburg in Breisgau: Ernst Guenther Verlag, 1920.

Grimpen, Alb. *Judentum und Sozialdemokratie.* Leipzig: Otto Maier, G. M. B. H., 1919.

Haenisch, Konrad. *Lassalle: Mensch und Politiker.* Berlin: Franz Schneider Verlag, 1923.

Iltis, Hugo. *Volkstuemliche Rassenkunde.* Jena: Urania Verlagsgesellschaft, 1930.

Kloth, Emil. *Dittmanns Enthuellungsschwindel: Nach Eingestaendnissen seiner Genossen.* Berlin: Brunnen-Verlag, 1926.

————. *Sozialdemokratie und Judentum.* Munich: Deutscher Volks-Verlag, 1920.

Krueger, Oskar. *Proletariat: Ein deutsches Arbeiter-Manifest.* Berlin: Brunnen-Verlag, 1928.

Kundgebung fuer das Werk des Hilfsvereins der deutschen Juden. Berlin: Siegfried Scholem, 1930.

Reichstags-Handbuch, IV. Wahlperiode 1928. Berlin: Buero des Reichstags, 1928.

Reichstags-Handbuch, VII. Wahlperiode 1932. Berlin: Buero des Reichstags, 1933.

Schweriner, Arthur. *Von Tillesen bis Schmelzer.* Berlin: Verlag Alfred Buchholz, 1928.

Tillich, Paul. *Die sozialistische Entscheidung.* Offenbach on the Main: Bollwerk-Verlag Karl Drott, 1948.

Weiss, Christoph. *Vom Juden-Sozialismus geheilt!* Lorch: Karl Rohm Verlag, 1920.

Winnig, August. *Europa: Gedanken eines Deutschen.* Berlin: Eckart Verlag, 1937.

————. *Das Reich als Republik 1918–1928.* Stuttgart and Berlin: J. G. Cotta'sche Buchhandlung, 1929.

————. *Vom Proletariat zum Arbeitertum.* 2nd ed. Hamburg, Berlin, and Leipzig: Hanseatische Verlagsanstalt, 1930.

GENERAL SECONDARY SOURCES

Abrahams, Israel. *Jewish Life in the Middle Ages.* New York: Meridian Books, 1958.

Arendt, Hannah. *The Origins of Totalitarianism.* New York: Harcourt, Brace and World, 1966.

Baron, Salo W. *A Social and Religious History of the Jews*. 12 vols. New York: Columbia University Press, 1952–67.

Beer, Max. *Fifty Years of International Socialism*. London: George Allen and Unwin, 1935.

Bergstraesser, Ludwig. *Geschichte der politischen Parteien in Deutschland*. 9th ed., rev. Munich: Isar Verlag Dr. Guenter Olzog, 1955.

Bernstein, F. *Der Antisemitismus als Gruppenerscheinung: Versuch einer Soziologie des Judenhasses*. Berlin: Juedischer Verlag, 1926.

Bronder, Dietrich. *Bevor Hitler kam*. Hanover: Hans Pfeiffer Verlag, 1964.

Butler, Rohan D'O. *The Roots of National Socialism*. New York: E. P. Dutton and Co., 1942.

Chakotin, Serge. *The Rape of the Masses: The Psychology of Totalitarian Political Propaganda*. London: George Routledge and Sons, 1940.

Clark, Robert Thomson. *The Fall of the German Republic: A Political Study*. London: George Allen and Unwin, 1935.

Cole, George Douglas Howard. *A History of Socialist Thought*. 5 vols. New York: St. Martin's Press, 1953–60.

Elbogen, Esmar. *A Century of Jewish Life*. Philadelphia: Jewish Publication Society of America, 1944.

Eschenburg, Theodor. *Die improvisierte Demokratie: Gesammelte Aufsaetze zur Weimarer Republik*. Munich: R. Piper and Co., 1963.

Fraser, Lindley. *Germany between Two Wars: A Study of Propaganda and War-Guilt*. New York: Oxford University Press, 1945.

Friedensburg, Ferdinand. *Die Weimarer Republik*. Berlin: Carl Habel Verlagsbuchhandlung, 1946.

Halperin, S. William. *Germany Tried Democracy: A Political History of the Reich from 1918 to 1933*. New York: W. W. Norton and Co., 1946.

Hoegner, Wilhelm. *Die verratene Republik: Geschichte der deutschen Gegenrevolution*. Munich: Isar Verlag, 1958.

Kampmann, Wanda. *Deutsche und Juden: Studien zur Geschichte des deutschen Judentums.* Heidelberg: Verlag Lambert Schnei-der, 1963.

Kaznelson, Siegmund, ed. *Juden im deutschen Kulturbereich.* Ber-lin: Juedischer Verlag, 1959.

Landauer, Carl. *European Socialism: A History of Ideas and Move-ments.* 2 vols. Berkeley and Los Angeles: University of Cali-fornia Press, 1959.

Long, Emil J. *Two Thousand Years: A History of Anti-Semitism.* New York: Exposition Press, 1953.

Lowenthal, Marvin. *The Jews of Germany.* New York: Longmans, Green and Co., 1936.

Marcus, Jacob R. *The Jew in the Medieval World: A Source Book.* Cincinnati: The Union of American Hebrew Congregations, 1938.

————. *The Rise and Destiny of the German Jew.* Cincinnati: The Union of American Hebrew Congregations, 1934.

Mosse, George L. *The Crisis of German Ideology: Intellectual Origins of the Third Reich.* New York: Grosset and Dunlap, 1964.

Neumann, Sigmund. *Die deutschen Parteien: Wesen und Wandel nach dem Kriege.* Berlin: Junker und Duennhaupt Verlag, 1932.

Osterroth, Franz. *Biographisches Lexikon des Sozialismus.* Vol. I: *Verstorbene Persoenlichkeiten.* Hanover: J. H. W. Dietz Nachf., 1960.

Parkes, James. *Antisemitism.* Chicago: Quadrangle Books, 1963.

Pinson, Koppel S., ed. *Essays on Anti-Semitism.* New York: Con-ference on Jewish Relations, 1946.

————. *Modern Germany: Its History and Civilization.* New York: Macmillan Co., 1954.

Quigley, Hugh, and Robert Thomson Clark. *Republican Ger-many: A Political and Economic Study.* New York: Dodd, Mead and Co., 1928.

Rosenberg, Arthur. *A History of the Weimar Republic.* Trans-lated by Ian F. D. Morrow and I. M. Sieveking. London: Me-thuen and Co., 1936.

Ruppin, Arthur. *The Jews in the Modern World.* London: Mac-millan and Co., 1934.

———. *Soziologie der Juden.* 2 vols. Berlin: Juedischer Verlag, 1930–31.

Sachar, Abram Leon. *A History of the Jews.* New York: World Publishing Co., 1958.

Scheele, Godfrey. *The Weimar Republic: Overture to the Third Reich.* London: Faber and Faber, n.d.

Schwarz, Stefan. *Die Juden in Bayern im Wandel der Zeiten.* Munich and Vienna: Guenter Olzog Verlag, 1963.

Shirer, William L. *The Rise and Fall of the Third Reich: A History of Nazi Germany.* New York: Simon and Schuster, 1960.

Stampfer, Friedrich. *Die vierzehn Jahre der ersten deutschen Republik.* Karlsbad: Verlagsanstalt Graphia, 1936.

Theimer, Walter. *Von Bebel zu Ollenhauer.* Munich: Lehnen Verlag, 1957.

Tramer, Hans, ed. *In zwei Welten: Siegfried Moses zum fuenfundsiebzigsten Geburtstag.* Tel Aviv: Verlag Bitaon, 1962.

Ulbricht, Walter, and others. *Geschichte der deutschen Arbeiterbewegung.* 8 vols. Berlin: Dietz Verlag, 1966.

Vermeil, Edmond. *Germany in the Twentieth Century.* New York: Frederick A. Praeger, 1956.

Viereck, Peter. *Metapolitics: The Roots of the Nazi Mind.* New York: Capricorn Books, 1965.

Vogt, Hannah. *The Burden of Guilt: A Short History of Germany, 1914–1945.* Translated by Herbert Strauss. New York: Oxford University Press, 1964.

Wirth, Louis. *The Ghetto.* Chicago: The University of Chicago Press, 1928.

MONOGRAPHS AND SPECIAL STUDIES

Abel, Theodore. *Why Hitler Came into Power.* New York: Prentice-Hall, 1938.

Adler, H. G. *Die Juden in Deutschland. Von der Aufklaerung bis zum Nationalsozialismus.* Munich: Koesel Verlag, 1960.

Adler-Rudel, S. *Ostjuden in Deutschland 1880–1940.* Tuebingen: J. C. B. Mohr, 1959.

Allen, William Sheridan. *The Nazi Seizure of Power: The Ex-

perience of a Single German Town, 1930–1935. Chicago: Quadrangle Books, 1965.

Anderson, Evelyn. *Hammer or Anvil: The Story of the German Working-Class Movement.* London: Victor Gollancz, 1945.

Asaria, Zvi, ed. *Die Juden in Koeln von den aeltesten Zeiten bis zur Gegenwart.* Cologne: Verlag J. P. Bachem, 1959.

Bausch, Hans. *Der Rundfunk im politischen Kraeftespiel der Weimarer Republik.* Tuebingen: J. C. B. Mohr, 1956.

Beck, Earl R. *The Death of the Prussian Republic.* Tallahassee: Florida State University, 1959.

Becker, Howard. *German Youth: Bond or Free?* London: Kegan, Paul, Trench, Trubner and Co., 1946.

Berlau, Abraham L. *The German Social Democratic Party, 1914–1921.* New York: Columbia University Press, 1949.

Bevan, Edwyn. *German Social Democracy During the War.* London: George Allen and Unwin, 1918.

Bracher, Karl Dietrich. *Die Aufloesung der Weimarer Republik.* 2nd ed., rev. Stuttgart and Duesseldorf: Ring-Verlag, 1957.

Brecht, Arnold. *Prelude to Silence: The End of the German Republic.* New York: William Morrow and Co., 1933.

Bruck, W. F. *Social and Economic History of Germany from William II to Hitler, 1888–1938.* Cardiff: Oxford University Press, 1938.

Cohn, Norman. *Warrant for Genocide: The Myth of the Jewish World-Conspiracy and "The Protocols of the Elders of Zion."* New York: Harper and Row, 1966.

Coper, Rudolf. *Failure of a Revolution: Germany in 1918–1919.* Cambridge: At the University Press, 1955.

Dickinson, John K. *German and Jew.* Chicago: Quadrangle Books, 1967.

Drechsler, Hanno. *Die Sozialistische Arbeiterpartei Deutschlands (SAPD). Ein Beitrag zur Geschichte der deutschen Arbeiterbewegung am Ende der Weimarer Republik.* Meisenheim on the Glan: Verlag Anton Hain, 1965.

Edinger, Lewis J. *German Exile Politics: The Social Democratic Executive Committee in the Nazi Era.* Berkeley and Los Angeles: University of California Press, 1956.

Fischer, Ruth. *Stalin and German Communism: A Study in the Origins of the State Party.* Cambridge, Mass.: Harvard University Press, 1948.

Flechtheim, Ossip K. *Die Kommunistische Partei Deutschlands in der Weimarer Republik.* Offenbach on the Main: Bollwerk-Verlag, 1948.

Fuchs, Eduard. *Die Juden in der Karikatur. Ein Beitrag zur Kulturgeschichte.* Munich: Albert Langen Verlag, 1921.

Gay, Peter. *The Dilemma of Democratic Socialism: Eduard Bernstein's Challenge to Marx.* New York: Columbia University Press, 1952.

Geyer, Curt. *Macht und Masse: Von Bismarck zu Hitler.* Hanover: Verlag Das andere Deutschland, 1948.

Hamburger, Ernest. *Juden im oeffentlichen Leben Deutschlands: Regierungsmitglieder, Beamte und Parlamentarier in der monarchischen Zeit 1848–1918.* Tuebingen: J. C. B. Mohr, 1968.

Heberle, Rudolf. *Landbevoelkerung und Nationalsozialismus: Eine soziologische Untersuchung der politischen willensbildung in Schleswig-Holstein 1918–1932.* Stuttgart: Deutsche Verlags-Anstalt, 1963.

Heidegger, Hermann. *Die deutsche Sozialdemokratie und der nationale Staat 1870–1920.* Goettingen: Musterschmidt-Verlag, 1956.

Hertzman, Lewis. *DNVP, Right-Wing Opposition in the Weimar Republic, 1918–1924.* Lincoln, Neb.: University of Nebraska Press, 1963.

Hilberg, Raul. *The Destruction of the European Jews.* Chicago: Quadrangle Books, 1961.

Hoover, Calvin B. *Germany Enters the Third Reich.* New York: Macmillan Co., 1933.

Hunt, Richard N. *German Social Democracy, 1918–1933.* New Haven and London: Yale University Press, 1963.

Jacob, Herbert. *German Administration since Bismarck.* New Haven and London: Yale University Press, 1963.

Die Juden in Deutschland. Munich: Verlag Franz Eher Nachf., 1939.

Kantorowicz, Ludwig. *Die sozialdemokratische Presse Deutschlands.* Tuebingen: J. C. B. Mohr, 1922.

Kaufmann, Walter. *Monarchism in the Weimar Republic.* New York: Bookman Associates, 1953.

Kisch, Guido. *The Jews in Medieval Germany: A Study of their Legal and Social Status.* Chicago: University of Chicago Press, 1948.

Klemperer, Klemens von. *Germany's New Conservatism: Its History and Dilemma in the Twentieth Century.* Princeton: Princeton University Press, 1957.

Koszyk, Kurt. *Zwischen Kaiserreich und Diktatur: Die sozialdemokratische Presse von 1914–1933.* Heidelberg: Quelle and Meyer, 1958.

Kupisch, Karl. *Das Jahrhundert des Sozialismus und die Kirche.* Berlin: Kaethe Vogt Verlag, 1958.

Lamm, Hans, ed. *Von Juden in Muenchen: Ein Gedenkbuch.* Munich: Ner-Tamid-Verlag, 1958.

Lidtke, Vernon L. *The Outlawed Party: Social Democracy in Germany, 1878–1890.* Princeton: Princeton University Press, 1966.

Lutz, Ralph Haswell, ed. *The German Revolution, 1918–1919.* Palo Alto, Calif.: Stanford University Press, 1922.

Marburg, Fritz. *Der Antisemitismus in der Deutschen Republik.* Vienna: Kommissions-Verlag, Josef Brenner, 1931.

Maser, Werner. *Die Fruehgeschichte der NSDAP: Hitlers Weg bis 1924.* Frankfurt on the Main: Athenaeum Verlag, 1965.

Massing, Paul W. *Rehearsal for Destruction: A Study of Political Anti-Semitism in Imperial Germany.* New York: Harper and Brothers, 1949.

Matthias, Erich, and Rudolf Morsey, eds. *Das Ende der Parteien 1933.* Duesseldorf: Droste Verlag, 1960.

Mehring, Franz. *Geschichte der deutschen Sozialdemokratie.* 4 vols. Stuttgart: J. H. W. Dietz, 1919.

Mitchell, Allen. *Revolution in Bavaria, 1918–1919: The Eisner Regime and the Soviet Republic.* Princeton: Princeton University Press, 1965.

Mohler, Armin. *Die konservative Revolution in Deutschland 1918–1932.* Stuttgart: Friedrich Vorwerk Verlag, 1950.

Mosse, Werner E., ed. *Entscheidungsjahr 1932: Zur Judenfrage in der Endphase der Weimarer Republik.* Tuebingen: J. C. B. Mohr, 1965.

Mowrer, Edgar Ansel. *Germany Puts the Clock Back.* New York: William Morrow and Co., 1933.

Opel, Fritz. *Der deutsche Metallarbeiterverband waehrend des ersten Weltkrieges und der Revolution.* Hanover: Norddeutsche Verlagsanstalt, 1957.

Osterroth, Franz. *100 Jahre Sozialdemokratie in Schleswig-Holstein.* Kiel: Haase-Druck, [1963].

Paucker, Arnold. *Der juedische Abwehrkampf gegen Antisemitismus und Nationalsozialismus in den letzten Jahren der Weimarer Republik.* Hamburg: Leibnitz-Verlag, 1968.

Pohle, Heinz. *Der Rundfunk als Instrument der Politik: Zur Geschichte des deutschen Rundfunks von 1923/38.* Hamburg: Verlag Hans Bredow Institut, 1955.

Pulzer, Peter G. J. *The Rise of Political Anti-Semitism in Germany and Austria.* New York: John Wiley and Sons, 1964.

Reichmann, Eva G. *Hostages of Civilisation: The Social Sources of National Socialist Anti-Semitism.* London: Victor Gollancz, 1950.

Rohe, Karl. *Das Reichsbanner Schwartz Rot Gold: Ein Beitrag zur Geschichte und Struktur der politischen Kampfverbaende zur Zeit der Weimarer Republik.* Duesseldorf: Droste Verlag, 1966.

Roloff, Ernst August. *Buergertum und Nationalsozialismus 1930–1933: Braunschweigs Weg ins dritte Reich.* Hanover: Verlag fuer Literatur und Zeitgeschehen, 1961.

Runes, Dagobert D. *A World Without Jews.* New York: Philosophical Library, 1959.

Schay, Rudolf. *Juden in der deutschen Politik.* Berlin: Welt Verlag, 1929.

Schorske, Carl. *German Social Democracy, 1905–1917: The Development of the Great Schism.* Cambridge, Mass.: Harvard University Press, 1955.

Silberner, Edmund. *Sozialisten zur Judenfrage.* Translated by Arthur Mandel. Berlin: Colloquium Verlag, 1962.

Schulz, F. O. H. *Jude und Arbeiter: Ein Abschnitt aus der Tragoedie des deutschen Volkes.* 3rd ed. Berlin: Nibelungen Verlag, 1944.

Sontheimer, Kurt. *Antidemokratisches Denken in der Weimarer Republik: Die politischen Ideen des deutschen Nationalismus zwischen 1918–1933.* Munich: Nymphenburger Verlagshandlung, 1962.

Stern, Fritz. *The Politics of Cultural Despair.* Berkeley and Los Angeles: University of California Press, 1961.

Sturmthal, Adolf. *The Tragedy of European Labor, 1918–1939.* New York: Columbia University Press, 1943.

Tenenbaum, Joseph. *Race and Reich: The Story of an Epoch.* New York: Twayne Publishers, 1956.

Toury, Jacob. *Die politischen Orientierungen der Juden in Deutschland. Von Jena bis Weimar.* Tuebingen: J. C. B. Mohr, 1966.

Turner, Henry Ashby, Jr. *Stresemann and the Politics of the Weimar Republik.* Princeton: Princeton University Press, 1963.

Waite, Robert G. L. *Vanguard of Nazism: The Free Corps Movement in Postwar Germany, 1918–1923.* Cambridge, Mass.: Harvard University Press, 1952.

Wolbe, Eugen. *Geschichte der Juden in Berlin und in der Mark Brandenburg.* Berlin: Verlag Kedem, 1937.

BIOGRAPHIES

Bullock, Alan. *Hitler: A Study in Tyranny.* 2nd ed., rev. New York: Harper and Row, 1962.

Edinger, Lewis J. *Kurt Schumacher: A Study in Personality and Political Behavior.* Stanford, Calif.: Stanford University Press, 1965.

Haase, Ernst. *Hugo Haase: Sein Leben und Wirken.* Berlin: J. J. Ottens Verlag, n.d.

Haschke, Georg, and Norbert Toennies. *Friedrich Ebert: Ein Leben fuer Deutschland.* Hamburg: Antares Verlag G. Hermann and Co., 1961.

Heiber, Helmut. *Joseph Goebbels.* Berlin: Colloquium Verlag, 1962.

Heiden, Konrad. *Der Fuehrer: Hitler's Rise to Power.* Boston: Houghton Mifflin Co., 1944.

––––––. *Hitler: A Biography.* New York: Alfred A. Knopf, 1936.

Kessler, Harry. *Walther Rathenau: His Life and Work.* Translated by W. D. Robson-Scott and Lawrence Hyde. New York: Harcourt, Brace and Co., 1944.

Kotowski, Georg. *Friedrich Ebert: Eine politische Biographie.* Vol. I. Wiesbaden: Franz Steiner Verlag, 1963.

Kuttner, Erich. *Otto Braun.* Leipzig: R. Kittler Verlag, 1932.

Peters, Max. *Friedrich Ebert: Erster Praesident der deutschen Republik.* 2nd ed., rev. Berlin: Arani Verlag, 1954.

Siemsen, August. *Anna Siemsen: Leben und Werk.* Hamburg: Europaeische Verlagsanstalt, 1951.

Wheeler-Bennett, John W. *Wooden Titan: Hindenburg in Twenty Years of German History, 1914–1934.* New York: William Morrow and Co., 1936.

Zeman, Z. A. B., and W. B. Scharlau. *The Merchant of Revolution: The Life of Alexander Israel Helphand (Parvus), 1867–1924.* London: Oxford University Press, 1965.

PERIODICAL ARTICLES

Avineri, Shlomo. "Marx and Jewish Emancipation," *Journal of the History of Ideas,* XXV (July / September, 1964), 445–50.

Baumgardt, David. "Looking Back on a German University Career," *Leo Baeck Institute Year Book,* X (1965), 239–65.

Bein, Alexander. "Der moderne Antisemitismus und seine Bedeutung fuer die Judenfrage," *Vierteljahrshefte fuer Zeitgeschichte,* VI (October, 1958), 340–60.

Braunthal, Gerard. "The German Free Trade Unions During the Rise of Nazism." *Journal of Central European Affairs,* XV (January, 1956), 339–53.

Epstein, Klaus. "The End of the German Parties in 1933," *Journal of Central European Affairs,* XXIII (April, 1963), 52–76.

Feder, Ernst. "Paul Nathan, the Man and his Work," *Leo Baeck Institute Year Book,* II (1958), 60–80.

Hirsch, Felix E. "William Sollmann, Wanderer Between Two Worlds," *South Atlantic Quarterly*, LII (April, 1953), 207–27.

Landauer, Carl. "The Bavarian Problem in the Weimar Republic," *Journal of Modern History*, XVI (June–September, 1944), 93–115, 205–23.

Maehl, William Harvey. "Recent Literature on the German Socialists, 1891–1932," *Journal of Modern History*, XXXIII (September, 1961), 292–306.

Preuss, Ulf. "Von der Arbeiterpartei zur Volkspartei," *Die neue Gesellschaft*, XIII (September / October, 1966), 371–85.

Silberner, Edmund. "The Anti-Semitic Tradition in Modern Socialism," *Scripta Hierosolymitana*, No. 3 (1956), 378–96.

————. "German Social Democracy and the Jewish Problem Prior to World War I," *Historia Judaica*, XV (April, 1953), 3–48.

————. "Was Marx an Anti-Semite?" *Historia Judaica*, XI (April, 1949), 3–52.

Snell, John L. "Some German Socialist Newspapers in European Archives," *Journal of Modern History*, XXIV (December, 1952), 380–82.

Stillschweig, Kurt. "The Jews of Germany as a National Minority," *Historia Judaica*, XI (April, 1949), 53–76.

Tobias, Henry J., and John Snell. "A Soviet Interpretation of the S.P.D., 1895–1933," *Journal of Central European Affairs*, XIII (April, 1953), 60–66.

Weinryk, Bernard D. "Jews in Central Europe," *Journal of Central European Affairs*, VI (April, 1946), 43–77.

Whiteside, Andrew G. "The Nature and Origins of National Socialism," *Journal of Central European Affairs*, XVII (April, 1957), 48–73.

UNPUBLISHED STUDIES

Creekmore, Marion V. "The Left and the New Right in the 1928 German Reichstag Election." M.A. thesis, Tulane University, 1963.

Hallgring, Louis, Jr. "The German Reichstag Elections of September, 1930." Ph.D. dissertation, Columbia University, 1950.

Kele, Max H. "Nazi Appeals to the German Workers, 1926–1932." M.A. thesis, Tulane University, 1963.

Mishark, John W. "Friedrich Ebert and German Social Democracy, 1914–1919." Ph.D. dissertation, University of Michigan, 1954.

Niewyk, Donald L. "German Social Democracy and the Problem of Anti-Semitism, 1906–1914." M.A. thesis, Tulane University, 1964.

Spalding, William Livingston, Jr. "Social Imperialism: The Impact of Nationalism on German Socialist Thinking During the First World War, 1914–1918." Ph.D. dissertation, Cornell University, 1949.

Wiener, Alfred. "The Centralverein deutscher Staatsbuerger juedischen Glaubens—Its Meaning and Activities." Typescript on file in the Wiener Library, London.

Index

Abegg Committee, 190
Adler, Josef, 193
Africans, 136
Ahlwardt, Hermann, 21
Alarm, 150
Albert, Johannes, 140, 168–69
Allen, Frank, 186
Allgemeiner freier Angestelltenbund, 19
All Quiet on the Western Front, 178
Allwohn, Adolf, 116
Altenburg, 156
Altenfeld, 172
Altmann, Bruno, 130
America, 96, 103, 130, 172, 204
Angriff, Der, 148, 149, 150
Anthropology, Institute of (Berlin), 136
Anti-Anti, 190
Anti-modernism: source of anti-Semitism, 127–28
Anti-Nazi, 190
Anti-Semitism: historical development of, 5–10 *passim*, 20–27 *passim*; sources of, 5–6, 8, 9, 14–15, 20–21, 22, 26–32 *passim*, 45–50, 122–28, 169; postwar revival of, 8–10, 29; irrational nature of, 123–31; post-World War II, 220
Anti-Socialist laws, 11, 21
Arabs: and Jews in Palestine, 103, 187–88
Arbeiterfuersorgeamt. See Workers' Welfare Office of Jewish Organizations in Germany
Arco-Valley, Anton von, 74
Aretin, Erwein von, 207
Army: Jews in, 7, 42–43; anti-Semitism in, 23, 29, 60, 83, 86, 90–91, 216; general staff of, 43–44; un-

trustworthiness of, 79; mentioned, 13, 100
Aryan clause, 159
Aryan race. *See* Racialism
Aschau, 114
Aschenbrenner, Rosa, 180, 196
Aster, Ernst von, 34
Auer, Erhard: combats anti-Semitism, 35, 40, 41, 58, 97, 166; on Jewish workers, 48; on *Ostjuden*, 102; on anti-Semitism in SPD, 107–108; on Eisner, 207; mentioned, 37, 208, 217
Auerbach, Berthold, 170
Aufhaeuser, Siegfried, 19
August Wilhelm, 176
Australians, 136
Austria: anti-Semitism in, 93, 119, 159, 180; Socialists in, 138; Jews in, 153; mentioned, 25, 39*n*, 133, 158

Bach, 156
Baer, Fritz, 201
Baltic, 109, 172
Barmat Affair, 103–105, 120, 196
Basler, Adolf, 48
Bauer, Georg, 123
Bauer, Gustav, 26, 104
Baumgarten, Otto, 161
Bavaria: Nazis in, 58–59, 182–83; anti-Semitism in, 63, 80–81, 91, 114, 133; revolution in, 74; parliament of, 80–81, 92, 97, 159, 178*n*, 195; government of, 93, 97; SPD in, 107, 133, 142*n*, 166–67, 182–83, 195–96, 207; Jews in, 195–96; mentioned, 35, 40
Bavarian People's Party, 195
Bebel, August, 10, 11, 12, 26*n*
Beer Hall putsch, 74
Beethoven, Ludwig van, 40, 136
Behrend, E., 105